SUNDAY &
HOLY DAY
LITURGIES

YEAR B

SUNDAY & HOLY DAY LITURGIES

YEAR B

Flor McCarthy, S.D.B.

DOMINICAN PUBLICATIONS

First published (1984) by
Dominican Publications
42 Parnell Square
Dublin 1

ISBN 0-907271-37-5

© Dominican Publications

This reprint: 1993

Cover design by
David Cooke

Printed in Ireland by
The Leinster Leader Ltd
Naas
Co. Kildare

CONTENTS

FOREWORD

These liturgies have grown out of an experience, and most of them have already been tried out in practice. The story of how they came into existence is told in the foreword to volume one (Cycle A). Therefore I will not repeat it here. In the foreword to this volume all I want to do is to restate the general approach that has been followed, and make a few additional general points.

The liturgies are aimed mainly at the generation of Catholics who have grown up since the Second Vatican Council ended. All the changes that have occurred in the liturgy subsequent to that event are taken for granted. I have tried throughout to use a language the modern generation can readily understand. I have attempted as far as possible to avoid theological jargon and religious cliches. It is not up to the people to learn the language of the homilist, it is up to the homilist to learn the language of the people.

You will notice that there is *a single theme* running through each of the liturgies. The theme, which, naturally, is drawn from the readings of the day, is introduced briefly at the start of the Mass. It is developed in the homily. We are invited to pray about it in the prayer of the faithful. And it is reinforced in a short communion reflection. Occasionally, however, the communion reflection may touch on another aspect of the mystery being celebrated, one not contained in the chosen theme.

I would like to emphasise once again the need for introductions to be kept to a minimum. We have to know *exactly* what we want to say, otherwise we will begin to waffle, in much the same way as a man who is unsure of the right path tends to stray. The same applies with even greater force to the homily. The introductions to the readings which I offer here are meant to serve as an example of what I mean. In preparing them I relied heavily ON THE SAVING WORD (Year B) which provides an excellent scriptural background to the readings.

From time to time I recomend the shorter form of a particular reading (usually in the case of the Gospel). The reason for this is as follows. Sometimes a reading introduces two or more themes. Now, since the homily always deals with one theme only, it seems more logical to confine the reading to the same theme. Take for instance the Gospel reading for the Twenty-Seventh Sunday of the Year (Mk 10:2-16). There are two themes in this Gospel passage. The first deals with the question of divorce (vv. 2-12). The second deals with Jesus and the children (vv. 13-16). Since the homily deals with the indissolubility of marriage, the shorter form of the Gospel is recommended (vv. 2-12).

A special feature of this vilume is the large number of variations of the prayer for peace which are here suggested before the giving of a sign of peace. People, especially the young, get tired of hearing the same formula repeated over and over again. The variations I have offered are for the most part drawn directly from the Gospel. I feel they will help our congregations to appreciate not only different aspects of peace but the great richness we have at our disposal in the Gospel.

You may notice that on major feasts, Christmas and Easter for example, my homily is shorter than usual. In most churches on these occasions the liturgy tends to be fuller and richer than it normally is. Now, every part of a good liturgy speaks to people. Hence the homily can be somewhat shorter than usual. Besides, on occasions such as Christmas, there is an 'atmosphere' present that make the homilist's job a lot simpler.

Since the first volume appeared a number of kind people wrote to me or said to me that they were finding it helpful and thanked me for it. Their words of encouragement reached me in the dark depths of winter when I was immersed in the writing of the present volume. They helped me to persevere with it and to do the best job on it that I possibly could I want to thank those people. Now I know what Mark Twain meant when he said: "I can live for at least two months on a compliment."

Flor McCarthy.

Advent

FIRST SUNDAY OF ADVENT
The Doorkeeper

INTRODUCTION AND CONFITEOR

Today we start a new liturgical year. During it the whole of Christ's life and teaching will pass before us. We've made the journey before, even so we must try to embark on it as if for the very first time.

Advent, the beginning of the journey, calls us to *wake up,* to look at our service of God. We are his servants in whom he has placed enormous trust for our own lives, for those of others, and for the whole of his creation.

How are we fulfilling this trust? (Pause).

You call us to awake from the sleep of habit, custom, and routine. Lord, have mercy.

You rouse us from the sleep of indifference to you and to others. Christ, have mercy.

You lift us out of the ruts of laziness, selfishness, and sin. Lord, have mercy.

HEADINGS FOR READINGS

First Reading (Isaiah 63:16-17; 64:1, 3-8). This reading recalls God's past goodness to his people, while freely admitting the people's sinfulness. The dominant note, however, is one of confidence in God who alone can save his people.

Second Reading (1 Cor 1:3-9). As we await the coming of Christ in glory, the Holy Spirit will keep us steadfast as we bear witness to him in our lives.

Gospel (Mark 13:33-37). This urges us to stay awake at our appointed tasks, because we simply do not know the day or the hour when the Master will return.

HOMILY

It was about mid-November of 1979 in Dublin. One morning we woke to find that overnight a layer of fine dust had fallen. It was very noticeable. It covered cars, windows, clothes lines . . . In some areas it was heavier than in others. One man went out to look for his blue car, but so thick was the dust that he had great difficulty in finding it.

The dust caused quite a sensation. People reacted immediately. What was it and and where did it come from? Many were worried, fearing that it was caused by a fall-out of dangerous chemicals or radio-active material. There was a deluge of phone calls to the police, to weather centres, and motoring organisations. Finally the explanation came: it was sand from the Sahara Desert! This came as a great relief. It was still a nuisance but was readily accepted because the southerly winds that had brought it, also brought the warmest November in fifteen years.

Now suppose that same coat of dust had fallen, not in a single night as it did, but over a period of months, what would have happened? Nobody would have noticed it, much less feared it. Yet things can accumulate gradually, and for that reason can be all the more dangerous because we fail to notice them. C. S. Lewis said: "The surest road to hell is the gradual one".

In the Gospel today there is a short little parable. It's about a householder who had a number of servants. On one occasion he had to go abroad, which meant that he would be away a long time. Meanwhile the servants would have the place to themselves. Before leaving he called them together and gave each of them a job to do. He urged them to be responsible. To do their various jobs and not to fall asleep. He singled out the doorkeeper for a special warning. "When I return I want to find you awake," the Master said. This was not surprising since he would have control over all those entering and leaving the house.

Christ's story ends there with that warning ringing in our ears. Let us take it a little further, concentrating only on the doorkeeper. Perhaps the greatest danger facing him is not so much that he may fall asleep on the job as that he may grow so accustomed to it that it will become just a job and nothing more. Let us see.

In the beginning he is all excited about the task. He feels honoured that the Boss placed so much trust in him. He loves the uniform. As soon as he puts it on he feels important. He is somebody. He is conscientious to the point of being scrupulous. It is not so much a job for him as a labour of love which he does with joy and enthusiasm.

But time goes by. Opening and closing doors can get very monotonous. The novelty soon wears off. Slowly but surely the dust of custom begins to fall and accumulate on him and his world. A deadly routine takes over, snuffing out all joy and spontaneity. He becomes caged in by habits. Attitudes settle and harden. He is getting used to the job. A person can get used to anything, it just takes time. Smugness and complacency follow, and act like a blight on his personality. He is pursuing a descending and darkening path.

Since he holds the keys he is in a very powerful position. He owes nothing to anybody but many people owe a lot to him. He becomes cold and unfeeling in the exercise of his authority. His fellow servants have to bow and scrape to him before he will condescent to open the door for them. Unwittingly power corrupts him and he makes an idol of himself.

After a certain time it becomes just a job for him. He is still responsible, still unfailingly at his post. But he is only going through the motions. He is little better than a robot. His main reason for staying is the security it provides. The initial love and enthusiasm have faded away into nothing. When the Master will return he will undoubtedly find him at his post. He will not be asleep. He will be awake, but he will not be alive. He will be dead, for he has lost his soul.

Habit is a scourge which paralyses and in the end snuffs out all life. We need to be provoked, to be goaded from time to time like oxen. It is remarkable how easily we fall into a particular route, and make a beaten track for ourselves. Woe to the person who tries to disturb us! How worn and dusty are the highways of life. How deep the ruts of tradition and conformity. We forget we once had dreams. We sit in our armchairs practising idle and musty virtues, passing judgement on everything and everybody.

It can so easily happen that we become Christians by habit only. Over the years the dust of routine has been falling silently and secretly. Now perhaps it blots out everything or almost everything. We are only going through the motions, taking part in rituals have lost all freshness and meaning. We don't hear the Gospel anymore. It just goes in one ear and out the other. The face of Christ has vanished from our sight.

I am the doorkeeper. Each of us can say that. It was Christ who put me in charge, in charge first of all of my own house — the house of my soul. Then in charge of my fellow servants, in the sense that I am supposed to take an interest in them and in their welfare.

Advent calls us to wake up, to arise from sleep. To shake off the dust of routine, habit, custom . . . and to let Christ come alive in our lives once more. "The spiritual life is first of all a matter of keeping awake." (Thomas Merton). But to be awake means to be alive.

PRAYER OF THE FAITHFUL

Let us pray to our heavenly Father that during this season of Advent we may awake from the sleep of routine, indifference, and neglect and so come to follow the Son more closely and more generously.   R: Lord, hear us in your love.

For those people who with their lips call themselves Christians, but who deny it by the way they live. (Pause). We pray in faith.

For all those who hold positions of trust and honour in our country but who betray both by their deeds. (Pause). We pray in faith.

That those who find life a burden too heavy to carry may find strength and hope. (Pause). We pray in faith.

That the coming of Christ may find us steadfast in faith, joyful in hope, and untiring in love. (Pause). We pray in faith.

For local needs.

Let us pray:

Heavenly Father, grant that we may be faithful and true servants of Christ your Son, so that when he comes he may find us awake and at our tasks. We ask this through the same Christ our Lord.

SIGN OF PEACE

Lord Jesus Christ, you said to your apostles:
'I leave you peace, my peace I give you'.
We find it hard to give peace to others
because sometimes we don't have it ourselves.
Take pity on our weakness,
and grant us the peace and unity of our kingdom
where you live for ever and ever.

COMMUNION REFLECTION

Advent: a time of hope.

It is said that while there is life
there is hope.
This has even a deeper meaning in reverse:
while there is hope there is life.
Hope comes first, life follows on.

Hope gives power to life,
for hope is strength.
The amount of energy in the world
is equal to the amount of hope in it.

Hope sheds light into millions of despairing hearts.
It is the miracle medicine of the mind.
It inspires the will to live.
It is the doctor's most powerful ally,

It is a shield against defeat and failure.
It never sounds the retreat.
It revives ideals and renews dreams.
As long as there is hope,
no situation is impossible.

Advent summons us
to wait in joyful hope.
for the coming of our Saviour Jesus Christ.

Lord, in the final analysis,
you are our only hope.

SECOND SUNDAY OF ADVENT
Preparing The Way

INTRODUCTION AND CONFITEOR

In today's liturgy the Church enables us once again to hear the lonely voice of John the Baptist calling us to repentance, urging us to prepare a way so that Christ our Saviour can come to us. Let us pause for a moment to call to mind the goodness of God and our need of salvation. (Pause).

One thing Christ brings us is the Father's forgiveness. Let us, therefore, confess our sins with confidence in his mercy.

I confess etc. . . .

HEADINGS FOR READINGS

First Reading (Isaiah 40:1-5, 9-11). This contains a piece of good news. God is coming to save his people. The people are urged to prepare a way for him.

Second Reading (2 Peter 3:8-14). If the Lord appears to be slow in coming, Peter says it is only so that people may have a chance to repent and so be ready to meet him when he comes.

Gospel (Mark 1:1-8). John the Baptist appears on the scene to announce to the people the imminent coming of their Saviour and to prepare them for his coming.

HOMILY

Tolstoy has a story about a worldly careerist named Ivan. His one aim was to climb up the social ladder. He worked very hard and by middle age he is a successful and self-assured high court judge. But he is not happy. Far from it. He lives an unreflecting life and is totally given over to one long round of activity.

But then something happens which shatters his world into a thousand pieces. The crisis comes about in a very trivial way. He bumps himself slightly while hanging a curtain. A pain develops. At first he ignores it but it refuses to go away. He goes to see a doctor, but gets no relief or satisfaction. The pain persists. It even gets worse. Slowly it comes home to Ivan that he is going downhill, that in fact he is terminally ill.

He rebels against his illness. He sees himself as the victim of a blind fate. There is no reason, no explanation for what has happened to him. He is being cut off in the prime of life. It is absurd to be swept away by such a trifle.

He has no resources within himself to help him cope with the crisis. There hasn't been a trace of spirituality in his life. Previously he had never given as much as a thought to death, and now it is at his doorstep. To make matters worse, he is starved emotionally. His marriage was one of convenience. If there was some love in it once, that love has long since evaporated.

He is knocked from his pedestal. Unable to work and confined to bed, he knows that in effect he is no longer the head of the house. Instead of being a support to his family he is an obstacle. His life has been poisoned and was poisoning the lives of others. That life is now flowing through his hands like water from a leaking container, and he is powerless to stop it.

Worst of all, when he looks back on his life he realises that he has never really lived. The values on which he constructed his life were false. His smart lifestyle has been reduced to rubble. He has squandered all he was given and now has no chance of rectifying matters. He falls into a mood blacker than night.

He feels terribly alone, without a single person to either understand or pity him. There is no one to accompany him even a little way along the dark road that stretches out ahead of him. He is skeptical that there can be such a thing as real love in the false world he has lived in.

When he realises the hopelessness of his plight he begins to scream. He screams for three whole days. He has lived a life of vanity and meanness of spirit, and is now dying a death without dignity.

Yet salvation, or at least help, comes from a most unexpected source. Into this vacuum of horror love comes. First in the person of his pantry boy named Gerasim. Gerasim is a simple, kind boy, who is optimistic about his lowly life. He is not frightened by death. He stays at Ivan's side, nursing him with disinterested love, carrying out the most sordid tasks with complete naturalness. He becomes Ivan's sole source of strength.

But shortly before he dies further help arrives. His young son has stolen into the room. Suddenly Ivan's hand comes into chance contact with the boy's head. As soon as the boy feels his father's hand on his head, he takes it and kisses it. Ivan opens his eyes and sees that his wife is also in the room and that tears are running down her face. Thus in his last hour he experiences true love, and suddenly all that had been oppressing him begins to fall away. And he dies a peaceful death.

Ivan was powerless to help himself. His situation was hopeless. Furthermore, he has done nothing to deserve the help that arrived. Nevertheless, arrive it did, and that is what is so marvellous about Tolstoy's story.

In today's Gospel John the Baptist announces to the people the good news that the long-awaited day of salvation is about to dawn upon them. He urges the people to "prepare a way for the Lord". But it is clear that the Lord's coming does not depend on their efforts.

It is very easy to get the Gospel (the Good News) wrong, to turn it upside down, and say that God loves us and saves us only because we have earned his love and salvation. But this is not so. The Good News is that it was God who first loved us. "When we were lost and could not find our way to you, you loved us more than ever". (Eucharist Prayer of Reconciliation I). All that is asked of us is to try to return his love.

Is this so hard to believe? If you look back at Tolstoy's story, and consider how the boy Gerasim was able to love and care for his sick boss, then we ought to be more ready to believe in God's love for us, even though we know we do not deserve that love.

Happy are those who feel their need of God's help and salvation, even though they may not be as desperate as Ivan. All they have to do is reach out and they will get it. But of course it takes humility to recognise one's need and to accept help.

We have to allow ourselves to be loved by God. Then having experienced this love we will naturally want to share it with others. A fire that has a warm centre will naturally throw out heat all around it. Then people will know that they are not victims of a blind and often cruel fate, but that they are in the care of a loving Providence.

PRAYER OF THE FAITHFUL

Let us pray that we may make ready the way for Christ to come to us, bearing gifts for us from God our Father.   *R*. Lord hear our prayer.

That all those who believe in Christ may be saved from the blindness of materialism and self-sufficiency. (Pause).   We pray to the Lord.

That our political leaders may strive to level the mountains of injustice and fill in the valleys of poverty so that we may have a more just society. (Pause).   We pray to the Lord.

That we may realise that Christ is always trying to come to us in the person of the one we are ignoring or excluding, in the person who is in need and in want. (Pause).   We pray to the Lord.

That we may create a time and a space for Christ in our lives, so that he can come to us with his light, his healing, and his peace. (Pause).   We pray to the Lord.

For local needs.

Let us pray:

Almighty, ever-living Father, whose love surpasses all that we ask or deserve; open for us the treasures of your mercy; forgive us all that weighs on our conscience, and grant us more even than we dare ask. We make our prayer through Christ our Lord.

COMMUNION REFLECTION
Lonely voices

John's was a voice crying in the wilderness,
a lonely voice that many of his contemporaries ignored.
The voice of the prophet
is not the only voice that is ignored.
There are many lonely voices in our world
that go unheeded.

Somewhere at this moment a child is crying —
crying for love or maybe simply for bread.

Somewhere a young person is crying —
crying for a listening ear
or an understanding heart.

Somewhere a deserted wife and mother is crying —
crying for the support of a husband.

Somewhere old people are crying —
crying for a word from their children.

There are a thousand lonely voices,
a thousand unheard cries in our world,
coming from the victims of injustice or neglect.

Lord, help us to listen to these voices.
Above all, help us to listen to your voice
whispering to us in the wilderness of our hearts,
telling us that we are loved by the Father,
and that we are to love one another.

THIRD SUNDAY OF ADVENT
Witnessing to the Light

INTRODUCTION AND CONFITEOR:

In today's liturgy we will hear John the Baptist say to us: "There stands one among you whom you know not". The one he speaks of is Christ our Saviour. Christ is the unseen guest at our banquet. More than that — he is the host who welcomes us to this banquet given by the Father. Let us draw close to him and renew our faith in his presence with us. (Pause).

You work marvels for us. Holy is your name. Lord, have mercy.

Your mercy is from age to age on those who fear you. Christ, have mercy.

You fill the starving with good things. Lord, have mercy.

HEADINGS FOR READINGS

First Reading (Isaiah 61:1-2, 10-11). The writer declares that he has been anointed by God and sent to bring good news to the poor. Jesus used this passage to announce the programme of his own ministry.

Second Reading (1 Thess 5:16-24). St. Paul tells the Thessalonians how they ought to live as they wait for the second coming of Christ.

Gospel (John 1:6-8, 19-28). John the Baptist makes it clear that he is not the Saviour. His task is a humbler one — to prepare the way for the Saviour who is already among the people, though they do not recognise him.

HOMILY

There was a certain kingdom that had been blessed with a long line of kings who were both wise and good. The explanation was thought to lie in a magic ring. The ring had been passed down faithfully from father to son. Always it was the oldest son who inherited the throne. Consequently it was he too who inherited the ring.

But then a problem arose. A king came along whose wife gave birth to twins, both boys. They were christened Peter and Paul. The father loved both of them equally. But to whom should he leave the ring? He fell very ill, and thinking that he was about to die, he hit on the following plan. He got another ring made exactly like the first. It was so good that even he was unable to tell them apart.

Then he called in his two sons separately and gave each of them a ring. But when Peter found out that his brother had also got a ring he made a terrible scene. He had to be sure that he himself had the magic ring and not the look-alike. The king consulted a wise man to help him decide the issue. After examining the rings the latter declared: "I cannot tell which of you is wearing the magic ring. However, if you continue to wear the ring you've been given, in time you yourselves will be able to tell". "How?" they asked earnestly. "It's quite simple. Whichever of you displays the greater amount of goodness in his life will prove beyond doubt that he possesses the magic ring".

It was agreed. As it happened, the king recovered from his illness and reigned for many years more, years in which the kingdom was blessed with peace and prosperity. When at least he was nearing death he called in his two sons once more. Now was the time to finally decide which of them had the magic ring.

Peter was the first to come in. He began to claim adamantly that he possessed it. But then the people who knew him best were asked their opinion. His wife told how over the years he had shown her very little affection. His children said that he was never at home. His servants complained that he had been very hard on them and had paid them poor wages. His neighbours told how he was forever stirring up trouble among them. And so it went on.

Paul came in. He made no claims whatsoever. But when the people who knew him best were asked what kind of man he was they were loud in their praise of him. He had proved to be a loving husband, and a kind father to his children. He had treated his servants with respect and generosity. He had been a force for peace and goodwill among his neighbours. And so it went on. In fact, not a single one had a bad word to say about him.

Then the king spoke: "Peter, you have witnessed to the presence of the ring, but only with your words. Paul, on the other hand, has witnessed to it with his deeds, that is, with his life. To me it is obvious that his witness is the greater and the more convincing. Therefore, I declare that his ring is the genuine one. Now Paul I ask you to produce it. "I no longer have it", Paul answered. "What do you mean you no longer have it?" asked the King. "One day many years ago a poor woman and her child came to my gate and I gave it to her so that she could sell it and buy food and clothes."

Far from being angry, the king was very pleased on hearing this. It merely confirmed him in his belief that the verdict he had reached was in fact the correct one. And in due course Paul ascended the throne and donned the crown.

The second son in some ways reminds us of that great man John the Baptist. In today's Gospel we are told that John was a witness to the light. "He was not the light, but only a witness for the light". The light of course was Christ.

But what a wonderful witness John was. He witnessed not only with his words but especially with his deeds and his life. And when the light finally appeared John was quite content to fade from the scene and let Christ take over. That takes greatness.

For many people in the world today Christ has become a very dim and distant figure. The words of today's Gospel are literally true: "There stands one among you whom you know not". Christ has come into our world. And what's more, he remains with us as he promised. But he still needs witnesses, people who can effectively make him present to other people. No witness reaches our contemporaries more persuasively than the witness of those who do what Jesus did and who live as he lived.

If Christ is the light of my life then naturally I will let that light shine, simply by the way I live. But how can I witness to the light if I live by values that do not even remotely resemble those of the Gospel? Without the witness of Christians the face of Christ, already blurred, will continue to fade from our world. He will continue to stand among us, unknown and unrecognised. And hearts will remain broken, and people will remain imprisoned in darkness, and the good news will not be preached to the poor.

PRAYER OF THE FAITHFUL

Let us pray that the light of Christ our Saviour may shine in our lives and in our world.   *R.* Lord, graciously hear us.

That Christians, by the way they live, may show forth the light of Christ's love and mercy to all people. (Pause).   Lord, hear us.

For all rulers: that they may work for the good of those they govern. (Pause).   Lord, hear us.

That hearts that are broken with sorrow, disappointment, or loneliness may experience the gentle healing of Christ. (Pause).   Lord, hear us.

That we ourselves may witness to the Good News that there is forgiveness for sin, and that there is hope for our world, by the way we speak and act. (Pause). Lord, hear us.

For local needs.

Let us pray:

Heavenly Father, send your Son once more to us, that he may brighten up our dark lives, heal our wounds, and teach us to follow your way in freedom, joy, and love. We ask this through the same Christ our Lord.

COMMUNION REFLECTION

A six year old child whose parents were non-believers
one day asked his teacher
to take him to visit a nearby church.
During the visit he said to the teacher:

"This is God's house, so Grandma says.
She says that God is love.
She says she prays to him
which means she talks to him.

I have never prayed.
But I would like to talk to God.
I would like to hear what he has to say.

There's a boy in my class at school
who believes in God.
He's a Catholic.
But Papa and Mama are not God-believing people
and so I am not.
It makes me feel lonely not knowing God".

The words of a six year old:
"It makes me feel lonely not knowing God".
But sadly his parents were no help to him.
in search for God.

If we do not possess the light
we cannot give it to others.

FOURTH SUNDAY OF ADVENT
Saying Yes To God

INTRODUCTION AND CONFITEOR:

As the birth of a child draws near, naturally all attention focuses on the mother. We are nearing the celebration of the birth of Christ. Hence it should come as no surprise to find that Mary his Mother is at the centre of today's Gospel. Mary was a very humble person. A mere "handmaid of the Lord" was how she saw herself. Her only concern was to do the will of God in her life. She will help us to do it also. (Pause).

Lord Jesus, Prince of Peace, you call us to walk in the paths of peace. Lord, have mercy.

Lord Jesus, glorious Son of God, you teach us to obey the will of the Father. Christ, have mercy.

Lord Jesus, humble Son of Mary, you teach us humility and gentleness of heart. Lord, have mercy.

HEADINGS FOR READINGS

First Reading (2 Samuel 7:1-5, 8-11, 16). We read how King David had hoped to build a house (a temple) for God. But he is informed that it is God who will build a house (a dynasty) for him.

Second Reading (Romans 16:25-27). God's plan of salvation for Jews and Gentiles has come to fulfilment in Christ. The good news must be broadcast everywhere.

Gospel (Luke 1:26-38). Mary gives her consent to become the mother of the Redeemer, though she does not fully understand what is being asked of her.

HOMILY

The setting is a southern town in the United States. A father, a lawyer by profession, lives with his two young children, a son and a daughter. His wife is dead. Though he is strict on the children he is good to them and they love him. He is an upright man and an excellent lawyer. However, he has made himself very unpopular in the town by opting to defend a Negro who is charged with a very serious crime. Though the Negro is almost certainly innocent, he stands very little chance of getting a fair trial, for the town is rife with discrimination against blacks.

At the end of the street there lives an elderly woman. She spends her afternoons sitting in her front arden. She is very cranky and bad-tempered. She is forever giving out to the lawyer's two kids as they pass by on their way to and from school. But what hurts the kids most of all are the names she calls their father, simply because he is defending the Negro.

One evening the son decides he has taken enough from this cranky old woman. He hops over her garden wall and destroys some of her flowers. Then he runs home. When Dad comes home he sends for his son and says: "Son, you shouldn't have done that".

And he protests: "But she's not nice. She's always giving out to us. And you should hear the things she says about you. I really did it because of you".

"That woman is a very sick woman. Now go down and apologise to her for what you did".

Reluctantly the son goes down and apologises. The woman asks him if he would agree to come and read for her for an hour each evening. He is horrified at the thought, but when he gets home and tells his father, the father insists that he must say Yes to the old lady. So each evening the boy, accompanied by his little sister, goes to visit the old lady and reads for her. They both hate it, for she remains as contrary and cantankerous as ever, and still continues to insult their father. Each evening after they have read for about an hour the old woman gets a violent fit for trembling. They are forced to leave and a nurse takes over. However, as the weeks go by, the fits get less frequent and less severe.

Then one evening their father arrives home and tells them that the old lady has just died. They think 'thank God' but do not say it. But then the father tells them something which changes their whole attitude to the old lady. He tells them that several years previously a doctor had prescribed painkilling drugs for her and she had got addicted to them. Then she was told that she had only a short while to live, so she made up her mind that she would try to kick the habit and die free of drugs. Those fits they saw her getting — they were withdrawal symptoms.

"And did she succeed?" the kids asked earnestly.

"She did", the father answered. "And just before she died she told me that she would never have succeeded if you hadn't come and read for her. She wanted me to thank you".

The kids were flabbergasted on hearing this, and they cried out: "If only we had known what she was going through, we would have been nicer to her".

"It doesn't matter," the father said. "The main thing is you did what I asked you to do. You are two good children. I'm proud of you".

Those two children didn't realise the full significance of the task their father asked them to do. Nevertheless, they did it in a spirit of love and obedience.

In today's Gospel we see how Mary consented to become the mother of the Redeemer because she was a humble person and wanted to do the will of God. But when she said Yes to God, I wonder did she realise the full implications of what she was agreeing to? I think it's quite obvious that she didn't. She had no idea that at his birth every door would be closed in her face. That shortly after his birth she would be a refugee in a foreign country. That some thirty-three years later she would see him die the death of a criminal.

Mary didn't just say her 'Yes' once. She had to confirm that original Yes many times during her life. But all through her life, because she was poor and relied completely on God, he upheld her and enabled her to remain faithful. Without Mary's obedience to God we would not have a Redeemer.

Each of us has said Yes when we have undertaken commitments and responsibilities. When we said our original Yes we took a leap in the dark, for we didn't know the full implications of what we were undertaking. This was gradually revealed to us as we went along. It unfolded before us like a winding path. Hence, we too have to confirm our original Yes, not once but often, and ask God to help us to remain faithful.

Again, often in life we can't see the full meaning of what we do. Sometimes this meaning is completely hidden from us. as it was from the two children. In that case it becomes very difficult to go on, especially if the task is disagreeable or those for whom we do it are ungrateful. Once again we have to go on confirming our Yes, in a spirit of loving obedience to God.

It was in this way that Mary brought Christ to birth. It is by following the same path that he will be brought to birth in us.

PRAYER OF THE FAITHFUL

Let us pray that like Mary each of us may continue to say Yes to the will of God in our lives.   *R*. Lord, graciously hear us.

That the pope and the bishops may guide the people of God not only by word but by example. (Pause).   Lord, hear us.

For those in charge of civil affairs: that they may be found faithful to their commitments and obligations. (Pause).   Lord, hear us.

For those who are struggling to know and do the will of God: that they may find light and strength. (Pause).   Lord, hear us.

That each of us may strive to follow the example of Mary in her faith, humility, and obedience to God. (Pause).   Lord hear us.

For local needs.

Let us pray: Heavenly Father, in your gentle mercy, guide our
wayward hearts, for we know that, left to ourselves, we cannot do
your will. We ask this through Christ our Lord.

COMMUNION REFLECTION

The first crib

The appearance of the crib in our churches
is a sure sign that Christmas is at the doorstep.
St Francis of Assisi assembled the first crib
in a cave on an Italian hillside in 1223.
His aim was to make the Christmas story come alive
for the shepherds and farmers of the locality.

On Christmas eve the friars and the people assembled
with candles and torches to illuminate the night.
Then Francis arrived and was very happy
when he saw the preparations they had made.

The crib was put in place.
The hay was brought in.
The ox and donkey were led forward.
The woods rang with their prayers.
The rocks echoed with their hymns.

Francis spoke to them about God's Son coming among us
to help us to realise our splendid dignity
as sons and daughters of the same Father.

At the end of the vigil
they all returned to their homes,
full of peace and joy,
feeling very close to God
and to one another.

Christmastide

CHRISTMAS
God Is With Us

INTRODUCTION AND CONFITEOR:

This is a great night(day). It is a night (day) we should experience a closeness to one another. For Christmas is a time for taking off the masks: for admitting that we are fellow human beings, in fact brothers and sisters. Let us think about this for a moment. (Pause).

Now let us confess our sins to God and to one another: I confess.

HEADINGS FOR READINGS

Midnight Mass

First Reading (Isaiah 9:1-7). This reading looks forward to the coming of a Saviour-child who will rescue his people from darkness and oppression, and enable them to live in security and peace.

Second Reading (Titus 2:11-14). St Paul reminds us of what is expected of us if we are to enjoy the salvation won for us by Christ.

Gospel (Luke 2:1-14). This tells about the birth of Christ our Saviour in a manger and how the glad news of his birth was brought by angels to simple shepherds.

Dawn Mass

First Reading (Isaiah 62:11-12). With the birth of our Lord the Christian people can taste the joy of the exiles returning from Babylon.

Second Reading (Titus 3:4-7)). We ourselves did nothing to merit the birth of Christ; rather, God sent his Son out of compassion for us.

Gospel (Luke 2:15-20). With Mary we are invited to ponder on the deep meaning of the birth of Christ so that, with the shepherds, we may be moved to glorify and praise God.

Day Mass

First Reading (Isaiah 52:7-10). This great hymn of exultation at the return of the exiles from Babylon is also a poem of joy for our redemption.

Second Reading (Hebrews 1:1-6). This whole history of God's dealings with his people in the past was a preparation for the coming of his Son at a particular moment in history.

Gospel (John 1:1-18). This is a great hymn to the Word of God, the source of all life, whose coming among us makes us children of God.

Picture a man going through the desert. The heat of the sun beats down mercilessly on him. The glare from the burning sand almost blinds him. He is ready to collapse from exhaustion. But the worst thing of all is the thirst. It torments him.

But then to his great joy he sees an oasis up ahead. His spirits soar. He sees trees. These will give him shelter, perhaps food as well. But the one thing he desperately needs and desires is water. There will surely be a well there. He reaches the oasis, finds many other desirable things, but no water. The well has dried up.

Most people look forward to Christmas. It's a kind of oasis in the dark dreary desert of winter. However, we too might have all the outward trappings — the lights, trees, candles, cards, gifts, desorations — but no 'water'. There is no Christ. From a Christian point of view if Christ is not there, then Christmas is only a mirage. It is like an oasis without water.

I remember once as Christmas approached discussing its meaning with a group of young people. In the group was a middle-aged woman whom we unconsciously tended to ignore and omit from our discussion. When we each had said our piece she began to speak, and when she did we all listened very intently.

She told us that she was dreading the approach of Christmas. She had been an only child. But her parents were long since dead. She had no aunts or uncles. No close relatives. She was all alone, the last of her family. She had friends, yes. She exchanged cards and gifts with them at Christmas time. But somehow none of them ever thought of inviting her to their homes on Christmas Day. They did invite her on St Stephen's Day, but never on Christmas Day.

So how does she spend Christmas Day? Mostly on her own, though she is by no means a recluse. After an early morning Mass she goes out to help in some voluntary work for others. Then she comes back, cooks dinner, and eats it on her own. She switches on the TV, but even its bright shows fail to raise her spirits. TV is no substitute for having someone with you.

She cries a lot. She just can't help it. Towards evening, as darkness sets in and the lights of a million Christmas trees come on, she goes for a walk. But on Christmas evening it's lonely out of doors too. The streets and parks are deserted. All doors are closed. She tries the door of her local church but that too is firmly locked.

But then she told us how in the midst of her loneliness and tears she feels very close to Christ. She feels close to his sufferings. She realises that in a very real sense he was an outsider at the first Christmas — there was no room for him at the inn. And even though her tears continue to fall. she feels an inner happiness that is impossible to describe or explain. Why? Because Christ gives a meaning to her loneliness and pain. He is her Saviour and her Brother who came to share our lives, to help us carry our burdens, and to walk the road of life at our side. That is the meaning of Christmas.

Here was someone who had the core of Christmas. Christ was with her. And even though many of the trimmings were missing, she had the essential thing. She had found an oasis, and though it lacked some of the superfluous items, it had the one thing necessary — water.

Is Christ at the centre of our celebration of Christmas? If not, then for us too there is no water at the oasis.

PRAYER OF THE FAITHFUL

Jesus is Emmanuel, God with us. Let us then with confidence place our requests before the Father.   *R*. Lord, hear us in your love.

That through the coming of Christ their Saviour, Christians may walk in the light of sincerity and goodness. (Pause). We pray in hope.

For the world and for all mankind: that the birth of the Prince of Peace may spread understanding and unity among all peoples. (Pause). We pray in hope.

Christ took on our human weakness: may he be the eyes of the blind, the strength of the weak, the friend of the lonely. (Pause). We pray in hope.

That the coming of Christ may fill our hearts with joy and make us heralds of his Gospel as it did the shepherds. (Pause). We pray in hope.

For local needs.

Let us pray:

Father, Christ your Son made this night (day) radiant with his light. May we come to share in his divine life who came on earth to share our human lives. We ask this through the same Christ our Lord.

SIGN OF PEACE

Lord, at your birth the angels sang: 'Glory to God in the highest, and peace to his people on earth'. Yet they still fight for possession of the land where you were born. Grant to us who have heard the message of the angels, the peace and unity of your kingdom, where you live for ever and ever.

COMMUNION REFLECTION

In our times Christmas has become
very commercialised and very pagan.
Many people are lured into over-spending
as well as excessive eating and drinking.

However, these abuses should not blind us
to the true meaning of Christmas.
When thick smoke rises up,
catches in your throat,
and brings tears to your eyes,
it is because a fire has been lit.

Ever since the coming of Christ
a bright fire has been burning on our earth,
a fire that will never die.
At this fire we experience
the warmth of God's love,
as well as the glow of human fellowship.

Let us not be afraid to come in out of the cold
and warm ourselves at this fire.

So happy Christmas, everyone!

FEAST OF THE HOLY FAMILY

INTRODUCTION AND CONFITEOR

Through Christ God has made of us one family and he has bound himself even more closely to us by a bond that can never be broken. Today we celebrate the feast of the Holy Family. We think of our own families, which are coming under increasing pressure. We think too of the human family, scarred by so many divisions. We ask God to heal the wounds of sin and division. (Pause).

You open our eyes and our hearts to understand that we are brothers and sisters. Lord, have mercy.

Though we may abandon you, you do not abandon us. Christ, have mercy.

By the power of your Holy Spirit you make us one body, healed of all division. Lord. have mercy.

First Reading (Ecclesiasticus 3:2-6, 12-14). This reading could be seen as a brief commentary on the commandment to honour one's father and mother. This entails not only obeying them when we are young, but caring for them then they get old.

Second Reading (Colossians 3:12-21). This stresses the atmosphere of love that should reign in a Christian family. It places special emphasis on mutual forgiveness.

Gospel (Luke 2:22-40). This relates the presentation of the child Jesus in the temple, and also provides us with a brief glimpse of his life at Nazareth.

HOMILY

This is the time of year when the travel agencies begin to display their summer holiday packages. What a rosy picture their glossy brochures and TV ads paint! We are confronted with holiday spots that would make Paradise look drab. The sun is always shining from an azure sky, the beaches are one vast expanse of white sand, the sea is blue and beautiful, the water cool and refreshing, the food exquisite, the drink cheap, the accommodation first class, the night-life bright and exciting, and so it goes. The would-be traveller is promised a heaven where his days will be filled with sun and his nights with fun. There is not even the faintest hint of a dark spot such as inconvenience or discomfort, not to mention such things as nausea or boredom.

In the middle of winter to visit such a place even in one's fantasy is comforting. And it's easy to believe the propaganda when it's presented attractively. Yet we suspect, to some extent at least, that we are being conned. That the ads exaggerate. that it could not be quite as good as that. And we are right.

Take a typical resort and what do you find? The first thing is that you can take only so much sun. In any case, too much of it is actually bad for you, and if you're not careful it will cause you very nasty burns which will rob your nights of sleep. Sandy beaches are fun but the sand has a knack of getting into everything. The sea at times is filled with jellyfish who seem determined to keep it to themselves. In the evenings when at last a cool breeze blows the mosquitoes drive you indoors to swelter, the food doesn't agree with your delicate stomach, so that at times you long for such a simple thing as a decent cup of tea. The drink is cheap, okay, but you tend to overdo it, and a hangover spoils the fun. The accommodation is fine were it not for that noisy crowd on the floor above. And surprise! surprise! It rains here too.

In a word, you discover that though it has its good points, it also has its drawbacks. It's not quite the paradise the brochures made it out to be. The reality, and therefore the truth, lies somewhere in between.

Today is the feast of the Holy Family. We tend to have an idealised picture of the Holy Family. Angels whispering in the ears of Mary and Joseph telling them what to do in moments of doubt. We tend to see the home at Nazareth as a haven of uninterrupted calm, perfect harmony, and complete understanding. We see Jesus, Mary, and Joseph living as it were on a sunlit island, cut off from the storms and rains of the world. I haven't the slightest doubt but that such a picture bears less resemblance to the reality than do the glossy travel brochures.

We are not told very much about the life of the Holy Family in the Gospels. But we are given glimpses. With the help of these, as well as reading between the lines, we get quite a different picture. We see that the Holy Family had at least its fair share of storms, and in that respect was a normal and typical family. Let us look at a few examples.

When the time came for Jesus to be born, Joseph and Mary could find no accommodation. To have all doors shut in your face is not a nice feeling. Their joy at the birth of the child was short-lived. No sooner was he born than he became the target of Herod's murderers, so that Joseph and Mary had to flee to a foreign country. There they knew what is is like to be an alien.

Back home they had to find a place where they could begin life all over again. When Jesus was twelve, during a visit to Jerusalem, he got lost. Joseph and Mary sought him with fear and sorrow in their hearts. During his public life Mary did not always understand what he was doing. She saw him being taken over by the crowds. Once she made a vain attempt to rescue him. Later she saw the tide turn against him and the net of authority close around him. Finally came the ignominy of the crucifixion, when a sword of sorrow pierced her heart, and a real sword pierced the heart of her Son.

So after all this, can we still believe that the Holy Family lived a sheltered and trouble-free life? I do not see how we can. It is for this reason that the Holy Family is a model for us. If it had never known sorrow or trouble or pain, how could it serve as an example for us? Our families are often visited by sorrow, misunderstandings, and problems of one kind or another. Our lives together are often disrupted, sometimes perhaps broken up altogether.

We should not grow disheartened. I feel that Joseph and Mary would understand. Besides, there is more depth to relationships that have weathered some storms. Sorrow and problems can bring people together provided they are shared. Ideally there is no place like home. There I have a refuge where I'm always welcome. There forgiveness, love, and understanding always await me.

An impossible ideal? Difficult yes, but impossible no. Jesus and Mary and Joseph will help us grow in grace and favour with God and with one another.

PRAYER OF THE FAITHFUL

Let us pray to God our Father for the family, which is still one of the best and most important institutions in the world.   *R*. Lord, hear our prayer.

For all humankind: that the different races, realising that they form one family under God, may seek the way of peace together. (Pause).   Let us pray to the Lord.

For our civil leaders and legislators: that they may protect the family as the most important unit in our society. (Pause).   Let us pray to the Lord.

For broken families and families in hardship: that they may find support. (Pause).   Let us pray to the Lord.

For all parents: that they may love their children warmly, yet without possessiveness. (Pause). Let us pray to the Lord.

For local needs.

Let us pray:

Heavenly Father, Christ your Son, during his years at Nazareth, made holy the intimate relationships of family life. Keep our families together, and make our homes places where we experience love, acceptance, forgiveness, and peace. We ask this through the same Christ our Lord.

OUR FATHER

Let us pray to God, the Father of the whole human family, as Jesus our Brother taught us.

COMMUNION REFLECTION

Looking at authority from the child's viewpoint

Don't spoil me.
I know I ought not have all I ask for.
I'm only testing you.

Don't be afraid to be firm with me.
It makes me feel more secure.

Don't correct me in front of others.
I'll take more notice
if you correct me in private.

Don't nag, or I shall have to protect myself
by appearing deaf.

Don't make rash promises.
I feel badly let down when promises are broken.

Don't be inconsistent.
That completely confuses me.

Don't put me off when I ask questions,
Or I think be forced to seek my information elsewhere.

Don't think if beneath your dignity
to apologise if you're wrong. An honest apology
makes me feel surprisingly warm towards you.

But two things I need above all others —
understanding and love.
If you give me these,
the rest will take care of themselves.

SECOND SUNDAY AFTER CHRISTMAS
He Lived Among Us

INTRODUCTION AND CONFITEOR:

We all suffer from loneliness from time to time. Even the great Helen Keller who was blind said: "At times loneliness sits like a load on my shoulders". It is wonderful to have company, especially in moments of pain. Our companion may not be able to take away our pain, but at least we know that we are not alone. That someone cares about us. The message of today's liturgy is that God is always present with his people. He never abandons us. Let us draw close to him now. (Pause).   Let us ask his help in a spirit of deep faith and trust.

Lord Jesus, you are always thinking of your people. You never forget us. Lord, have mercy.

You came to save us and to give your life for us. Christ, have mercy.

Though we are sinners, you invite us to trust in your mercy. Lord, have mercy.

HEADINGS FOR READINGS

First Reading (Ecclesiasticus 24:1-2, 8-12). This is a poem in praise of wisdom, a wisdom that has pitched her tent among God's chosen people.

Second Reading (Ephesians 1:3-6, 15-18). This reading introduces the theme of God's loving plan of salvation for us.

Gospel (John 1:1-18). As the Son of God, Jesus existed from the very beginning, sharing the divine life of the Father. But then he became man, sharing our human lives in order to give us a share in his divine life.

HOMILY

Maxmilian Kolbe, a Franciscan priest, was arrested by the Gestapo on the 17th of February 1941. In May of that year he was transferred to Auschwitz concentration camp. There he quickly won himself a reputation for kindness and dedication to the needs of his fellow prisoners.

Towards the end of July a prisoner escaped from the camp. The camp commander was furious and ordered that ten of his companions should die in his place. He lined up the prisoners and went down the line picking out ten men at random. The tenth man to be chosen broke down and began to plead for mercy, on the strength of the fact that he had a wife and young family back home to support. It was then that the incredible happened: Maximilian Kolbe stepped forward and offered to take his place. After some hesitation the commander agreed, and the substitution was made.

The ten condemned men were then led to an underground bunker where they were left to starve to death as a deterrent to would-be escapers. In the days that followed the guards watched through a peep-hole the agony of the dying men. They could scarcely believe what they saw. The nine men were gathered around Fr Kolbe. At times they could be seen joking, at other times praying and singing hymns. Fourteen days went by. One by one they died. Last to die was Fr. Kolbe. On the night of August 14th he was still alive. A guard put an end to his agony when he gave him an injection of phenol.

The man whose place Kolbe took survived the camps and the war. Later he stated: "At first I felt terrible at the thought of leaving another man die in my place. But then I realised that he had done this, not so much to save my life, as to be with the other nine in their last terrible agony. His nearness to them in those dreadful last hours was worth more than a lifetime of preaching".

His presence was worth more than a lifetime of preaching. True love goes beyond the giving of gifts. It requires the giving of oneself. Fr Kolbe might have given those men advice and encouragement. He might have visited them in their death cell (supposing that it were allowed). But his presence with them, sharing in full their terrible ordeal, was worth more than anything else, even though in the end he could do nothing to save them from their cruel fate.

This is the note that is struck in today's liturgy. That God is present with his people. Christ came, as St John said, "and lived among us". He shared our lives fully. He knew what it was like to be human. In Christ we have a Brother who loves us to the extent that he came among us and shared our lives to the full. Not only our lives but our death as well. Let us reflect for a moment on this great mystery of love.

(Sit for a moment of reflection).

PRAYER OF THE FAITHFUL

God the Father loved us so much that he sent his Son to save us. With confidence let us place our requests before him.   *R*. Lord, hear our prayer.

Christ showed us how to live a life truly pleasing to God. May all his followers strive to follow his example. (Pause).   Let us pray to the Lord.

For leaders and governments: that God may guide them and give them wisdom and integrity. (Pause).   Let us pray to the Lord.

In the garden of Gethsemane Christ cried out: "My soul is ready to die with sorrow." May he be close to all those who suffer. (Pause).   Let us pray to the Lord.

Christ was not ashamed to call us his brothers and sisters. May we treat everyone in a Christlike way. (Pause).   Let us pray to the Lord.

For local needs.

Let us pray:

Father, your Son came to bring us hope. He not only shows us the road to your kingdom but travels that road with us. Help us always to be aware of his saving presence with us. We ask this through the same Christ our Lord.

SIGN OF PEACE

Lord, of what use is it if we extend our hand to our neighbour while all the time we exclude him from our heart? It is like talking to a person at the doorstep on a cold day without inviting him to enter into the warmth of the house. Grant us a warm and accepting heart so that we may truly enjoy the peace and unity of your kingdom where you live for ever and ever.

COMMUNION REFLECTION

Christmas can easily develop into a time
when we give gifts and send cards to people;
when we trade annual 'hellos',
and then forget all about one another,
feeling that we have done our Christian duty.

True love, however, goes far beyond the giving of gifts.
It requires the giving of oneself.
People want us to share their lives —
their hopes, frustrations, joys, and sorrows.
It is not easy to be present like that.
It calls for time, humility, and love.

The first thing is to know their names,
to eat and drink with them,
to listen to their stories,
to tell one's own story,
to let them know with words, handshakes, hugs
that you do not simply like them,
but that you truly love them.

"The Word became flesh and came to live among us".
This is the greatest news of all —
that God is present with his people,
that he is truly present in the person of Jesus his Son,
who is Emmanuel, God with us.

EPIPHANY
Searching For The King

INTRODUCTION AND CONFITEOR:

The Magi were almost certainly not kings, and we are not sure if they were rich. But one thing is certain — they were wise. They recognised Christ as the Saviour of the world. Whereas his own people, the Jews, for the most part rejected him. What does Christ mean to me? To what extent is he the 'star' that I follow? (Pause).

Lord, you reveal to us the love of the Father. Lord, have mercy.

You are the Good Shepherd. Christ, have mercy.

You are the light of the world. Lord, have mercy.

HEADINGS FOR READINGS

First Reading (Isaiah 60:1-6). The exiles returned from Babylon to find their beloved Jerusalem in ruins. The prophet cheers them up with a vision of a restored city.

Second Reading (Ephesians 3:2-3, 5-6). Paul reveals the fact that God invites all, Jew and Gentile, to share on an equal footing the salvation won by Christ.

Gospel (Matt 2:1-12). This relates how three strangers came from a far country to pay homage to the Christ-child while the Jewish leaders rejected him.

HOMILY

There is a legend that says there were not three but four Magi. The name of the fourth was Artaban. He too saw the star and decided to follow it, taking with him a sapphire, a ruby, and a pearl as gifts for the new King. Time was short. His three friends, Caspar, Melchior and Balthasar were waiting for him at an agreed spot. However, on the way there Artaban came across a traveller lying by the roadside stricken down with fever. Though he knew that if he delayed to help the man he would miss his friends, nevertheless, he stopped and brought the man to an inn and had him taken care of.

When he finally got to the agreed meeting place he found that his friends had indeed departed without him. So now he was on his own. He needed a camel and supplies to get him across the desert. Reluctantly he had to sell the sapphire to buy them.

When at last he reached Bethlehem, once again he was too late. Joseph and Mary had taken the baby and fled into Egypt to escape from Herod's killers. Artaban was staying at a house where there was a year-old baby boy. The mother feared for the life of her child. One evening soldiers came to the door. Artaban went out to meet them. With the ruby he bribed the captain not to enter. The captain took the ruby and left the child untouched. The mother was over-joyed. Artaban, however, was sad because now he had only the pearl left as a gift for the King.

During the long years that followed he searched in many places for the King, but all in vain. He always seemed to be late. Some thirty years later he came to the holy city of Jerusalem. He was now old and weary and dispirited. A number of crucifixions were taking place the very day he arrived. Artaban heard to his great surprise that Jesus was among those who were being executed. He hurried towards the hill of execution. Perhaps with the pearl he could save his life.

However, as he was on his way to Calvary he met a girl who was fleeing from a band of soldiers. The girl hurriedly told him her story. Her father had incurred large debts. As a result she was being sold into slavery. Artaban hesitated, but only for a moment. He took out his pearl, gave it to the soldiers, and the girl was allowed to go free. But now he had to face his King empty-handed.

Just then the sky began to get dark. An earthquake shook the ground under his feet. Houses began to rock. Roof tiles began to fly. One of them hit Artaban on the head. Mortally wounded he struggled onwards. But he died before reaching the hill of execution. He never quite succeeded in catching up with his King.

Yet in a sense Artaban always had his King. Ever since he saw the star had he not carried him with him in his mind and heart? The King had inspired in him deeds of love and generosity, and had lit up all his journeys with meaning and hope. They say that the person who is genuinely searching for God has already found him. In that sense Artaban certainly had found his God.

We believe that we have found the King, that is, Christ. But what difference does that make to us: to the meaning we find in life, to the goals we pursue, to the way we treat our companions?

(Sit for a short while to reflect on this).

PRAYER OF THE FAITHFUL

Let us pray to our heavenly Father who sent us Christ his Son as the star that guides us to our eternal home. *R*. Lord, hear us in your love.

For all Christians: that they may follow Christ unwaveringly, listening to his voice, and responding to his gentle call. (Pause). We pray in faith.

For all the human family: that Christ may be the star that will guide us to the Father's house, our eternal home where all our longings will be fulfilled. (Pause). We pray in faith.

For those who are still searching: that God will open their eyes to see, their minds to understand, and their hearts to love. (Pause). We pray in faith.

God has revealed his glory and his love to us: may we meet him face to face when our pilgrimage is ended. (Pause). We pray in faith.

For local needs.

Let us pray:

God our Father, source of all light, today you revealed your Son as
the light of all peoples. May we walk in the path of goodness and
come to the light that shines for ever. We make our prayers through
Christ our Lord.

OUR FATHER

Until Jesus came, people could think of God as, at best, a stranger,
and at worst, an enemy. But Jesus showed that he is a kind and
loving Father. Let us pray to him with the words and in the spirit he
taught us:

COMMUNION REFLECTION

*It is not so much we who are searching for God. It is God who is
searching for us, as this lovely psalm says.*

O God, you search me and you know me.
You know my resing and my rising . . .
All my ways lie open to you . . .

O where can I go from your spirit,
or where can I flee from your face?
If I climb the heavens, you are there.
If I lie in the grave, you are there.

If I take the wings of the dawn
and dwell at the sea's furthest end,
even there your hand would lead me,
your right hand would hold me fast.

If I say: 'Let the darkness hide me,
and the light around me be night'.
Even darkness is not dark for you,
and the night is as clear as the day.

It was you who created my being,
knit me together in my mother's womb . . .
See that I follow not the wrong path,
and led me in the path of life eternal.

(Ps 138, Grail translation, published by Collins/Fontana).

BAPTISM OF CHRIST
Fundamental Choices

INTRODUCTION AND CONFITEOR:

We celebrate birthdays with a lot of fuss. We celebrate many other events. But never our baptisms. How strange that Christians pay so little attention to their real birthday. In today's liturgy we celebrate the baptism of Christ. In celebrating his baptism we celebrate our own baptism too and we renew its grace within us. (Pause).

At our baptism we became your sons and daughters: born to live free from sin and wrong-doing. Lord, have mercy.

At our baptism your favour rested on us: we were born to return your love.   Christ, have mercy.

At our baptism your Spirit descended upon us: we were born to follow his call to a life of holiness and goodness.   Lord, have mercy.

HEADINGS FOR READINGS

First Reading (Isaiah 42:1-4, 6-7). Here we are given a picture of a true servant of God. He is gentle and humble of heart, and totally dedicated to his mission, which is to bring about true justice.

Second Reading (Acts 10:34-38). Here we are given a description of how the first Christians saw Baptism. The baptized person was said to have been 'anointed with the Holy Spirit and with power'.

Gospel (Mark 1:7-11). This tells how Jesus was baptized by John the Baptist in the river Jordan, and the signs that accompanied that baptism.

HOMILY

Many people, perhaps all people, experience moments which prove to be decisive turning points in their lives. They reach a cross-roads where they are confronted with radically different choices. They are forced to make a fundamental decision after which their life will never be the same again. That decision will be decisive for the entire person — for his fate, his convictions, his lifestyle. He will leave his old world behind and enter a new world. While that decision can be a positive or negative one, we will concentrate largely on the positive.

This moment of decision, this cross-roads, can be thrust upon a person like a bolt out of the blue. This happened to Matt Talbot. His life was going down the drain. He was drinking himself to death. One day he was standing outside a pub, begging the price of a drink from people he considered his friends. But they passed him by. Suddenly something happened inside him. The scales fell from his eyes and he saw the light. He saw that he was destroying himself, and he made a decision — he would give up drink, and with the help of God try to become a saint. He never looked back.

Or this moment may come at the end of a long growth process. A person may have been moving in that direction for a number of years. Then suddenly something happens and they make the choice to follow the inner voice which for a long time has been calling them in for a particular direction. This happened to Mother Teresa. For a number of years she had been working for well-off girls in a convent school in Calcutta. But all that time she had been hearing another voice — an inner voice calling her to serve the poor she saw lying like discarded refuse on the streets of the city. One day she could bear it no longer. She left her convent and went to work among the poor. Her name has long since become a byword for devotion to the abandoned.

It is intersting to note that Christ too knew such moments in his life. Today's Gospel shows us one of the most decisive of these — his baptism by John in the Jordan. This proved to be a real cross-roads in his life.

For close on thirty years he had lived at Nazareth, subject to Mary and Joseph. During most of those years he had lived the comparatively quiet and secure life of a village carpenter. But all the while he had been hearing an inner voice calling him to something more important. All the time the Father's hand was laid upon him and he was being gently guided towards his real work. He was just waiting for a sign.

Suddenly the sign was there. His cousin John was baptizing people in preparation for the coming of someone he said was far greater than himself. Jesus made a fundamental decision. He left his old life and opted for a new one — that of teacher, preacher, and healer to his brothers and sisters.

He knew that the hand of the Father was in his choice. That is the meaning of the voice: "This is my beloved Son, in whom I am well pleased". He made a fundamental decision to serve his brothers and sisters, God's children — all of them, but especially the poor. From that moment on his life would never be the same. Nor would he be the same. Suddenly he blossomed (we are using very human terms). He found himself and his real vocation. His love for God and his fellowman, which had been simmering for years, now boiled over. All his hidden qualities of care and love, which had been growing quietly like wheat in a field, now matured and manifested themselves. There was no going back to the old life.

Most of us on looking back over our lives can see that we have known such moments, moments that have proved decisive turning points. Perhaps at this moment some of us are standing at the cross-roads trying to decide which road to take. It takes longer for some than for others to find which road to take. Van Gogh spent twenty seven years groping before finding his way and discovering that he was a painter.

It's hard to know what these cross-roads are for others, but with a little reflection we ought to be able to pinpoint them in our own lives. But how many take the time and trouble to reflect on themselves and their strivings? Without such reflection we are in danger of becoming like a man blindly hacking his way through a jungle or like a piece of driftwood being carried along in a fast-flowing current. There are all sorts of pressures being exerted on us. We should try to be aware of these and look at where they are taking us.

Suppose that, on reflecting on our lives, we find that we have made decisions that have radically changed our lives for the worse. That we have taken wrong roads or made wrong decisions that have impoverished us spiritually. Are these decisions reversible? Of course they are. Where there's a will there's a way.

Baptism then for Christ was a turning point. What about our baptism? It is like a seed that was planted in our young hearts. But given time and a little care it can and will bloom into Christlike living. One day it will demand of us fundamental choices. We will be faced with a choice either to go our own way, the way of self-promotion and worldly values, or the way of Christ — to follow the call to live up to our dignity as children of the same Father, who consider the welfare of others as important as their own. This may not come to us in one dramatic moment. Rather, it may come as a series of little choices. But what we have always to look at is the direction of our lives. Are we being true to the direction in which we were pointed at our baptism?

PRAYERS OF THE FAITHFUL

Let us pray that we may understand the meaning of our Baptism and live up to it with joy and generosity.   *R*. Lord, hear our prayer.

For all Christians: that they may strive to live up to their Baptism. (Pause).   Let us pray to the Lord.

For all our leaders who have to make such difficult and important choices: that they may see truly and act rightly. (Pause).   Let us pray to the Lord.

For those who are at the cross-roads, faced with difficult and important choices for their own lives. (Pause).   Let us pray to the Lord.

That we may persevere in the right choices we have made, and that we may have the courage and strength to correct the wrong ones. (Pause).   Let us pray to the Lord.

For local needs.

Let us pray:

Father, you sent your Son into the world to show us the way to you. Help us to follow the road he travelled with courage and steadfastness, so that one day we may be where he is. We make all our prayers to you through the same Christ our Lord.

SIGN OF PEACE

Lord, here in church it is easy to give a sing of peace, but in the real world it is often very difficult. We pause to see if maybe there is one person who at this moment is waiting for a sign of peace from us. (Short pause). Lord, help us to give that sign of peace so that we may enjoy the peace and unity of your kingdom where you live for ever and ever.

COMMUNION REFLECTION

Out of his experience of Stalin's labour camps Solzhenitsyn wrote:

"Looking back, I saw
that for my whole conscious life
I had neither understood myself or my strivings.

What had seemed for so long to be beneficial
now turned out in actuality to be fatal,
and I had been striving to go in the opposite direction
to that which was truly necessary for me.

But just as the waves of the sea
knock the inexperienced swimmer off his feet
and keep tossing him back onto the shore,
so also was I painfully tossed back on dry land
by the blows of misfortune.

And it was only because of this
that I was able to travel the path
which I had always really wanted to travel".*

Lord, we ask you to keep on calling us
along the right path, no matter what the cost,
for life is slipping away from us,
and we cannot afford to get it wrong.

*Alexander Solzhenitsyn, *The Gulag Archipelago, II*. Published by Collins/Harvill. Used with permission.

Lent

FIRST SUNDAY OF LENT

INTROCUCTION AND CONFITEOR

Serious athletes prepare diligently, professional actors rehearse painstakingly, good teachers do their homework meticulously. Before starting his mission Christ went into the desert to prepare himself for it; to purify his mind and cleanse his heart. Lent is a time when all serious followers of Christ try to renew their lives. In a sense we go into the desert with Christ. But if this renewal does not touch our hearts it is only like putting a new patch on an old garment.

(Pause to think about what this Lent will mean for me).

Lord, at the start of Lent you say to us: "Harden not your hearts, but listen to the voice of the Lord". Lord, have mercy.

You say to us: "Rend your hearts, not your garments, turn to the Lord your God again". Christ, have mercy.

You say to us: "Beware lest you be a people that honours me with your lips while your hearts are far from me". Lord, have mercy.

HEADINGS FOR READINGS

First Reading (Genesis 9:8-15). This reading tells how after the flood God made a new friendship-agreement (covenant) with Noah and his descendants.

Second Reading (1 Peter 3:18-22). St Peter says that the waters of the flood of Noah's time were a type of the waters of our Baptism by which we are saved.

Gospel (Mark 1:12-15). After being baptised by John the Baptist Jesus spent forty days in the desert. While there he was tempted by Satan.

HOMILY

There is no doubt about it but Lent touches something in us all. The sight of Jesus, the sinless one, fasting and praying in the desert in order to be able to say No to Satan and Yes to God, moves us. But it also disturbs us. It forces us to look at our lives and to seek to correct what needs to be corrected.

Some people *give up* something for Lent. Others *take up* something. This is good. But did you ever feel that when you came to the end of Lent you had achieved anything worthwhile, anything lasting? Rather have you not felt that nothing has really changed. You are still the same person, with the same defective attitudes, afflicted with the same temptations, burdened with the same weaknesses, and so on. Perhaps the reason is that our efforts to renew ourselves, while sincere and well-intentioned, do not go deep enough. We are like a doctor who continues to treat a serious internal illness as if it were no more than a skin rash. Thoreau said: "There are a thousand hacking at the branches of evil to every one who is working at the roots".

There is a story about a man who had an apple tree in his garden. He loved apples and believed that he could not live without them. However, while the tree never failed to supply him with apples, apples which tasted good, there was definitely something lacking in their quality. One essential thing was missing — there was no nourishment in them.

He consulted a friend who was an expert on apple trees. The expert took a look at the tree. He pointed out some obvious deficiencies in it. It needed to be sprayed, for its branches were encrusted with moss. The branches needed pruning. It could do with having the earth around it dug up and fertilised. Our friend listened well and acted on the expert's recommendations.

Yet the following autumn the apples, though slightly more plentiful, were no more nourishing. The quality remained unchanged. Our friend was very disappointed. Once more he consulted the expert: "What more can I do?" he moaned. "You're wasting your time", the expert answered. "What do you mean?" "Obviously the only thing to do is cut the tree down and plant a new one in its place". "But what will I do in the meantime for apples?" "You'll have to do without them, won't you?" came the answer.

The man was faced with a radical decision: to go on making do with the unsatisfactory apples, or to plant a new tree and wait for the new apples. The question was: was he prepared to go to such lengths in order to have new and wholesome apples to eat?

Christ confronted people with that kind of decision. He said it was no use trying to put a new patch on an old garment. If you want a new garment then the old one has to be cast aside. If you want new wine you have to get a new wineskin. The old wineskin simply will not do. It cannot hold the new wine.

Lent, for all our goodwill, can so easily be a time when we put a new patch on the old garment of self. Or a time when we attempt to put the new wine into an old wineskin. Or when we spray the old defective tree and prune it a little, but we lack the courage to cut it down and plant a new one. But this is no good. It doesn't work. At the end of the day we are back to square one. We need to penetrate through the surface of past and present behaviour and to understand the forces that are driving us, and do something about them.

To make something of our lives from a spiritual point of view demands effort and sacrifice, in cooperation of course with God's grace, without which we are powerless to change ourselves. Even a drunken man can draw a crooked line. But to draw a straight line calls for care and requires instruments. So it is with the line of life.

We miss a great opportunity if we let Lent go by without trying to renew ourselves. The example of Christ in the desert, struggling with the tempter, stirs something in us. He too was faced with radical decisions at the start of his mission, about the kind of kingdom he should set up, his motives in doing so, and the methods he would employ.

The prophet Joel said to the people: "Rend your hearts and not your garments". If Lent does not touch our hearts then it will have no lasting effect on us. Thomas Merton says: "Rending our garments lets in nothing but the cold. But rending our hearts lets out our sins and lets in the clean air of God's spring".

In its original meaning Lent was seen as the Church's "holy spring". During this spring the catechumens were prepared for their Baptism, for their rebirth in Christ. It was a time of penance and effort. But it was also a time of great joy. It was like springtime. As we progress towards Easter the sun gets brighter and warmer.

This rebirth in Christ (our Baptism) does not happen once and for all. It is something we grow into. There is no better time for growth than springtime. Lent is the springtime of the spirit.

PRAYER OF THE FAITHFUL

On this the first Sunday of Lent, we think of Christ God's Son fasting and praying in the desert before starting his mission on our behalf. We pray for the discipline which will enable us to follow his example so that we too may be victorious over the evil one. *R*. Create a new spirit within us, O Lord.

For all Christians: that they may not be content with a superficial renewal of their lives but that they may strive after conversion of heart this Lent. (Pause). Let us pray to the Lord.

For the leaders of our government: that they may have the courage and the wisdom to tackle the root causes of poverty and crime in our society. (Pause). Let us pray to the Lord.

From those who are struggling with temptations: that the grace of Christ may help them to be victorious. (Pause). Let us pray to the Lord.

For local needs.

Let us pray:

Heavenly Father, look upon us in our weaknesses and reach out to help us with your loving power. Guide the penance we have begun and help us to persevere with love and sincerity. We ask this through Christ our Lord.

OUR FATHER

One day the disciples came to Jesus and said: "Lord, teach us how to pray". And he said: "When you pray, pray like this: Our Father

COMMUNION REFLECTION

If we wish to change the outer aspects of our lives
we must first change the inner attitudes of our minds.
The miracle of inner change is possible.
History and literature are full of examples:
Paul on the road to Damascus,
Charles Dickens' miser Scrooge,
Matt Talbot the alcoholic.
Something happened inside each of these,
and they became new people.

Change requires the substituting
of new habits for old ones.
It calls for self-discipline.
You have to command yourself
and make yourself do what needs to be done.

The change of heart to which Lent calls us
can be accomplished most of all
through the power of prayer.

Lord, each spring you renew the face of the earth.
May you also renew each of us,
so that we may be able to celebrate Easter
in newness of mind and heart.

SECOND SUNDAY OF LENT
The Transfiguration: No Shortcut To Glory

INTRODUCTION AND CONFITEOR

In today's liturgy we celebrate the mystery of Christ's transfiguration on Mount Tabor. It was a wonderful experience for the three apostles who witnessed it, so much so that Peter cried out: "Lord, it is good for us to be here". It is surely good for us to be here this morning — to draw close to one another and to Christ. Here our lowly and often humdrum lives are filled with meaning, light, and hope. (Pause).

The things that demean us, that disfigure our lives, are our sins. Let us now confess them:

I confess to almighty God . . . etc.

HEADINGS FOR READINGS

First Reading (Genesis 22:1-2, 9-13, 15-18). This reading shows how complete was Abraham's obedience to God. He was even ready to sacrifice his son Isaac if God so wished it.

Second Reading (Romans 8:31-34). God the Father has shown his love for us by giving up his Son to death for our sake.

Gospel (Mark 9:2-10). Jesus is transfigured before the eyes of three of his apostles on Mount Tabor. This glimpse of his glory was meant to sustain their faith in him during his passion and death.

HOMILY

We live in the age of *the instant product*. Thus we have instant soup, instant tea, instant photos . . . pretty well instant anything. We know that the quality suffers but we are willing to sacrifice that for time saved. We have the four-minute car wash, and shoes repaired while we wait. We know that the job is only a half job, but we are ready to make do with it because we are in a hurry. We have instant relief from boredom through TV or the pub. We have instant relief from pain through drugs, though we know they may well cause a new and worse problem. There is instant beauty for girls through the use of cosmetics. Though once again they know that it is not the real thing, it is not even skin-deep. Today there is instant marriage — well, almost! Young people simply cannot wait. Thus they rush headlong into the most important decision of their lives.

The result of living in a world like this is that we want results and we want them fast. "Everything must be grabbed from life immediately and with both hands". (Solzhenitsyn). We grow impatient and frustrated if we have to wait. But how many accidents happen, how many mistakes are made because of hurry. Besides, we forget that certain things simply cannot be rushed. They need time and patience.

If you plant a seed you must wait for it to grow. To grow to maturity as human beings is the job of a lifetime. To build a good relationship with someone takes time. To get to know one's marriage partner takes time. To get to know and understand your children takes time. To overcome our sins and weaknesses takes time.

Our age might also be called the age of *the push button.* You buy the can of food that says 'warm up'. You know that pre-cooked food is not the same but you are willing to put up with it because it takes less effort to prepare it. You opt for the tea bag. It saves you the trouble of bothering with a teapot, though once again you know that the quality suffers greatly. Why walk to the shops or the church if you can take the car, even though your destination is just down the road? Why bother to visit that old or sick person if you can phone them? You know a phone call is a very poor substitute for a visit, but you settle for it because it saves you time and trouble. Why bother to go to the match and brave the crowds and the weather if you can watch it on TV in the comfort of your living room, though again you know it is not the same?

Thus often today all we have to do is press a button or turn a switch and things begin to happen without any further effort on our part. Many of today's labour-saving devices are good. They take some of the monotony and drudgery out of life and work. But there is a danger in living in the world of the push button.

The push button encourages the minimum effort, the least cost, the shortcut approach to everything. It can easily succeed in luring us into always seeking the easy option, even when there is no easy option — at least not if we want the genuine article.

For the truth is that the old problems remain with us in the age of the push button. There is the problem of bringing up one's children well. There is no magic switch for that. There is the problem of passing an exam or acquiring a skill. There is no button you can press that will make these happen painlessly. There is of course the age-old problem of getting on with one another. In fact, all the really worthwhile things in life require a lot of patient effort. There are no shortcuts. But then an easy victory gives little joy. And at the end of the day, we really possess as our own only those things for which we have laboured and paid the price.

What has all this got to do with the mystery we are celebrating in today's liturgy, the mystery of Christ's transfiguration? We can easily get the impression that everything was different for Christ. After all, he was God's Son. So, we presume that all he had to do was to go up that hill, turn on the magic, and in an instant, without pain or effort, he was transfigured with glory. But all the evidence of the Gospels goes against such an interpretation.

St Paul tells us that the glory which belonged to Christ as the Son of God he put aside when he assumed our condition. The glory that finally came to him was a glory he won by a life of obedience to his

Father, a life that ended in pain, shame, and death. It was his passion and death that transfigured him with glory.

There is no shortcut to glory, to that goal which God intends, not only for Jesus, but also for us. But when things are difficult, when the haul seems very long, we too need a vision, a glimpse of the glory to which we are called. I believe that if we reflect on our lives, and if we are trying to live lives of quality, these glimpses, these 'Tabors', will be granted to us. If we know the glory that awaits us, that every single one of our pains and struggles has a meaning and a value, that is a tremendoud help.

Let us then beware of going for the quick result, or taking the false shortcut. Let us not settle for the cheap imitation instead of the real thing. Christ took no shortcuts. Neither should we.

PRAYER OF THE FAITHFUL

Let us pray that in our efforts to follow Christ we may never drop out of the race or seek false shortcuts.   *R*. Lord, hear our prayer.

For all those who follow Christ: that they may never choose the cheap and passing things, and so let go of the things that last for ever. (Pause).   We pray to the Lord.

For our leaders: that they may never take the easy way and so abandon the right way. (Pause).   We pray to the Lord.

For those who are finding life difficult through hardship, illness, or death, that the Lord may change their sorrow into joy. (Pause).   We pray to the Lord.

That we may never forget that sweat is the price of all great things, and that without the cross there can be no crown. (Pause).   We pray to the Lord.

For local needs.

Let us pray:

Father, give us a love for what you command and a longing for what you promise, so that amid this world's changes our hearts may be set on the world of lasting joy. We ask this through Christ our Lord.

OUR FATHER

On Mount Tabor the Father said to Jesus: "This is my beloved Son. Listen to him". We are his beloved sons and daughters. Let us pray to him as Jesus taught us:

COMMUNION REFLECTION

Jesus loved hills and mountains.

We read in the gospels
how he often went into the hills to pray.
He preached his most famous sermon from a hilltop.
He was transfigured on Mount Tabor,
he died on Mount Calvary,
and he ascended from Mount Olivet.
He was, after a manner of speaking,
a mountain man.
Why was this?

Was it because heights cause the spirit to soar?
Down in the valley
we often can't see the wood for the trees.
We can't see the pattern of our lives.
But the hilltop restores our vision,
and we find our way again.
A problem which down below seems like an elephant,
from up here seems no bigger than an ant.

Lord, we all need the view from the hilltop.
It is indeed good for us.
For then, even though we may have to walk
through valleys of darkness,
we will fear no evil,
for we will know that you are with us there too,
to guide us, to give us comfort,
and to transfigure our lowly lives.

THIRD SUNDAY OF LENT
The New Decalogue

INTRODUCTION AND CONFITEOR

"My house is a house of prayer", so says the Lord. It is only we who can make of this church a true house of prayer. We come here each Sunday to pray, not just individually, but collectively as members of a family should. Let us reflect for a moment on the attitude we bring here. (Pause). God's commandments are for our good. Yet we fail to keep them. Let us ask his forgiveness.

Lord, your laws are to be trusted; they give wisdom to the simple. Lord, have mercy.

Your commandments are right; they gladden the heart and give light to the eyes. Christ, have mercy.

Your decrees are just and true; they are more precious than silver and gold. Lord, have mercy.

HEADINGS FOR READINGS

First Reading (Exodus 20:1-17). (Shorter form recommended). This reading deals with the ten commandments. They are a map of life for a people that has a special relationship with God.

Second Reading (1 Cor 1:22-25). To some the idea of a crucified Saviour makes no sense whatsoever. But to those who can grasp it, it is a sign of the wisdom of God.

Gospel (John 2:13-25). This deals with the incident in which Christ cleared the money changers and sellers of sacrificial animals out of the Temple.

HOMILY

Introduction

Many Catholics are quite happy to use the old yardstick when examining their lives, namely, the ten commandments God gave to Moses. But is this good enough? The answer is No. Christ gave us a new yardstick. If the old was good enough then there was no need of Christ. But the old was not good enough.

The person who is still content with the old yardstick is like a man who is still going around in candlelight even after the advent of electricity. Such a man is left behind. Something new and better has happened. So it is since the coming of Christ. But do we let the new light shine into our lives? Do we examine our lives, not against the teaching of Moses, but against the teaching of Christ? In what follows we take another look at the ten commandments in the light of Christ's teaching. Notice that the Commandments were spoken, not so much to individuals, as to a people. They were meant to be not just a code of conduct but a whole way of life for a people who had entered into a very special relationship with God. So too with the new commandments.

In presenting what follows two pulpits could be used. A lay reader could do one of the parts.

Old: Listen Israel! I am the Lord your God who brought you out of the land of Egypt, out of the house of slavery.

New: Listen followers of Christ, new people of God! I am the Lord your God who brought you out of the land of darkness, error, and evil, and led you into the land of light, truth, and goodness. You were once slaves to sin and wrong-doing. Now you are to live in the freedom of the children of God.

Old: I am the Lord your God, you shall not have strange gods before me.

New: I am the Lord your God. But I am not a strange and distant God. I am your friend, guide, and cousellor. If you let me have the first place in your lives you will never be disappointed. All idols will eventually betray you. Money is the most common of all idols. You cannot serve me and money.

Old: You shall not take the name of the Lord your God in vain.

New: From now on I want you to call me by a new name. Call me 'Father'. Let it be the first word on your lips in the morning and the làst at night. Pronounce it not in fear but in love. Invoke it in praise, in thanks, as well as in making your needs known to me. Your names are written on the palm of my hand.

Old: Remember to keep holy the Sabbath day.

New: Remember that all days belong to the Lord and are to be made holy by the lives you live. But let the first day of the week, Sunday, be a sign that God has the first place in your life. This is the day Christ your Brother broke the chains of death and rose in triumph from the grave. On this day you should assemble in prayer and worship, to remind yourselves that you are a people on pilgrimage to the Promised Land of the resurrection. The Sabbath is already a foretaste of the joy to come.

Old: Honour thy father and thy mother.

New: Love your father and mother, those precious souls through whom you were invited to the banquet of life. Take care of them when they get old and feeble and fall victims of loneliness. But do not love your own family to the exclusion of others. All those who listen to the Word of God and live it, are members of a wider family — the family of the followers of Jesus.

Old: Thou shalt not kill.

New: You must not hurt your brother in any way. Be compassionate as your Father is compassionate. Do not judge, and you will not be judged. Do not condemn, and you will not be condemned. Give a full measure, and you will receive a full measure from God in return. And do not limit your love to your friends only. Love your enemies too. Do good to those who hate you. Bless those who curse you. Pray for those who speak evil against you.

Old: Thou shalt not commit adultery.

New: It is not enough to be faithful to your marriage partner. You must love him or her as you would your other self. Mere physical fidelity is no longer enough. Aim at fidelity of the heart and soul. If there is no love then even with fidelity, marriage is like a fireplace without a fire.

Old: Thou shalt not steal.
New: There are various ways of stealing besides the obvious one. If you pile up and hoard goods that you do not need, while at the same time your brother is in need — that is a form of stealing. The goods of the earth were meant for all of God's children. Each is entitled to what he or she needs in order to be able to lead a life of dignity. So I say to you: give to everyone who asks. Share your bread with the hungry. Clothe the naked. Open your doors to the lonely and the homeless, and God's light will shine on you.

Old: Thou shalt not bear false witness against thy neighbour.
New: Be a light to your brother, not a source of darkness, causing him to stumble and fall. Let your words build him up, support him, comfort him, console him. Then you will be like manna in his desert. If you can find nothing good to say about him, then remain silent.

Old: Thou shalt not covet thy neighbour's wife.
New: You can commit adultery in thought and desire as well as in deed. Adultery is in the heart — in the desire to possess. Strive, therefore, to keep your heart pure. All a person's thoughts and words and deeds flow from what is in the heart, like water from a hidden spring. If a spring is clean then the water that flows from it will be good to drink. If your heart is unpolluted by evil, then you will be able to see God in all that is good, beautiful, and desirable in the world.

Old: Thou shalt not covet thy neighbour's goods.
New: I say to you: do not covet any goods at all. Do not lay up treasures here on earth. Be on your guard against greed of any kind. What good would it do you to gain the whole world if you lost your soul? Strive, rather, to make yourselves rich in the sight of God. If you covet anything that is your neighbour's, let it be his kindness of heart and gentleness of manner.

Conclusion:

Do not obey these commandments out of fear but out of love. And if you find ten of them too many to remember, you can reduce them to two: Love God with all your heart and all your soul; love your neighbour as yourself. However, it is not a question of whether or not you can recite the commandments by heart, but whether you live by them.

PRAYER OF THE FAITHFUL

Let us pray to our heavenly Father that we may obey his commandments out of love and not out of fear.   *R*. Lord, graciously hear us.

For the pope and the bishops: that they may teach God's people to walk in his commandments in a spirit of love and freedom. (Pause).   Lord, hear us.

For all governments: that they may respect the laws of God in all their decisions. (Pause).   Lord, hear us.

For those who are walking in the darkness of error and sin: that they may discover the light of Christ's truth and love. (Pause).   Lord, hear us.

That when we examine our lives we may use no yardstick other than the teachings of Christ our Good Shepherd. (Pause).   Lord, hear us.

For local needs.

Let us pray:

Father, you know our weakness. Give us a love for what you command. May we reach out with joy to grasp your hand and walk more readily in your ways. We ask this through Christ our Lord.

OUR FATHER

Jesus said: "My Father's house is a house of prayer". It is therefore with confidence that we pray to our Father as Jesus taught us.

SIGN OF PEACE

Lord Jesus Christ, you said to your disciples: 'Blessed are the peacemakers, they will be called the children of God'. We are better at making war than at making peace. Help us to put an end to war and strife so that all humankind may enjoy the peace and unity of your kingdom where you live for ever and ever.

COMMUNION REFLECTION

This is the house of our heavenly Father.
Here we draw close to him
in whom we live and move and have our being.
It is above all a house of prayer.

We can pray in many ways
and at many different levels.

We pray first of all by being here.
Then we pray with our lips.
But most of all we pray with our heart.
Unless our heart is behind what we say,
than our words are no better
than a gong booming or a cymbal clashing.

Here we also draw close to one another.
Therefore we pray together as members of a family should.
The quality of our prayer
depends on the bond that exists between us.

If we are united in heart and mind
our prayer will ascend to heaven
like fragrant incense.
But if we are not reconciled with one another
our prayer will be like the singing of a choir
in which some members are out of tune.

Lord Jesus, help us to make this house
a true house of prayer.

FOURTH SUNDAY OF LENT
Accepting or Rejecting the Light

INTRODUCTION AND CONFITEOR

Generally speaking people welcome the light. But St John says that when the light of Christ came into the world there were some who did not welcome it. Why not? Because their deeds were evil and they were afraid the light would expose them. Alas, we ourselves often dabble in darkness. We do not always welcome the light of Christ and live joyfully in it. (Pause).

Lord, you bring the light of truth into the world. Lord, have mercy.

You bring the light of goodness into the world. Christ, have mercy.

You bring the light of forgiveness into the world. Lord, have mercy.

HEADING FOR READINGS

First Reading (2 Chronicles 36:14-16, 19-23). It was because of their sins that God allowed his people to be exiled to Babylon. But his mercy is seen in their home-coming.

Second Reading (Ephesians 2:4-10). It is not through our own efforts that we are saved but through the love and mercy of God.

Gospel (John 3:14-21). John speaks about the Father's great love for us. This love is so great that he sent his Son into our world, not to condemn us, but to save us and to be the light of our lives.

HOMILY

Some years ago when I was doing a course in London I got involved in a small way in the work of the Simon Community. We would meet in the night shelter around eleven o'clock to prepare soup and sandwiches. On the stroke of twelve we would take these and go in search of poor unfortunates who for one reason or another did not want to come to the shelter. These spent their nights mostly in derelict buildings.

The most important aid we took with us was a torch. Without this we would be lost, for there was no light in the haunts and hovels of the winos and meths-drinkers. When you opened a door you never knew what to expect. Perhaps the room was empty, perhaps not. But there were two main reactions to the light when you shone it into a room where some of these people were gathered.

Some knew at once that we were from Simon, and they welcomed us as friends. To them the light meant hot soup, food, and friendly chat. It meant goodbye, at least for a while, to darkness and loneliness. Some of them would cling to us so that it was often difficult to get away from them.

But others did not want to know us. As soon as the light shone into the room where they were, they shouted at us to switch it off. Light was the last thing they wanted. They were fearful and suspicious, as they were on the run from the police. Generally they refused our offer of soup and food, and told us to clear off in no uncertain terms.

There were those then who welcomed us and our offer of help, and those who refused to have anything to do with us. You could tell at once which group you were dealing with by their reaction to the light. Though the last thing we intended was to judge them, yet in a sense the light did judge them. Confronted with the light they gave themselves away. The light revealed where they stood.

That's what St John in his Gospel said about the coming of Christ. Christ came into the world as an envoy of the Father's love and mercy. He did not come to judge people but to save them — "to seek out and to save the lost", as he put it himself. He came bearing a light — the light of truth, goodness, love . . . Love comes more naturally with two basic reactions to his light.

There were those who longed for his light and who welcomed it with generosity and enthusiasm. These were the people who believed in him and who came to him. The Gospel is full of examples. Surprisingly, it was people who were living in darkness who welcomed him most warmly. Think of the tax collectors and sinners with whom he shared himself.

But others rejected him. His light was a threat to them. It was not only really evil people who didn't want to know him, but people who considered themselves holy, such as the Pharisees. His light proved a threat to these. It showed up the darkness of their pretence, self-righteousness and pride.

As for us: in a very real way light and darkness (good and evil) are fighting for possession of our souls. We are divided within ourselves. There is darkness in each of us — the darkness of pride, selfishness, lust, anger . . . Evil exercises a hold over us. It has a certain fascination for us. We must not be afraid to confront the darkness within us. We must let the light of Christ shine into it and scatter it.

But there is goodness in us too. We are also attracted to the light — the light of truth, goodness, love . . . Love comes more naturally to us than hate. We should trust this goodness and try to follow it. The light of Christ will help us to do so.

But perhaps the greatest danger facing us is that we might settle for some in-between state — a kind of twilight existence. Twilight has a certain attractiveness about it. It is a world of blurred edges. It guarantees us anonymity, while at the same time providing us with enough light to see.

In practice this means that we would try to have the best of both worlds. We would have a foot in either camp. We never decisively declare for the light. We never totally opt for the dark, but we do dabble in it. What are we left with? A mediocre person. Neither a great saint nor a great sinner. A person incapable of either great cowardice or great courage. Those who are in darkness may one day see the light and welcome it. But the twilighters? Who can teach them the glory of the light?

At some stage in our following of Christ we must opt to follow his light fully and generously. If we do we will find that our lives will be lit up by his grace, peace, love, and freedom. As a friend of mine who made such an option said: "The darkness lifted from my life".

We follow Christ the Light of the world, who made a tremendous promise. He said: "Those who follow me will never walk in darkness but will always have the light of life".

PRAYER OF THE FAITHFUL

Let us pray to the Father that we may welcome the light his Son Jesus brought into our lives and our world.   *R*. Lord, hear us in your love.

For the followers of Jesus: that they may shun the darkness of sin, and walk in the light of truth and goodness. (Pause).   We pray in faith.

For all those holding public office: that the light of truth and justice may shine in their words and actions. (Pause).   We pray in faith.

That the light of Christ may shine gently on the sick, the lonely, and those who are going astray. (Pause).   We pray in faith.

That the words and deeds of Christ may be a lamp for our steps and a light for our path. (Pause).   We pray in faith.

That eternal light may shine on all our departed brothers and sisters who have left the shadows of this world behind them. (Pause)   We pray in faith.

Let us pray:

Father, you call us your children to walk in the light Christ your Son brought into the world. Free us from darkness and keep us in the radiance of truth. We ask this through the same Christ our Lord.

OUR FATHER

Let us pray to God our Father, in whom there is no shadow or trace of darkness, in the words Jesus taught us.

COMMUNION REFLECTION

In Christ there is no trace of darkness.
He is always in the light
And his light shows up the darkness in us.

His truth shows up our lies.
His integrity shows up our falseness.
His generosity shows up our selfishness.
His peace shows up our conflicts.
His openness to others shows how closed we are.
Therefore, we should not be surprised
if we sometimes feel uncomfortable in his presence.

We do not always follow his light.
We follow other lights —
mere flares in the night
or candles in the wind.
When these lights go out the darkness is greater
than if they had never shone.

Christ, radiant Light of the world,

Messenger of the Father's love.
guide our steps in the way of truth.
Lead us through the gloom of this world
until the Father's eternal light shines upon us.

FIFTH SUNDAY OF LENT
Losing and saving life

INTRODUCTION AND CONFITEOR

At this time of year new things are being born all around us in nature. This happens because the old things have died. Christ said that the old self, the false self that is in each of us, has to die if the new self, the true self made in God's image, is to be born. In other words we have to die to sin so as to be able to live the new life Christ won for us. Are we dying to sin — to selfishness pride, anger, envy . . .? (Pause). Let us ask the Lord's mercy and help.

In your kindness, God, you take pity on us. In your compassion you blot out all our offences.   Lord, have mercy.

You create new hearts for us, O God. You put a steadfast spirit within us.   Christ, have mercy.

Again and again you give us the joy of your help; with a spirit of fervour you sustain us.   Lord, have mercy.

HEADINGS FOR READINGS

First Reading (Jeremiah 31:31-34). The prophet Jeremiah tells a shattered people that God will not forsake them. The day is coming when he will make a new and more intimate convenant with his people.

Second Reading (Hebrews 5:7-9). This speaks of the pain and anguish Christ endured during his life and especially during his passion. In this way he not only gave us an example but became for us the source of eternal life.

Gospel (John 12:2)-33). Jesus talks about his imminent death — how he fears it, yet desires it, for the hour of his shame will also be the hour of his glory. He talks also about how his followers will have to die to themselves.

HOMILY

Long ago there lived a dinosaur by the name of Pondus. He was by far the largest animal in the forest. And how he loved to throw his weight about! When he moved through the forest all the other animals got out of his way in double quick time.

Because of his size everybody was forced to take notice of him. Pondus lapped up the attention, admiration, and acclaim that was heaped on him on account of his size and strength. But he was feared rather than loved by the other animals. He was respected, yes, but for all the wrong reasons.

Pondus was extremely self-centered. There was one great love in his life. He himself was the object of that love. He lived for himself and by himself. He never once put himself out for others except when there was some clear advantage for himself.

Yet, in spite of his size, Pondus suffered from feelings of insecurity, with the result that he was deeply unhappy. He was allergic to sacrifice of any kind. He feared the slightest pain, and absolutely dreaded death. So what was he to do? To shield himself against these evils he proceeded to put on layer upon layer of protective shell. The result was that he got even bigger, so big that eventually he had a problem merely in getting around.

Even so, the feelings of insecurity persisted. If anything they got worse. Though he looked down on and despised the other animals, he couldn't help noticing that even the smallest of them had something he didn't have, namely, a carefree and joyous attitude to life. The birds sang and twittered merrily from the branches of the trees, as if the hawk never existed. The multi-coloured butterflies flitted crazily about, inebriated with joy, as if they were immortal. But the animals that best typified this spirit were the squirrels. These seemed to do nothing all day long but chase one another up and down trees in frolics of fun.

They say that in times of crisis people reveal what is inside them, for crisis does not create character but merely reveals it. So it was with the animals. One day a fire broke out in the forest. The squirrels, thanks to their lofty perches, were the first to spot it. They quickly sounded the alarm. Panic spread through the forest. Pondus, naturally, immediately thought of his own safety, and headed for the watering hole, believing he would be safe there. The other animals followed the squirrels as they hopped from branch to branch and from tree to tree. And what a magnificent job the squirrels did! They stayed up there even though the air was full of smoke and sparks, so that they might be visible to all the little creatures on the ground. And so, after much hopping and puffing, the colony reached open space and were spared — all but the very lazy ones among them who were surprised by the fire and perished.

The following day the animals went back into the forest to inspect the damage. They found their home in ruins. Everything was black and devastated. Naturally they wondered what had happened to Pondus. When they came to the watering hole, to their great surprise, they found that he had drowned. In his efforts to put as great a distance as possible between him and the fire he had ventured too far into the hole and had sunk into its soft bottom. On seeing his enormous carcase stuck in the mud they realised how fortunate they were to be alive. And one and all turned to the squirrels whose unselfishness had saved them from so terrible a fate.

This story I think illustrates the paradoxical saying of Christ we find in today's Gospel: "He who saves his life will lose it, and he who loses his life will save it". Pondus, in trying to save his own life, had lost it. The squirrels, in trying to save the lives of others (and in that sense dying to themselves), had saved their own.

In the Gospel we see that the moment of crisis, his "hour" as he called it, had come for Christ. A terrible death was staring him in the face. Naturally he recoiled from it. He could have thought of himself and tried to save himself — and could have done so. But No. This was to be his moment of unselfish greatness and of glory. Now was the time for the Good Shepherd to prove his love for his sheep. In doing so he was also being true to the task his Father had given him. So he overcame his fear. In this he showed real courage. Real courage does not mean never being afraid. It means doing what has to be done in spite of being afraid.

The world would be a very bleak place indeed if there were no people who were prepared to die to personal gain, safety, security, advancement, for the sake of others. Yet often today the attitude is: what's in this for me? If the answer is 'nothing', then forget it! It is easy to make the wrong choice, for we are selfish by nature. Every instinct in us urges us to follow the path of personal fulfilment. But in doing so we can so easily be merely building up the false self. We are being puffed up by pride and end up with an inflated ego. And all the while our true self, made in God's image, is being smothered under layers of foolishness, absurd pretence, and childish pride and vanity.

The old self must die for the new and true self to be born. Only in this way can we produce the harvest of goodness Christ spoke about and which he exemplified in his own life — not by saving it for himself but by giving it to us.

PRAYER OF THE FAITHFUL

Let us pray that like the grain of wheat we may be prepared to die so that we may be reborn and produce the fruits that God expects from us.   R. Lord, hear our prayer.

For Christians: that they may realise that it is by giving that we receive; it is by forgiving that we are forgiven; it is by dying that we are born to eternal life. (Pause).   We pray to the Lord.

For all those who hold positions of responsibility: that they may set aside their personal aims and ambitions and work unselfishly for justice and peace. (Pause).   We pray to the Lord.

For those who live only for themselves and whose spirit is suffocating under layers of pretence and vanity. (Pause).   We pray to the Lord.

That we may never forget that each of us carries within us a divine spark which makes us capable of higher things such as acts of generosity and self-sacrifice. (Pause).   We pray to the Lord.

For local needs.

Let us pray:

Heavenly Father, your Son died that we might live; that we might live lives that are worthy of our great dignity as your sons and daughters. Grant that his death for us may not be in vain. We ask this through the same Christ our Lord.

SIGN OF PEACE

Lord Jesus Christ, you said to your disciples: 'Love your enemies, and pray for those who persecute you: in this way you will show that you are true children of your Father in heaven'. Help us to be merciful and forgiving towards those who make life difficult for us, so that we may enjoy the peace and unity of your kingdom where you live for ever and ever.

COMMUNION REFLECTION

Each of us is like a grain of wheat
planted by the heavenly Father.
That grain must die if it is to produce a harvest.
This dying to self is a gradual process
and happens in very ordinary ways.

Every act of kindness involves dying to meanness.
Every act of love involves dying to selfishness.
Every act of humility involves dying to pride.
Every act of courage involves dying to cowardice.
Every act of forgiveness involves dying to bitterness.

When a person's life is producing
a rich harvest of such acts,
it means that the grain of wheat

has well and truly died.
The false self is dying,
and the true self, made in God's image,
is slowly being born.

It is the true self alone
that will inherit eternal life.
for there is no place for what is false
in the presence of God.
It would melt like snow before the sun.

PASSION (PALM) SUNDAY
He took our sins upon himself.

INTRODUCTION AND CONFITEOR

This week, all over the world, Christians will be celebrating the great mystery of Christ's love for us. "Greater love no man has than he who lays down his life for his friends". (Jn 15:13). This is the week Christ lived out the truth of these words. He took on himself our sins and the sins of all the world. (Pause).

Lord, you have pierced for our faults and crushed for our sins. Lord, have mercy.

You, the innocent one, bore our sufferings and sorrows. Christ, have mercy.

You were led like a lamb to the slaughter, but through your wounds we are healed. Lord, have mercy.

HEADINGS FOR READINGS

Gospel for Procession (Mark 11:1-10 or John 12:12-16). This tells of the entry of Jesus into Jerusalem as the humble king and gentle Messiah. His followers greet him with joy.

First Reading (Isaiah 50:4-7). The prophet suffers in carrying out his mission, but he is convinced that God will eventually save him.

Second Reading (Philippians 2:6-11). Because Jesus took on himself our human condition and accepted death on a cross, the Father has made him Lord of heaven and earth.

Gospel (Mark 14:1-15:47). St Mark stresses the cruel trial and the shocking details of our Lord's suffering. But a sudden light appears

when a pagan soldier makes a profession of faith in the crucified Son
of God.

HOMILY

I remember once being in a so-called good neighbourhood in New
York City. It was early November and the leaves from the trees that
lined the streets lay scattered on the ground. One day a week the
garbage collectors made a special collection. The idea was that each
household would have their leaves gathered into plastic bags for
removal. That was the idea but it didn't quite work out like that.

A few people on the street didn't bother at all. They saw the leaves
fall and cover lawn, flowerbeds, and driveway. They saw them begin
to rot and must have noticed the stench they soon gave off. But they
continued to walk over them, not once but several times every day, as
if they never existed.

There was one man at the corner who got a blower and simply
blew the leaves off his lawn and driveway out onto the street. There
they soon became an unsightly mess and somewhat of a traffic
hazard. But he couldn't care less. Let someone else clean up the mess.

There was a kid who bagged them and then proceeded to dump
them over his nextdoor neighbour's fence. When challenged he
replied: "They belong to him. We don't have any trees of our own".
That was true, but what he forgot was that in summer he was often
glad to sit in the shade provided by those trees in his neighbour's
garden.

Most people took care of their own leaves. Outstanding among
these was an old lady who went out each morning with a brush and a
pan. She wouldn't tolerate even one leaf on her lawn. But at the same
time she wouldn't dream of taking a leaf off her neighbour's lawn.
That was his territory and his responsibility.

Finally there was one truly remarkable man. I had to see him for
myself, to see if perhaps he had secret wings. But of course he looked
just like everybody else. In fact he looked rather sickly, which was
not surprising, as he had only recently come out of hospital where he
had undergone surgery for cancer. What made this man stand out
like a pine among shrubs was the fact that he not only collected up
the leaves off his lawn but collected leaves off the street also. And he
did so quietly and without complaining.

Now if we take the leaves as a symbol of sin, then these people in
their various attitudes to the leaves can remind us of the characters
we meet in the Passion Story, a story which is re-enacted for us in the
liturgy of this week.

Firstly you had those who left their leaves to rot and foul the air
with their stench. These are the people for whom there is no such

thing as sin or wrong-doing. Herod was one of these. When Christ was brought to him he just made fun of him.

Next there was the man who blew his leaves out onto the street. He stands for those who hump their sins and the consequences of their sins onto other people. Let others take the rap for them. These remind us of Barabbas who, though he was a murderer, got off scot-free.

There was the kid who was dumping the leaves over his neighbour's fence. He stands for those who blame others for their own sins. These remind us of Pilate who wanted to wash his hands of the whole thing. The soldiers and the crowd would fit into this category too. The former would not doubt say that they were merely obeying orders. The latter would protest that they did not really know what was happening.

Then came those who cleaned up their own leaves. These stand for the people who accept responsibility for their own sins. They remind us of Peter, who when he realised that he had denied his Master, went out and wept bitterly.

Lastly there was the man who not only collected up his own leaves but collected up leaves off the street as well. He reminds us of those rare people who not only accept responsibility for their own sins but who feel responsible also for the sins of their neighbours and indeed of the whole world. They remind us of Christ. Christ died for the sins of humankind. But what makes Christ unique is the fact that he alone is sinless. He is the innocent Lamb who bears the sins of the world, yours and mine and everybody's, on his back.

This Holy Week gives us an opportunity to look at their own lives. It is not a week to hide behind other people. First of all we must make sure to accept responsibility for our own sins. To stop trying to blame circumstances or other people. If we acknowledge our sins we have nothing to fear, for Christ came to take them away. Then we can try to feel at least some responsibility for the sins of our neighbours and of the world in general. No man is an island — he is a part of the continent.

But what shines out from this dark week is the bright light of Christ's love for us. I was truly amazed when I heard about the man who not only collected his own leaves but those off the street as well. Should we not be much more amazed at the story of Christ, who took our sins upon himself because of his love for us. Let the Passion Story inspire us to try in our own small way to imitate Christ. It may be difficult, but it is not impossible. I saw it happen with my own eyes.

PRAYER OF THE FAITHFUL

God the Father did not even spare his own Son but gave him up to death on our behalf. Let us then with confidence place our requests before him. *R.* Lord, hear us in your love.

For the Christian community, the flock for which Christ died: that Christ the Good Shepherd may heal in it the wounds of sin and division. (Pause).   We pray in faith.

For all world leaders: that Christ may help them in the exercise of their grave responsibilities so that the world .may find the way to justice and peace. (Pause).   We pray in faith.

For those who have lost their faith in God and in man: that Christ the Good Shepherd may seek them out and lead them to his fold. (Pause).   We pray in faith.

That the power of Christ's death and resurrection may help us to abandon the ways of darkness and walk in the bright light he brought into our world. (Pause).   We pray in faith.

For local needs.

Let us pray:

Heavenly Father, during this holy week we see your love for us displayed in the sufferings and death of your Son. Help us to believe in your love and try to return it. We ask this through Christ our Lord.

OUR FATHER

    Jesus taught us to pray during life and at the moment of death. He taught us how to speak to God our Father. Let us now pray to our Father as Jesus taught us:

SIGN OF PEACE

    Lord Jesus Christ, on this day we recall how you wept over Jerusalem and said: "If only you knew the way that leads to peace". Well might you weep over our modern world on seeing our many wars and countless killings. Take pity on us and help us find the way to peace, so that all humankind may enjoy the peace and unity of your kingdom where you live for ever and ever.

COMMUNION REFLECTION

    This prayer was found in a German concentration camp at the end of the last war. It was written on a scrap pf paper. We know the terrible things that happened in the camps. Yet this prayer speaks, not of revenge, but of forgiveness.

Lord,
remember not only people of good will
but also those if ill will.
Do not remember only the sufferings

that have been inflicted on us,
but remember too the fruit we have bought
as a result of this suffering:

the comradeship and loyalty,
the humility and courage,
the generosity and greatness of heart
that has grown out of it.
And when they come to judgement,
let all the fruits we have borne
be their forgiveness.

Father, forgive them,
for they know not what they do.

Eastertide

INTRODUCTION AND CONFITEOR

For Christians there is no day that compares with Easter Day. This is truly the 'Day of the Lord'. This is the day Christ, our Brother, was victorious over the powers of death. But it is meant to be our day too, for Christ wants to share with us the fruits of his victory. And which of us would not wish to share in so great a victory? (Pause). Let us ask the risen Christ to set us free from the chains of sin.

I confess . . . etc.

HEADINGS FOR READINGS

First Reading (Acts 10:34, 37-43). This is part of an early sermon of St Peter. He tells us how he was a witness to the life, death, and resurrection of Jesus. The risen Jesus is the Saviour of all those who believe in him, as well as the Judge of the living and the dead.

Second Reading (Colossians 3:1-4). Through our Baptism we already share in the risen life of Christ, though in a hidden and mysterious way.

Gospel (John 20:1-9). Early on Sunday morning some of the disciples discover that the tomb in which Jesus was buried is empty. Then the truth of what the Scriptures had foretold begins to dawn on them, namely, that Jesus would rise from the dead.

HOMILY

It is not easy even to imagine the joy the disciples experienced on Easter Day. The following story may help a little.

There was a Russian Cossack who had two sons in the first world war. Their names were Peter and Gregory. One day the father got a letter from the front. Being unable to read, he handed it to his daughter. It was from Gregory's commanding officer and began like this:

> "I regret to have to inform you that your son Gregory was killed in action on July 10th. Gregory was an excellent soldier and died the death of the brave. You have every reason to be proud of him . . . etc.

The effect of this news on the father was immediate and alarming. He seemed to wilt visibly. In a matter of days he aged, turning grey almost overnight. His memory began to fail and even his mind was affected. He went around under a terrible mental strain. He began to drink to excess.

He kept the letter under the icon in the kitchen. Each day he would take it down and ask his daughter to read it to him once more. But as soon as she began: "I regret to inform you that . . ." he would take it from her and put it away again. After the local priest had offered a Requiem Mass for his son he felt a little better, only a little.

Twelve days went by like this. On the thirteenth day a second letter arrived from the front. It contained a fantastic piece of good news. His son wasn't deat after all! He had been wounded and left for dead on the battlefield. Next morning he had come to and crawled four miles back to his own lines, dragging a wounded officer with him. He was to be raised to the rank of corporal, and had been awarded the Cross of St George in recognition of his bravery. Right now he was recovering from his wounds in hospital, and they could expect a visit from him in a month's time.

Once again the effect on the father was immediate, except this time it was for the better. He was a sight to see. He was scalded with joy. He grabbed the letter and went into the village with it. He stopped everyone he met, forcing all who could read to read it. "What do you think?" he would ask. "My son is alive! He's been awarded the St. George's Cross for bravery!" And he would be off to find someone else.

This should give us some idea of the joy the disciples experienced on Easter Sunday morning. The Cossack's son hadn't actually died. Jesus had died. They had witnessed his death with their own eyes. And now the tomb was empty and Jesus had been seen alive!

Naturally there was some confusion as the news spread. Nothing like this had ever happened before. At first they were puzzled. Some doubted. Some, like Thomas, simply refused to believe it. But slowly they took it in. Not, however, until each of them had experienced for himself an encounter with the risen Jesus. Then their joy bubbled over. Jesus their leader and friend had broken the chains of death through the power of the Father. Death, the last and greatest enemy. had been overcome.

The joy of the apostles is meant to be ours too. It does not immediately remove from us the fear of death, for like Jesus we have to go through it. But it was by going through it, by submitting himself to it, that Jesus overcame it. So it is for us who believe in him.

Without the message of Easter the story of Jesus would still be inspiring, but it would only be like a flare in the night. The darkness would still have had the last word. But with the resurrection we know that the darkness will not have the last word. As St John said: "Christ's was a light that shines in the dark, a light that darkness could never overpower".

Let us walk this day with joy in the bright light the risen Christ has brought into our world and into our lives.

PRAYER OF THE FAITHFUL

Let us pray to God our Father, who raised Jesus from the dead and who will raise us too, for a share in the joy and hope of this Easter Day. *R*. Lord, graciously hear us.

For all believers in Christ: that they may be messengers of joy and hope to a world that often seems to be filled with sadness and despair. (Pause). Lord, hear us.

For the world and all humankind: that all God's people scattered far and wide may experience the fruits of the victory Christ won over sin and death. (Pause). Lord, hear us.

For those who travel in darkness: those who have no faith and who have given up hope. (Pause). Lord, hear us.

That we may try to live like Jesus so that one day we may come to share fully in his Easter victory. (Pause). Lord, hear us.

For local needs.

Let us pray:

God, our Father, the power of this holy day drives away all evil, washes away all guilt, restores lost innocence, and brings joy to those who mourn. May we who celebrate the resurrection of your Son experience its power in our lives and in our world. We ask this through the same Christ our Lord.

OUR FATHER

This is the day the light of the Father's love shone on his Son, rescuing him from the powers of death. Let us pray to our Father as Jesus our crucified and risen Brother taught us:

SIGN OF PEACE

Lord Jesus Christ, on Easter evening, the doors being shut, you came and stood among your disciples and said: "Peace be with you". Then you showed them your wounded hands and feet, and they were filled with joy. Grant us the peace and joy of your kingdom where you live for ever and ever.

COMMUNION REFLECTION

This is a description of an Easter ceremony in Russia where it is highly dangerous to be a believer.

"Someone at the back of the church lit a candle,
a single point of light not able to pierce the darkness.
But there there was another, and another,
for each of the worshippers carried a candle.
Swiftly the flame was passed from one to another.
In less than a minute the church was a blaze of light —
no, not the impersonal glare of electricity—
it was a thousand individual flames united in a single faith.

Each candle lit up the face behind it.
That face bore the deep lines of suffering.
Yet it was illuminated,
and the suffering turned into joy,
because of the certain knowledge
that the Lord has risen.

These people do not debate the resurrection.
They have experienced it in their lives.
They have not persevered the faith in hostile surroundings;
it has preserved them.
Their joy is a glimpse throught the curtain
which divides us from heaven".*

Lord, may your Easter light shine on us this day,
and chase the shadows of the night of death away.

* From Michael Bordeaux, *Risen Indeed,* Darton, Longman and Todd. Used with permission.

SECOND SUNDAY OF EASTER
The Healing Power Of Touch

INTRODUCTION AND CONFITEOR

Faith is a delicate thing. It is exposed to the harsh winds of doubt, cynicism, and despair which frequently blow through the modern world. It is like a candle burning in an exposed place. Here on Sunday we ought to experience a great strengthening of our faith — our faith in each other, in ourselves, in life, in God, and especially in the presence of the risen Christ among us. (Pause).   Renewing our faith in God's love and mercy, let us confess our sins.

I confess . . . etc.

First Reading (Acts 4:32-35). This paints a glowing picture of the first Christian community. It is a community ideally faithful to the Gospel message.

Second Reading (1 John 5:1-6). The Christian is a child of God. He shows his love for God by keeping his commandments.

Gospel (John 20:19-31). By touching the wounds of the risen Jesus Thomas' doubt is turned into belief.

HOMILY

Touching plays a very important role in human life. Children get their first taste of life from the way they are touched. If they are handled gently, they begin to feel that they are worthwhile and that the world is a friendly place. But if they are handled roughly, they begin to feel bad about themselves and the world. When someone has won something we want to clap him on the back to show him we are happy for him. When someone has suffered a bereavement we clasp his hand to show solidarity with him in his sorrow. Whe we love someone we want to touch that person to let him know how we fell about him.

When we are feeling good we are quite happy to let others come near us and touch us. But when we are in pain, especially if this pain has been caused by others, the opposite happens. We want to cut ourselves off from others. We want to hide away and cover up our wound, while at the same time continuing to brood over it. Mentally we put up a sign: "Fragile: do not touch". We just want to be left alone. Our wound is hurting so bad that we have difficulty looking at it ourselves, Not to mind letting others touch it. Yet, while this is perfectly understandable, it is a mistake. Wounds are not things to be ashamed of. Anyway, how can healing happen if we will not allow our wounds to be seen and touched?

A priest was going from the United States to Latin America. He tells how on the plane he found himself sitting beside a woman from Peru. They got talking. The woman told him how she was returning home with her mother who had undergone three operations in the United States. "Is your mother feeling better now?" he asked. "Oh yes", the woman replied. "She is completely cured. When we get home the whole family will be waiting at the airport to welcome her back". Then the woman asked him why he was going south. He told her that he was a priest and that he was going there to do missionary work. On hearing that he was a priest her face changed dramatically.

She leaned over, grabbed him by the arm, and whispered in an agonised voice: "Oh Father, mother has cancer and there is no hope for her".

Why did she feel that she had to keep up the pretence that all was well? Why did she have to hide, not only the mortal physical wounds of her mother, but her own emotional wounds as well — the deep wounds of sorrow and anxiety? Surely they were not things to be ashamed of? Her own wounds were caused by love. These, like trophies, should be placed quietly on display. Only when she discovered that he was a priest, that is, someone from whom she might expect comfort, did she come out with the truth, allowing herself to touch and to be touched.

The disciple at the centre of today's Gospel (Doubting Thomas) was a deeply wounded man. He was wounded by grief, loneliness, unbelief, and despair. All this happened to him when Christ, his Master and Friend, was put to a cruel and unmerited eath. In his pain Thomas wanted to be alone, so he fled from the company of the other apostles.Thus he missed the first appearance of the risen Lord. But someone must have got through to him for he was there for the next appearance.

It is interesting to see how Christ dealt with him. The first thing he did was to show him his own wounds. Christ felt no need to hide these for they were the proof of his love for his disciples. They were the mortal wounds the Good Shepherd suffered in defending his flock from the wolf. Then he invited Thomas to touch those wounds. Thus it was by touching and being touched that he was healed of his unbelief as well as of his other wounds.

It is by showing our wounds, by touching and being touched, that we are healed. However, only children and the mentally handicapped are good at letting themselves be touched. Little children want one thing about all others — they want to be touched, hugged, stroked and caressed. Many of us adults have the same need but we no longer have the innocence and spontaneity to allow it to happen to us. Many people are starving for affection, tenderness, care, love, acceptance, forgiveness, and gentleness. But often they are afraid to let people come near them, perhaps because someone has let them down or hurt them. Or it may be that the people who are close to them are totally unaware of their needs. Or it may be that they are indeed aware of their needs but are simply incapable of responding to them.

The world today is full of Doubting Thomases. In fact a little of Thomas lurks in us all. Many today simply do not believe that Christ is risen and that he can be encountered. And they will not be converted and believe unless they can touch his wounds (those of love) and see the radiance of his face.

How can this happen? It can happen only if Christ is seen to be alive in us his followers. He must be seen to dwell in us and among us. For it is only in us, and through us, that others can see and touch him, and be touched by him and so healed of their unbelief.

Without the Church (that is, Christians), the risen Christ would remain invisible, untouchable, faceless. He lives in his Church. There he can be encountered, that is, he can be touched and he can touch us, and healing can take place.

PRAYER OF THE FAITHFUL

Let us pray to God our Father in the spirit of today's Gospel, so that his risen Son may touch our lives and heal in us the wounds of separation and of sin. *R*. Lord, hear our prayer.

For all who celebrate the Eucharist: that they may experience the presence of Christ among them as the apostles did on Easter Day. (Pause). We pray to the Lord.

For our leaders: that Christ may touch their minds and hearts, and so enable them to build a human society based on love, justice and peace. (Pause). We pray to the Lord.

For all those who are wounded emotionally or physically: that their wounds may be touched and healed by those who care for them. (Pause) We pray to the Lord.

For local needs.

Let us pray:

God our Father, you give strength to the weary, and new courage to those who have lost heart. Hear the prayers of all who call on you in any trouble, that they may have the joy of receiving your help in their need. We ask this through Christ our Lord.

OUR FATHER

Jesus said: "Not one sparrow falls to the ground without your heavenly Father knowing. So there is no need to be afraid of what might happen to you, for you are worth more than many sparrows". We pray to our Father now as Jesus taught us.

COMMUNION REFLECTION

Aristides, a non-Christian, when defending the Christians before the Emperor Hadrian made the following statement:

"Christians love one another.
They never fail to help widows.
They save orphans from those who would hurt them.

If a man has something,
he gives freely to the man who has nothing.

"If they see a stranger,
Christians take him into their homes
and treat him as a brother.
Not that they consider themselves brothers
in the usual sense,
but brothers instead through the Spirit, in God.

"And if they hear that one of them is in jail,
or persecuted for professing the name of their redeemer,
they all give him what he needs.
If it is possible, they bail him out.

"If one of them is poor
and there isn't enough food to go around,
they fast several days to give him the food he needs.
We are dealing with a new kind of person.
There is something divine in them".

THIRD SUNDAY OF EASTER
Rebirth of a Collapsed Dream

INTRODUCTION AND CONFITEOR

The crucifixion of Christ was a sin and a terrible crime. Today's liturgy doesn't deny this, yet it says that from it God drew a great good. Indeed, it even suggests that it was somehow necessary. Through it we have forgiveness for our sins. Our sins cost Christ his life. But he died only because he cared about us. (Pause).

You were sent to heal the contrite of heart. Lord, have mercy.

You came to call us sinners to repentance. Christ, have mercy.

You plead for us now at the right hand of the Father. Lord, have mercy.

HEADINGS FOR READINGS

First Reading (Acts 3:13-15, 17-19). Peter lays the blame for the death of Jesus fairly and squarely on the Jews. Nevertheless, he excuses them on the strength that they did not know who Jesus really was.

Second Reading (1 John 2:1-5). In spite of everything, Christians are still prone to sins. If we sin Christ will come to our aid if we have recourse to him.

Gospel (Luke 24:35-48). The risen Jesus appears to his apostles. As in all his appearances, words and gestures are needed to help them believe that he is real and not a ghost.

HOMILY

There was a train driver whose job it was to drive up and down the same line every day. In time the job became so routine that he was able to do it almost with his eyes closed. Hence he had lots of time to observe the passing scenery. There was this lovely little cottage which caught his imagination. It was set in a little distance from the track. Its white walls shone in the sun. In front of it grew the most gorgeous roses he had ever seen. There were geraniums on the window ledges. It was surrounded by shady trees and exotic shrubs. It was like something one imagines exists only in picture postcards. He fell in love with it. "What a lovely place to live!" he said to himself. "Maybe one day when I retire I will live in a cottage like this".

One afternoon as he was passing the cottage he saw a little girl playing on the front lawn. She waved to him as the train swept past. He hooted the horn in response. The same thing happened next afternoon. Thus began an innocent and beautiful friendship between him and the child. Every afternoon she was there and waved to him, and he hooted the horn in reply. Sometimes the little girl was joined by her mother, and they both waved to him. It made him very happy. It also made the monotonous journey seem short. He looked forward to seeing them. If for some reason neither of them appeared he was very disappointed. His heart would sink and the journey seemed interminable.

Years passed. The child grew up. Nevertheless, most days she or her mother still waved to him. The bond that had been forged over the years was still intact. Then he retired and went to live quite a distance away. But he could not get the cottage and his two waving friends out of his mind. So one day he decided to visit them.

When he got there things were very different from what he had imagined. The walls of the cottage were not nearly as white as he had thought. Cracks were clearly visible in the plaster. The roses were not as beautiful as they seemed. In fact they were quite ordinary. The garden had weeds growing through it. The trees and shrubs had a rather battered and windswept look about them.

But the biggest disappointment of all came when he met the woman and her daughter. They were polite to him when he told them who he was. They led him into a gloomy parlour. They chatted. But it was hard to keep the conversation going. They really had very little in common. Tea was duly brought in. But he felt out of place. He couldn't really explain why he had come, and they didn't seem to be all that anxious to know.

So as soon as he could politely do so he withdrew. As he left, he felt a terrible emptiness. His dream-world dissolved into thin air. The lovely castle that he had built up over the years now crumbled and slipped through his fingers like fine sand until there was nothing left. The bond that had existed between them, and which had given so much meaning to his life, was shattered — shattered beyond repair. Yet as he went away deep down he knew that the fault lay, not with them, but with himself.

We cannot but feel sorry for that train driver. Yet, was he not rather foolish to live in a dream-world rather than the real world? The dream-world was indeed beautiful, but it was only a figment of his imagination. Yet the real world could have been even more beautiful, precisely because it was real, if only he had reached out and grasped it. Its beauty lay in the bond that had grown up between him and his two friends. The fact that there were cracks and weeds in their world could have brought them closer instead of separating them for good. There is no defeat as final, no despair as total, as that of the man who pursues a mirage.

Many people nurture illusions and pursue them with all their hearts. The apostles did. For three years they had been pursuing an illusion — the illusion of a Messiah who could not suffer, much less die a humiliating death. So when Christ died the illusion was exposed and their world fell apart. Their reaction was to cut themselves off from the real world and live behind closed doors. This is not a good way to live.

It was only when Christ appeared to them and opened their minds to a new truth that hope returned and their collapsed dream was reborn. The new truth consisted in the fact that it was precisely through his suffering and shameful death that he had attained to his glory. He showed them his wounds. He forced them to look at them. It took some time for this to sink in, but when it did, they knew that even death had not succeeded in breaking the bond that had been forged between the Master and them over three years.

The resurrection is all-important. It is a pity, however, that we tend to see it only as something that belongs to another time and another place — Palestine of two thousand years ago. If the Easter proclamation is true, then we too can encounter the risen Christ. He will not insulate us from reality. He will not lift us out of the tears, the sweat, and the grime of our humanity, and take us into a dream-world. But he will be with us where we are, helping to give meaning and beauty to our lives, especially to the painful and dark parts.

For us then the resurrection will not be just something that happened to Christ a long time ago, or something we hope will happen to ourselves in the next life. It will be *a present reality*. It will be a country we have already entered and whose light and warmth we are already experiencing. The risen Christ will have entered our closed world too. He will have calmed our fears and agitation, and brought us his peace, hope and light.

PRAYER OF THE FAITHFUL

Christ is alive. Death has no more power over him. Let us renew our faith in the belief that he walks the road of life by our side. *R*. Stay with us, Lord.

For the leaders of the Christian community: that the risen Christ may sustain their faith, their courage, and their love. (Pause).   We pray.

For the leaders of our country: that the Lord will help them to fulfil their responsibilities worthily and well. (Pause).   We pray.

For the unemployed, and for all those who walk on the edge of despair: that they may find understanding and support. (Pause).   We pray.

That we may experience the presence of the risen Christ with us in all the realities of life, but especially in the painful and dark parts. (Pause).   We pray.

For local needs.

Let us pray:

Lord, don't walk ahead of us, we may not follow; don't walk behind us, we may not lead; just walk beside us and be our friend. We make all our prayers to the Father through you, Christ our Lord.

COMMUNION REFLECTION

The apostles talking to us about the Easter experience.

For three long and joyous years we followed him.
We followed his every move.
We drank in his every word.
We knew neither doubt nor hesitation.

We were like sunflowers.
During the day these keep turning their heads
so that they are always facing the sun.
But when the sun goes down
they close their petals and hang their heads.

That's how it was with us.
When the sun went down on the Master's life
we wilted.
Without him our days lacked all charm.
Our lives became a desert.

But how can we tell you that joy that flooded our souls
when we discovered that the Lord had risen?
We cannot do so.
Only he, by his touch,
can do for you what he did for us,
the day he broke through the walls
behind which we were hiding,
bemoaning our shattered dreams.

Risen Lord, help us to believe
that you are always with us,
and that nothing in life or in death
can separate us from you.

FOURTH SUNDAY OF EASTER
The Good Shepherd Versus the Hireling

INTRODUCTION AND CONFITEOR

Of all the images we have of Christ, the one which is dearest to us and with which we are most familiar, is probably that of the Good Shepherd. This is not surprising. It is such a lovely image and is deeply rooted in Scripture. Besides, it is one of the images Christ used to describe himself.

How well do we trust Christ our Good Shepherd? (Pause).

You, O Lord, are our Shepherd, there is nothing we shall want. Lord, have mercy.

You guide us along the right path; you are true to your name. Christ, have mercy.

Even if we walk through the valley of darkness, we will fear no evil because you are with us. Lord, have mercy.

HEADINGS FOR READINGS

First Reading (Acts 4:8-12). Peter tells the people that the crippled man had been cured, through the power of the risen Jesus, and not through any power of Peter's. Jesus is the only one who can save us.

Second Reading (1 John 3:1-2). Through his love God has made us his children. In the next life he will do even greater things for us. Then we shall see him as he is.

Gospel (John 10:11-18). Jesus compares his role to that of a good shepherd who, unlike the hireling, is ready to give his life for his sheep.

HOMILY

Two bricklayers are at work on separate projects. Let's observe them for a moment.

Take the first. Though not as skilful as his comrade, he gets more work done. He picks up each brick as if it was as light as a feather. He places it on the wall, taps it with his trowel until it fits exactly where he wants it, then makes it secure. And straightaway he reaches for another.

Though his face often wears a serious look, you can detect a joy there too. If he stops, it is rarely to examine his blisters, real or imaginary, but rather to draw his breath or to wipe the sweat from his brow. He seems utterly oblivious to pain and hardship. You'll never hear a word of complaint from his lips.

His wife has to call him, not once but several times, to come to his meals. I imagine that those meals are often cold by the time he gets to them. Every time he gets off the scaffolding he steps back and takes a good look to see how things are shaping up.

Rain or shine he's there, as faithful as a sentinel. If he tires, you'd never notice. He's totally absorbed in what he's doing. Even should a low-flying jet pass directly overhead and shake the ground around him, you cannot be sure that he will look up. His enthusiasm never seems to wane. Each morning he attacks the job with the same alacrity as on the first morning. Each evening it is with reluctance that he puts his tools away. It's obvious that for him time flies.

Here then you have a truly dedicated man. He has made a total gift of himself to his work, and like a master craftsman he puts a part of his soul into it. He is a man with a vision. He knows what he's aiming at. He's like an arrow in full flight towards its target. What is he building? A new home for his family. That explains a lot.

Take the second man. He obviously knows his job. In fact, you can tell at once that he is a man of considerable skills. When he puts his mind to it he can make it all look so simple. But he's not killing himself. He's only half-hearted.

There is a weariness about his every movement. Every effort has to be dragged out. He lifts each brick as if it weighed a ton. You cannot detect as much as a shred of enthusiasm or joy in him. He stops frequently to examine his hands for blisters that are clearly imaginary. He takes advantage of the slight mist to down tools. The most insignificant event around him, such as the passing of a pedestrian, distracts him. At times you can see him gazing into space. At such moments his mind appears to be a million miles away. It's as if his real life was somewhere else, and his work was interfereing with it.

He anticipates his tea-breaks, and invariably prolongs them beyond the allotted time. In the morning it takes him ages to get warmed up. In the evening it takes him only seconds to finish off. In between he keeps glancing at his watch or looking at the sky to follow the path of the sun or its journey towards its setting. Time weighs like a load upon his shoulder.

Rarely will you see him stand back to see how things are shaping up. He doesn't seem to care how the job will turn out. Neither satisfaction nor disappointment show on his face. It's clear that for him it's only a job. He takes no pride in what he's doing. He gets no feeling that he is accomplishing anything worthwhile. His output is only a fraction of what it could be. Indeed, were it not for the fact that he has a foreman standing over him, he would do even less. The only thing that concerns him is the size of his pay packet at the end of the week. What's he building? The wall of a factory. That too should explain a lot.

Christ put a name on the first man. He likened him to a good shepherd, who owns the sheep and who knows and cares for every single one of them. He also put a name on the second man. He called him a hireling. The hireling does not own the sheep and is not concerned about them. His one concern is himself. He's only in it for the money. It is possible to go through the whole of one's life with the mentality of the hireling, and the damage done to one as a person hardly bears thinking about. "If the worker gets no more than the wages which his employer pays him he is being cheated and is cheating himself". (Thoreau).

Christ called himself the Good Shepherd. He cared about his disciples. He cared about people, especially the weak, the wounded and the lost. The evidence is there on every page of the Gospels. We should draw great comfort from this. This is the kind of Saviour we have. Someone who really cares about us, even to the point of giving his life for us.

The person who has experienced Christ's love will naturally want to return it. But we cannot return it to him personally. However, in our various jobs and professions, we can be people who care about those around us. It is a fact of life that most of us are hirelings, in the sense that we do not work for ourselves. But that does not mean that we have to have the mentality of the hireling. By all means we have a right to a decent wage. Apart from other considerations, it is good for

our dignity. But as Christians we ought to try to see our work
(whether we be bus drivers, or builders, or teachers or prison officers
. . .) as a service to our brothers and sisters.

If we do this, then we too in our own way are being good
shepherds. We have left the ranks of the hirelings. We are members of
a sacred band — those who perform needful but irksome drudgery in
a spirit of service. Honest, manly toil makes a man's bread taste
sweet.

The Christian who is not concerned about those around him is like
a lamp that doesn't give light.

PRAYER OF THE FAITHFUL

Christ is the Shepherd of his flock, the Church; he loves and cares
for his people. We turn to him in trust with our prayers.   *R.* Good
Shepherd, hear our prayer.

For all the leaders of the Church: that Christ may give them warm
and caring hearts so that they can be true shepherds to his flock.
(Pause).   Let us pray.

For those who make our laws and who apply them: that the Lord
may guide them with his wisdom and discernment. (Pause).   Let us
pray.

For the sick and the hungry, for prisoners and all those who are cut
off from society and who feel that nobody cares about them.
(Pause).   Let us pray.

That wherever we are and whatever we do, we may be people who
care about those around us and so imitate the love of the Good
Shepherd. (Pause).   Let us pray.

For local needs.

Let us pray:

Heavenly Father, help us to be people who follow Christ, the Good
Shepherd who first loved us, out of the joy that love gives to service.
Let us not seek any rewards, lest we become mere hirelings and
mercenaries. We ask this through the same Christ our Lord.

COMMUNION REFLECTION

Jesus said:
"I know my own and my own know me".

How can we be good shepherds
to those under us or those in our care,
if we don't try to get to know them?

Often, alas, we don't even know their names,
not to mind their life stories.
Can we blame them, then,
if they look upon us as mere hirelings
who are just interested in their salaries?

And how can we form a bond with them
If we keep our distance from them
thus preventing them from getting to know us?
Can we blame them
if they too keep their distance from us,
and if as a result they distrust or fear us?

Don't tell me that you care about me
if you haven't even bothered to get to know my name.
Don't tell me that you love me
if you have kept your distance from me.

Caring is risky.
Love is risky.
It means getting close to people,
as Christ, the Good Shepherd, got close to us.

FIFTH SUNDAY OF EASTER
The Vine and The Branches

INTRODUCTION AND CONFITEOR

There is no such thing as a solitary Christian. Every Christian is linked to Christ and to all other Christians by an invisible bond. This bond is very precious. It was Christ who wished it, and it was he who best described it. He said: "I am the vine, you are the branches".

Alas, we often live as if this bond never existed. We live for ourselves. We ignore and sometimes even hurt each other. (Pause).

Lord, you are the vine, we are the branches.   Lord, have mercy.

You make our lives fruitful.   Christ, have mercy.

You bind us to one another so that the world will know that we are your disciples.   Lord, have mercy.

HEADINGS FOR READINGS

First Reading (Acts 9:26-31). This tells how Barnabas introduced the converted Paul to the Christians living in Jerusalem. They accepted him but the Jews tried to kill him.

Second Reading (1 John 3:18-24). If we wish to live as God wants, we must keep his commandments, especially the commandment to love one another.

Gospel (John 15:1-8). Christ uses the image of a vine and its branches to illustrate the closeness of the ties that exist between him and his disciples.

HOMILY

In moments of danger people draw close to each other. Between people who up to that point may have felt indifferent towards each other, or who may have been divided off from each other by apathy, fear, or jealousy, a bond is suddenly created. All barriers fall down, and they are drawn to one another.

A French pilot tells how in the early days of World War II three small reconnaissance planes came down in a remote part of the Sahara desert, at exactly the spot where a year earlier two of their comrades had been murdered by the tribesmen of that region. As darkness set in the ten crewmen made ready for the night. They unloaded six large wooden boxes from the hold, emptied the merchandise out of them, and then arranged them in a circle. At the deep end of each case, as in a sentry box, they set a lighted candle. So in the very heart of the desert, feeling as alone on the earth as a group of aliens from outer space, they build a little community of men.

They sat huddled on this little island, lit by the flickering light of the candles, and waited for the rescuing dawn or for the hostile tribesmen. However, they lived to tell the tale. How did they spend that night? They told stories, joked, and sang songs. Outwardly they possessed practically nothing, yet in other ways they felt they had invisible riches to share with one another — the kind of things that make life worthwhile — comradeship, loyalty, and love. They felt that at last they had truly encountered one another.

Often it takes a common danger to bring people close to one another. People travel side by side for years, each locked up in his or her silent world, or exchanging words that carry no real significance, until danger strikes. Then they stand shoulder to shoulder. They discover that they belong to the same family. They wax and bloom in the recognition of each other as fellow human beings. They look at one another and smile.

If there is any happiness on this earth. it is not to be found in possessions or even in achievements, but in the warmth of human relationships. Often our individual interests and concerns imprison us within walls and cut us off from others. It is only the grasp of a warm and friendly hand that sets us free from this prison of our own making.

On Holy Thursday night Jesus ate a very special meal with his friends — the Passover meal. It was to be his last meal with them before he died. Death was in the air. Danger lurked in every corner. It was hard to tell who could be trusted. He felt this more keenly than they did. In his moment of darkness and danger Jesus felt closer than ever to his apostles. To show them how he felt about them he got down and washed their feet. Then he spoke to them with great sadness in his heart about how one of them would betray him, and how the rest would desert him.

The bond that Jesus felt that night with his friends had always been there on his part, though he felt it more keenly then. Even the knowledge of their weakness failed to weaken it. Not surprisingly, while at table, he spoke to them about love — about how they were to love one another the way he loved them. On the way to the garden he found the ideal symbol for the bond he felt with them. He stopped by a vine and said: "See this vine! See the bond that exists between the vine and its branches! That's how it is between me and you. I am the vine, you are the branches. If you remain attached to me you will produce much fruit. But if you cut yourselves off from me you will wither and die". Even as he spoke one of their number had already cut himself off, and would end his life with that most barren of all acts — suicide.

This is how Jesus felt. This is how he wanted it to be between him and his disciples. This is the way he wants it to be between him and us. He is the vine, we are the branches. We should not wait for danger to threaten before we experience and live this reality. It should be the climate in which we live.

There is much loneliness in the world. Psychiatrists in America say that an increasing number of their patients when asked who they love most or are closest to, reply: "My dog!" Isn't it very sad. Yet who can blame them if they look to books or to pets for the love that is absent from their lives?

Jesus wanted his disciples to realise that they were branches of the same vine, and that therefore they should form a community of love. There should be no such thing as a solitary Christian. The fruit which Christ desires from us is primarily that of unity among ourselves. But if an outsider were to look at our local community, would it be clear to him that we are branches of the same vine? That the good of one is the good of all, and the pain of one is the pain of all? I do not think so. Often we, Christ's followers, live and act as if we had nothing in common. If we are indifferent towards one another, or worse still, if we are divided, then will it not be clear to the world that we have cut ourselves off from the true Vine?

It is Christ himself who unites us. It is in him that we become one. His life is the 'sap' that gives life to us the branches. By this all men will know that we are living branches of the Vine — by the bond that exists between us.

Of course it's an ideal, but surely it's what the modern world is most in need of.

PRAYER OF THE FAITHFUL

Christ wanted his disciples to be united to him and to one another like a vine and its branches. Let us pray for this unity for ourselves and for all of God's people. *R*. Lord, hear us in your love.

For the Church: that its leaders may build it into a true community, producing the fruits of love and peace. (Pause). We pray in faith.

For our civil leaders: that they may promote the well-being of all members of society so that all, and not just a privileged few, may enjoy the fruits of freedom and justice. (Pause). We pray in faith.

For the lonely, for shut-ins, for outcasts — who belong to no community: that Christians may reach out to them. (Pause). We pray in faith.

That we may realise that we cannot be united with one another or do the works of love unless we are united with Christ, the true Vine. (Pause). We pray in faith.

For local needs.

Let us pray:

Father, may we the followers of your Son be fruitful witnesses to his compassion, love, and joy, not only to those nearest to us but to the world in which we live. We ask this through the same Christ our Lord.

OUR FATHER

The Father is the one who takes care of the vine. He prunes it so that it may produce more fruit. Let us pray to him as Jesus taught us:

SIGN OF PEACE

Lord Jesus Christ, the night before you died, in order to let the apostles know the bonds of love that existed between you and them, you said to them: 'I am the vine, you are the branches; separated from me you can do nothing; united with me you will bear much fruit'. Strengthen the bonds that unite us to you and to one another, so that we may enjoy the peace and unity of your kingdom where you live for ever and ever.

COMMUNION REFLECTION

We need Christ — that is no surprise.
But he also needs us.
Vine and branches need each other.
But our need of him is the greater.
"Cut off from me you can do nothing", he says.

It is not he who cuts himself off from us.
It is we who sometimes cut ourselves off from him
through indifference, selfishness, or pride.
And when we cut ourselves off from him,
we automatically cut ourselves off from one another.
Is it any wonder then that our lives
are sometimes barren and lonely and empty?

Thank you, Lord, for forming such a bond with us.
Thank you too for the bond
that exists among us because of you.
Thanks to this bond we have invisible riches
to share with one another.

Grant that we may never be separated,
so that together we may produce in the world
the fruits of faith, hope, and love.

SIXTH SUNDAY OF EASTER
Love One Another

INTRODUCTION AND CONFITEOR

A lamp that gives no light is useless. A fruit tree that produces no fruit is worthless. A Christian who doesn't love his neighbour is in the same category. But it was God who first loved us. He wants us to repay his love by loving one another. We know we fail to love others as we should. Let us have the courage to look at our failures and to admit them. (Pause).

You bring us back even when we stray from your love.   Lord, have mercy.

You gave yourself up to death so that we might turn again to you and find our way to one another.   Christ, have mercy.

You are the hand you stretched out to sinners; you are the way that leads to peace. Lord, have mercy.

HEADINGS FOR READINGS

First Reading (Acts 10:25-26, 34-35, 44-48). This tells how Cornelius, a Roman Centurion, became the first pagan to receive the grace of Baptism. It shows that God is not selective in his love. His salvation is offered to all.

Second Reading (1 John 4:7-10). This contains what is probably the most important statement ever made about God, namely, that he is love.

Gospel (John 15:9-17). Jesus is talking to his friends the night before he died. He leaves them his supreme commandment: "Love one another, as I have loved you".

HOMILY

Every afternoon as they were coming home from school the children used to play in the Giant's garden. It was large and beautiful, with soft green grass and fragrant flowers. Twelve apple trees grew there, which in spring broke out in lovely blossoms, and in autumn were loaded down with large red apples.

The children were enjoying it greatly until the Giant returned home, having been away for seven years. When he saw them playing in the garden he was very angry. "Get out of here!" he cried. "My garden is my own. No one plays in it but me".

Now the children had nowhere to play. They tried using the road but it was full of sharp stones and dust. They used to wander round the high walls but were always afraid when they came to the big sign over the gate which said: TRESPASSERS WILL BE PROSECUTED. "How happy we were", they said sadly, "when we were in there".

Then spring came, and all over the land there were lovely blossoms and the birds sang happily. Only in the Giant's garden it was still winter. There no green leaf or blade of grass or flower appeared. There the birds refused to sing. The only ones pleased were the snow and frost. "Spring has forgotten this garden", they said, "so we will come here all the year round". The snow covered the grass with a great white cloak, and the frost painted all the trees silver. Then they invited the north wind to stay with them, and he was glad to come. And they invited the hail, and he too came. Every day for hours he rattled on the roof of the castle till he broke most of the slates.

"I cannot understand why the spring is so late in coming", said the Giant, as he sat by the window and looked out at his cold white garden. "I hope there will be a change in the weather". But the spring never came, nor the summer. The autumn gave fruit to every garden but none to his. It was always winter there, and the north wind, and the hail, and the frost and snow danced about among the trees.

One morning, however, the Giant awoke to find that the hail had stopped dancing, and the north wind had ceased blowing. A lovely perfume came to him. "I believe that spring has come at last", he said, and he jumped out of bed. He saw a wonderful sight. Through a little hole in the garden wall the children had crept in and they were sitting in the branches of the trees. In every tree there was a child. And the trees were so glad to have them back that they covered themselves in blossoms.

It was a lovely scene. Only in one corner was it still winter. A little boy stood there on his own. He was too small to climb up into the branches. He was crying bitterly and the tree was covered with frost and snow. The Giant took pity on him. "How selfish I have been!" he exclaimed. "Now I know why spring would not come to my garden. I will lift this little boy into the branches".

He crept out but as soon as the children saw him coming they fled in fear, and winter came back to the entire garden. Only the little boy did not run away for he didn't see the Giant coming. So the Giant took him gently by the hand and placed him up in the tree. At once the tree broke into blossoms and the birds came and sang in it. When the other children saw this they came running back, and with them spring returned to the garden.

"It is your garden now", said the Giant smiling broadly. With that he took an axe and knocked down the wall. When the people were going to the market they saw the Giant playing with their children in the most beautiful garden they had ever seen.

It is not difficult to see Oscar Wilde's beautiful story as a commentary on Christ's commandment to love. When we are selfish and refuse to love and share as Christ urged us, we build a wall around ourselves. We ourselves are the first to suffer. We condemn ourselves to a winter of loneliness, surliness, and bitterness. In this hard climate it is impossible to grow as people. Everything that is lovely within us, our God-given capacity to love and to care, is stifled or stunted. And of course others, especially those nearest to us, feel nothing but coldness coming from us, and not surprisingly, they are put off and avoid us.

But when we show love and care as Christ showed us and commanded us, then the wall falls down. We open ourselvs to others. And we ourselves are the first to benefit. We experience a springtime of friendship, joy, goodwill, and peace. In this favourable climate we grow and blossom as persons. And others are attracted to us and rejoice in the warmth that emanates from us.

To love another person calls for maturity. First we have to be able to see the need of the other person. Next we have to be able to forget ourselves and respond to that need. To love means to open oneself out to others. This makes us very vulnerable, because others will often take without a thought for giving back. This means that love is risky.

There are some people who, by their attitudes, bring winter around with them. Discontent, surliness, selfishness, and meanness of spirit follow them around. But then there are others who, by their attitudes, bring spring around with them. Peace, friendship, joy, and generosity of spirit follow them around. The first are the ones who haven't learnt to love. The second are the ones who have.

"Love one another", said Jesus, "as I have loved you". For those who obey this commandment the winter is over for good. "In the evening of our lives we shall be examined on love". (John of the Cross).

PRAYER OF THE FAITHFUL

Let us pray that spring may come to our hearts through the power of Christ's glorious resurrection, so that we may be able to live his great commandment of love.   *R*. Lord, hear us in your love.

For all Christians: that they may banish the winter of apathy and selfishness and show the kind of love for one another that followers of Christ should. (Pause).   Let us pray to the Lord.

For all those who have power and who hold positions of authority: that they may banish from their hearts all spiteful and rejecting attitudes, and work to ensure justice for all their brothers and sisters. (Pause).   Let us pray to the Lord.

For those who are unable to love, either because they have never known love or because they have been very badly hurt. (Pause).   Let us pray to the Lord.

That we may show love in little ways, especially towards those we rub shoulders with each day. (Pause).   Let us pray to the Lord.

For local needs.

Let us pray:

Heavenly Father, your Son commanded us to love one another, and he set us a marvellous example in his own life: he laid down his life for his friends; he prayed for those who put him to death. Help us your sons and daughters to follow his way of love. We ask this through the same Christ our Lord.

SIGN OF PEACE

Lord Jesus Christ, you said to your disciples: 'A new

commandment I give you: love one another, as I have loved you.
All men will know that you are disciples of mine if you love one another'.
Lord, touch our hearts, so that we may be people who are able to love,
and thus we will enjoy the peace and unity of your kingdom where you
live for ever and ever.

COMMUNION REFLECTION

A fifty year-old Greek was dying in a New York hospice.
He had a good life, so he said.
He would have it all over again.
He would gladly forgo money and health
and making it in America,
if only he could have the same wife,
the same family,
the same love again.
Love — that was what was important in life.
It was love which kept things together and made sense.

The day before he died
he sent for the members of his family, who were, he said,
quarrelsome and at odds with one another.
He told them solemnly
that they must learn to love one another,
they must try harder.
It was everything, everything.
They must believe this,
for it was the word of a dying man.

Christ spoke similar words to his friends
the night before he died.
He gave them a simple. clear message:
"Love one another, as I have loved you".
His words were meant for us too.

THE ASCENSION
Lift Up Your Hearts!

INTRODUCTION AND CONFITEOR

Today we celebrate the glorious Ascension of Christ, our Brother
and our Saviour, into heaven. It is not a day for sadness or narrowness. It is a day for joy and openness. It is a day for renewing our
hope in the goal towards which Christ leads us, namely, a share in his
own glory in the Father's kingdom.

But the things that drag us down and keep us down are our sins. Let us confess them humbly and trustingly.

I confess to almighty God . . . etc.

HEADINGS FOR READINGS

First Reading (Acts 1:1-11). This describes the ascension of Jesus into heaven, and his promise to send the Holy Spirit on his apostles.

Second Reading (Ephesians 1:17-23). Paul describes the meaning of the ascension, which is that God has raised Jesus above all earthly powers, and made him, not only head of the Church, but Lord of creation.

Gospel (Mark 16:15-20). Before ascending to his Father Christ instructs his apostles to preach the Gospel to the whole world.

HOMILY

The Pygmies of the Congo region in Africa live in very dense rain forests. They spend their entire lives surrounded by trees and all kinds of vegetation. This vegetation is so dense and difficult to keep in check that the largest open space a pygmy is likely to see is the 30 or 40 yards between him and the far side of a clearing or river.

Consequently, the Pygmies have no real concept of space or distance. They enjoy very little freedom of movement, their world is small and extremely enclosed. Their horizon is severely limited. In such a world even comparatively small objects can appear larger than life because of one's nearness to them.

Colin Turnbull, an anthropologist who has spent years studying the Pygmies of the Congo region, tells how once he took one of them, a man called Henge, out of the forest and up to the top of a high mountain overlooking Lake Edward. Henge couldn't get over what he saw.

The things that impressed him most of all were the wide open spaces that existed beyond the forest, the immensity of the sky, and the vastness of the horizon. He was greatly surprised at discovering that a world existed in which there were no trees and very little vegetation.

He was like a little child in his excitement. "Oh, look at the river!" he cried out. For the very first time he was able to see its path as it snaked its way through the forest on its long journey to the great ocean. But then he made the classical mistake when he said to his guide: "What are those insects down there on the plain?"

What a surprise he got when he was told that the 'insects' were in fact a herd of buffalo! He simply had no idea how small things get when viewed from a distance. He was so thrilled with the experience that he wanted to remain up there. But of course he had to go back down to his small, enclosed, narrow world. However, he never forgot his visit to the mountain top. It had a wonderful effect on him. It helped him to take a broader view of his world and his life, especially when things were getting him down and the world was closing in on him.

Above all he remembered the river. In the forest he was far too close to it to be able to see either where it came from or where it was going. But from the mountain top he had got a clear view of its winding path. He learned that it originated in great snowy peaks away to the north, and that it entered the ocean (something he had never seen and could scarcely imagine) some hundreds of miles to the south. He came to look on the river as a symbol of his life. He believed that though often his life appeared to be going nowhere, this was not so. Like the river, his life too had a goal, and that goal was what gave meaning and direction to his life.

Christ, our Brother and our Saviour, lived like we do in the 'rain forest' of this world. But, unlike us, he always seemed to have this perspective on his life. Thus, the night before he died, he said: "It was from the Father I came out when I entered this world; now I am on my way back to the Father". (John 16:28).

And yet, it is obvious that at times the forest closed in on him too, and there were moments when he found it hard to see his way or to find a meaning in his life and work. When the time came for him to leave this world, he took his apostles up to the top of Mount Olivet. There they caught a glimpse of the glory towards which he was going, a glory which he had promised would one day be theirs too if they remained faithful to what he had taught them. And of course they too wanted to remain up on that hill, so that a voice had to call them back to reality: "Men of Galilee. who do you stand here looking up into the heavens?" Even though they had to go back down into the real world, their lives would never be the same.

Often, as Thoreau said, "we live meanly, like ants, and our lives are frittered away by detail". We get caught up in trivialities, bogged down in our everyday problems, so that we lose direction and are unable to see things in perspective. It is then we need to recall the vision our faith gives us of the goal and meaning of our lives.

We live in expectation of that goal. We live in the hope that the words of Jesus will come true for us, when he said: "Where I am, you too shall be". Surely this vision, this promise, and this hope cannot fail to inspire us and to ligut up our lives?

PRAYER OF THE FAITHFUL

Today the Church invites us to lift up our minds and hearts to contemplate Christ our Brother ascending to the right hand of the

Father. Let us pray for the grace to be able to rise above the things
that keep us bogged down, closed in, and enslaved. *B*. Lift us up
where we belong.

For all who follow Jesus: that they may rise above the sins that
enslave them. (Pause).   Let us pray to the Lord.

For the human family: that people may rise above their prejudices and
see the world as their common home and all people as their brothers and
sisters. (Pause).   Let us pray to the Lord.

For those who cannot see beyond the narrow horizons of this
materialistic world: that they may hear the voice of Christ calling
them to eternal life and an everlasting kingdom. (Pause).   Let us
pray to the Lord.

That we may rise above the problems and worries that get us down,
and above the grudges, jealousies and meanness of spirit which
prevent us from loving each other. (Pause).   Let us pray to the
Lord.

For local needs.

Let us pray:

Lord, you are now exalted at the right hand of the Father. Help us to
follow the path you traced out for us, so that we too may one day be
where you now are, living and reigning with the Father and the Holy
Spirit, one God for ever and ever.

OUR FATHER

    Jesus now sits at the right hand of the Father where he intercedes
for us. Let us pray to the Father in the words he taught us, knowing
that he prays with us:

COMMUNION REFLECTION

This is the day of the Lord's ascension.
This is the day of his triumphant
return to his Father.

It is no day for narrowness or sadness.
It is a day for openness and joy.
Therefore, lift up your hearts.
Raise up your minds.
Let your spirits soar and be free.
For death the leveller
has been put out of business.

We know nothing of the mystery of the beyond.
We have no maps of the other side.
All we have is his word.
His word assures us of its existence.

He has gone before us.
For the time being a 'cloud'
hides him from our view.
But he has told us that where he now is
we shall one day be.

On the strength of that word
let us go forward in joyful hope.

SEVENTH SUNDAY OF EASTER
Praying For The Spirit

INTRODUCTION AND CONFITEOR

We, the disciples of Jesus, are gathered here this morning in his name. We are doing what he asked his apostles to do: to wait in prayer for the coming of the Holy Spirit.

Without the Spirit the apostles were like a sail boat without the wind. If they needed the Holy Spirit, how much more do we need him? We who are weak and cowardly, and who find it so hard to disentangle ourselves from sin and to follow Christ without counting the cost. (Pause).

You create a pure heart for us, O Lord, You put a steadfast spirit within us. Lord, have mercy.

You do not cast us away from your presence, nor deprive us of your Holy Spirit. Christ, have mercy.

You give us again the joy of your help; with a spirit of fervour you sustain us. Lord, have mercy.

HEADINGS FOR READINGS

First Reading (Acts 1:15-17, 20-26). The defection of Judas left a gap which had to be filled. This reading tells us how Matthias was chosen to fill that gap.

Second Reading (1 John 4:11-16). Since God has loved us, we too must love one another.

Gospel (John 17:11-19). The disciples are being sent into the world to carry on the work of Jesus. Jesus prays to his Father for them and for us.

HOMILY

The scene in today's Gospel is the Last Supper. Jesus is about to leave his apostles. He is concerned about what will happen to them when he is gone. He gives expression to this concern by praying to his heavenly Father for them. In praying for them it is nice to know that he also prayed for us. In this prayer we are given a precious insight into the mind and heart of Jesus. When he prayed for his apostles, what kind of things did he pray for?

He prayed that they would remain *faithful:* "Keep those whom you have given me true to your name".

He prayed for *unity among them:* "May they be one, as you and I are one".

He prayed that they might be *preserved in the truth:* "May they be consecrated in the truth".

And he prayed that they might be *victorious over evil:* "I do not ask you to remove them from the world, but to protect them from the evil one".

So he prayed for: faithfulness, unity, truth, and victory over evil.

The latter may come as somewhat of a surprise: "I pray, not that they may be spared trials and tribulations, but that they may be victorious in all their trials and difficulties". Jesus foresaw that life would not be easy for his apostles. Many times, in fact, he forwarned them that the opposite would be nearer the truth. He told them that they would even be hated by some people, just as he was hated by some people. But what is interesting to note is that Jesus did not pray that they might be spared trials and sufferings, but that they might remain faithful in spite of them. He did not offer a release from problems but the strength to cope with them. We could learn from this. Often we think that God has abandoned us when we run into troubles.

There is an ancient story about a young woman who lost her only son. She was heart-broken and didn't know what to do. She felt that life wasn't worth living. God obviously didn't like her and had abandoned her. As a last resort she went to see a holy man who lived in a cave up in the mountains. There she poured out her sad tale, blaming God for her pain and grief. The holy man listened patiently, then said: "It is wrong to blame your misfortune on God. God did not take your son from you, rather he is the one who will help you to cope with your great loss".

What did he suggest? He suggested that she go down into the town and countryside and bring back a mustard seed from the house that had never been visited by sorrow or death. She set off at once in search of the magical mustard seed. First she knocked at the door of a rich family. "I am looking for a home that has never known sorrow," she said. But they answered: "You've come to the wrong place". With that they told her about a recent tragedy that had befallen them. On hearing their story she said to herself: "Who can help these unfortunate people if not me?" And she stayed and helped to comfort them.

Later she set out once more in quest of a house that had never known sorrow. But wherever she turned, whether to the homes of the wealthy or of the poor, she was confronted with tale after tale of sorrow and tragedy. And in every case she tarried to bring what comfort she could. Unknownst to herself, she became so involved in trying to minister to the needs of others in their grief that she completely forgot her own.

And when at last she returned to the holy man he asked her: "And did you find the mustard seek?" "No," she replied, "but I found something infinitely better. I found a means of coping with my own sorrow. I have found that God was with me in my sorrow, and I have been able to help others find him also".

It is wrong to blame our troubles on God. We are well able to manufacture them for ourselves. But God is the one to whom we turn in our troubles, for comfort, strength, patience and hope, and he will not disappoint us. We do not have to beg him or to bribe him. All we have to do is admit that we can't manage on our own.

This attitude and approach is illustrated very beautifully in the famous psalm: The Lord is my Shepherd. One verse of it goes like this: "Even if I should walk in the valley of darkness, no evil would I fear, for you are there with your crook and your staff; with these you give me comfort". Notice that it doesn't say that the person who puts his trust in God will be spared the "dark valley", but that even in the middle of it, he will not fear because God will help him make his way through it.

This is how Jesus prayed. This is how we should pray. Besides, without pain no real growth or Christian maturity is possible. We pray then, not to be spared trials, but rather that with God's help we will be able to cope with the trials life sends us. God did not send us Auschqitz. We created that little gem for ourselves. It would be blasphemy to blame it on God. But it was God who helped people walk into the gas chambers with the Lord's Prayer or the *Shema Yisrael* on their lips.

PRAYER OF THE FAITHFUL

Jesus promised to send the Holy Spirit to his disciples. Let us pray

for the coming of the Spirit and for those things that Jesus prayed
for.   *R*. Come, Holy Spirit.

For the Church: that it may be a sign of unity and an instrument of
peace in the world. (Pause).   Let us pray.

For all our leaders: that they may be true to their word and faithful to
their obligations. (Pause).   Let us pray.

For those Christians who have strayed from the path of Christ's truth
and who are living in the darkness of prejudice and bigotry.
(Pause).   Let us pray.

For those who are struggling against evil or against pain and despair.
(Pause).   Let us pray.

For local needs.

Let us pray:

Heavenly Father, in your goodness and love for us, give us the Spirit
who alone can teach us to think and to do what is right, so that we,
who without you cannot exist, may live in loving obedience to your
will. We ask this through Christ our Lord.

OUR FATHER

Jesus prayed to his heavenly Father: "Father, I have made your
name known to them, and I have loved them as much as you have
loved me". Let us then pray to the same Father in confidence, with
the words Jesus taught us:

SIGN OF PEACE

Lord Jesus Christ, during the last supper, you prayed for your
apostles in these words: 'Father, may they be one as we are one'.
Heal the divisions among us; make us one in mind and heart, so that
we may enjoy the peace and unity of your kingdom where you live
for ever and ever.

COMMUNION REFLECTION

Choosing a replacement for Judas: Cf. first reading.

In choosing a replacement for Judas
the early Church realised they were picking
someone who would be a leader in the community.
What qualities did they look for?
Basically two.

First of all: faithfulness.

He would have to be someone who was there from the start.
that is, not some recent 'blow-in',
but someone who had already proved himself.
This was an exterior thing.
something therefore they could judge for themselves.

Secondly: integrity of heart.
This is an interior thing,
something therefore God alone can judge.
Hence the need for prayer.
Matthias was the man they chose.

Lord, you call each of us
to be a witness to your resurrection,
that is, to prove to the world by the way we live
that you are alive in us.
Send your Holy Spirit to dwell in us,
so that we may be like Matthias:
people of integrity of heart,
who follow you through thick and thin.

PENTECOST SUNDAY
Birthday of the Church

INTRODUCTION AND CONFITEOR

Pentecost saw the birth of a new community, the new People of God. Today then is the birthday of the Church. This is the day the apostles left the supper room, where they had been hiding for fear of the Jews, and went out fearlessly to preach the Gospel. They could not have done this without "power from on high", that is, the Holy Spirit.

We too need the Holy Spirit in order to live as Christians in the world of today. He comes to us, not just as individuals, but as members of a community. (Pause).

Lord, your Holy Spirit heals in us the wounds caused by sin and division.   Lord, have mercy.

Your Holy Spirit binds us together in ties of love.   Christ, have mercy.

Your Holy Spirit guides us into the fulness of the truth of the Gospel. Lord, have mercy.

HEADINGS FOR READINGS

First Reading (Acts 2:1-11). Here we have an account of the coming of the Holy Spirit on the apostles on Pentecost Sunday and the effects of that coming on them.

Second Reading (1 Cor 12:3-7, 12-13). People have different gifts, but it is the same Spirit who gives these various gifts for the building up of the Christian community, which is the Body of Christ.

Gospel (Jn 20:9-23). On Easter Sunday evening Jesus breathes the Holy Spirit upon his apostles, a Spirit of forgiveness and of peace.

HOMILY

Once upon a time a group of rich and powerful men came together. They conceived a very ambitious project — to build a tower that would reach from earth to heaven. They prepared well. Humanly speaking no stone was left unturned. They assembled learned architects, skilled masons, and an army of able-bodied labourers. They brought in a huge supply of the finest granite and cement in the whole land. The organisers were of one mind and spoke the same language. The plans were drawn up, a toast was drank, and the project got underway.

However, it was in trouble from the word go. A whole series of things began to go wrong. Straightaway the bosses aroused a lot of resentment because they showed not the slightest interest in the plight of the workers. It was clear that they were interested in one thing only — their own glory. The tower was to be a monument to them.

There was a lot of jealousy among the architects, each of whom was determined to leave his own mark on the tower. Some of the masons were downright lazy, but when the foreman tried to fire them the others threatened to go out in sympathy. There was a rash of strikes over worker demands for higher wages and better working conditions. There were numerous accidents and workers frequently were killed or injured.

Besides, the workers were constantly fighting among themselves. Bitter quarrels broke out over politics and nationalities. Jews and Arabs refused to work side by side. So too did Irishmen and Englishmen, Russians and Americans, and various other groups. On top of all this there were inevitable setbacks. A large section of a wall would collapse overnight. This was blamed on outside saboteurs. Materials were constantly disappearing, stolen by workers who were building little towers of their own on the quiet.

Costs mounted. The banks began to kick up. Sponsors grew harder to find. Misunderstandings multiplied. Mistrust was rampant. They no longer spoke the same language, literally or metaphorically.

Despair raised its ugly head. The result was that the tower, which began with such high hopes, was abandoned. In time even the part of it that had been completed fell into ruins. In a way it was not surprising, for it was built on very shaky foundations. It was built on the sands of pride and arrogance.

The tower is a symbol of man's attempts to create here on earth a paradise without any recourse to God. The effort is still going on. Modern man with his massive highways, supersonic planes, nuclear power stations, manned space flights is still in pursuit of an earthly paradise. Yet he still cannot live at peace with his fellow man. His very existence is now threatened by the 'tower' he has been building (think of the bomb). It's not that we are powerless if left to ourselves. Part of the reason for our failure is that we don't know the right goals.

Now there was another group of men who came together, very ordinary men who had little faith in their own abilities. They too were to build a tower to heaven, well maybe not so much a tower as a spiritual stairway. It was not they who conceived the idea, but their Master. Before his death he told them not to begin until he sent them 'power from on high'.

On Pentecost Day the Spirit descended on these men, the apostles, and they set forth to build a new community, the community of the new People of God. They spoke a new language. It was the language of love and cooperation, a language all men of goodwill understand. For love transcends speech. It shines in the face and is felt in the clasp of a hand. Hence it can unite people of different languages.

Today is the birthday of this great happening. It is the birthday of the Church, the community of the followers of Jesus. On this day the infant Church left the cradle and took its first steps, not falteringly but boldly, thanks to the power of the Holy Spirit. God knows down the ages it has seen its fair share of troubles, problems, and setbacks. But it is still being built.

It is assembled here in front of our eyes this morning, and it is something marvellous. Not that it is made up of saints. It is rather like the field Jesus spoke about — a mixture of wheat and weeds. When we assemble here we do so, not as rivals, but as friends. Here those factors that have traditionally divided people, such as class, colour, age, wealth, and so on, count for nothing. There is a great levelling off, a great coming together. We realise that before God we are all equal.

And all this is only as it should be and as Christ intended. The things that divide us are trivial, the things that we have in common are tremendous. Deep down we all have the same needs — to be valued and to belong. On week days we worship our own gods so to speak. On this day we worship the one true God. During the week we

pursue our separate goals. On Sunday we become one family —
members of God's people on pilgrimage to the Kingdom of Heaven.

This is the wonderful thing that began on Pentecost Sunday. We
not only find shelter in this tower, we are also builders of it. Let us
pray for an outpouring of the Holy Spirit on this community founded
by Christ.

PRAYER OF THE FAITHFUL

On this day we celebrate how at Pentecost Christ sent the Holy
Spirit on the first community of his followers. Let us pray that he may
send the same Spirit on us, on our Church, and on our world.
R. Spirit of the living God, fall afresh on us.

For the Christian community: that it may enjoy the gifts of unity,
love, and peace. (Pause).   Let us pray.

For the world community: that it may enjoy the gifts of freedom,
justice, and peace. (Pause).   Let us pray.

For those who have never belonged to the flock of Christ, and for
those who have cut themselves off from it: that they may hear the
gentle voice of Christ. (Pause).   Let us pray.

That as with the apostles on Pentecost Day, the Holy Spirit may help
us to profess our faith openly by word and deed in the world.
(Pause).   Let us pray.

For local needs.

Let us pray:

God, our Father, may your Holy Spirit come to us to enlighten our
minds, purify our hearts, and strengthen our wills so that we, the
community of believers in Jesus, may give effective witness to him in
the world. We ask this through the same Christ our Lord.

OUR FATHER

United by the Holy Spirit, let us pray to our Father in the words
Jesus left us:

COMMUNION REFLECTION

Thoughts from St Paul

My friends,
let me remind you that you were called to freedom,
the freedom of the children of God.

If you want to be free

you must let yourselves be guided,
not by the spirit of self-indulgence,
but by the Spirit of God.

Look at the legacy self-indulgence produces:
bad temper, fighting, jealousy,
cruelty, meanness, revenge,
fornication, idolatry, and drunkenness.
These are ugly things.
They make life miserable,
and make slaves of us.
Besides, those who live like this
do not belong to the kingdom of God.

But consider the legacy the Spirit brings:
love, joy, peace,
patience, kindness, goodness,
faithfulness, gentleness and self-control.
These are beautiful things.
They make life worthwhile,
and those who live like this are free agents.
They already belong to the kingdom of God,
but what they enjoy now is only a foretaste
of the joys to come.

Spirit of the living God,
fall afresh on us.

TRINITY SUNDAY
The Mystery Of God

INTRODUCTION AND CONFITEOR

Today the Church invites us to celebrate the mystery of the Trinity. We begin and end each Eucharist with the names of the Father, the Son, and the Spirit on our lips.

This is a mystery to be celebrated with childlike love and trust. God is a Father to us; he is a Brother to us; he is a Consoler and and Guide to us. This should be the atmosphere in which we live, move, and have our being. Yet we often relegate the Father, the Son, and the Spirit to the margins of our lives. (Pause).

I confess to almighty God . . . etc.

HEADINGS FOR READINGS

First Reading (Deuteronomy 4:32-34, 39-40). Moses reminds the people that the great God of heaven and earth has entered into a close and loving relationship with them. They should respond by doing his will.

Second Reading (Romans 8:14-17). By the fact that the Holy Spirit dwells within us, we become children of the Father, and co-heirs with Christ his Son.

Gospel(Matthew 28:16-20). This contains the final instructions of Jesus to his apostles.

HOMILY

Once there was a king who at the end of his life was beset by melancholy. He reflected sadly: "During my life I have seen and experienced everything any mortal man can experience or grasp with his senses. But there is still one thing that I haven't seen. I haven't seen God. How I would dearly love to see him before I die".

He called in his wise men and priests, and consulted them. All he wished, he stated, was to get one glimpse of God, then he would die happy. He offered them all kinds of rewards if they could make his dream a reality, but they were unable to do so. He was very disappointed and gave in to an even deeper melancholy.

But then a kind shepherd who lived out in the hills heard of the king's plight. He approached the king and said: "Allow me to help your Majesty". The king was overjoyed and followed the shepherd into the hills, rough places he had never before set foot in. When he saw how poorly and simply the shepherd lived he had pity for him. As he went along he rubbed his eyes in anticipation of what he hoped to see. But the shepherd turned to him and said: "Your Majesty, if you want to see God, it's your heart that you have to purify, not your eyes". The king was puzzled by this remark but made no reply.

At last the shepherd stopped on a hilltop and, pointing towards the sun, said: "Look up!" The king raised his eyes and tried to look directly at the sun, but the glare dazzled him. "Do you want to blind me?" he said. And the shepherd answered: "But, my king, this is only part of creation, only a small reflection of the glory of God, a tiny spark of his radiant light. How then can you expect to look at God with your weak and imperfect eyes? You must begin to search for him with eyes other than your physical ones".

The king liked the idea and said: "I thank you for having opened the eyes of my mind. Now if you would be good enough to answer another question: where does God live? I've searched for him everywhere, especially in shrines and temples, but I haven't found him". The shepherd pointed once more to the sky. Above them wild birds were flying about. "Look at these birds", he said. "See how they live surrounded by the air. In the same way we live surrounded by God. So stop searching. Just be still. Open your eyes and look. Open your ears and listen. You can't miss him".

The king stopped and looked and listened. As he did so a peaceful expression came over his sad face. Then the shepherd added: "There is something else your Majesty ought to know". "What's that?" asked the king eagerly. Then the shepherd led him to a well. He stood there looking into its calm deep water in silence. Growing impatient, the king asked: "Who lives down there?" "God does", the shepherd answered. "Can I see him?". "Sure. Just take a look".

The king then gazed intently down into the well. But all he saw in its still water was his own reflection. Then he raised his head and said: "But all I see is me".

"Now your Majesty knows where God lives. He lives in you. If a person has the misfortune of losing God in his heart. he may search the entire universe for him but he will not find him.. The world, O king, is God's temple, but the human heart is his sanctuary".

Suddenly the king realised that this simple shepherd possessed the only riches worth owning, and that it was he, for all his wealth, that was the poorer of the two. He thanked the shepherd and returned to his palace. No one knew if he had seen God, but they could tell that something had happened to his heart. This was evident from the kindly way he dealt with even the least of his servants, people who prior to this he hardly knew existed.

God is everywhere. He is all around us. This is something we were taught since our earliest years. But until we look into the inner well and discover him there, he will always be remote from us, and perhaps even appear unfriendly and uncaring. When we have experienced the God within us, we need no longer feel alone anywhere in the world. And we can look with love and excitement at creation as the work of an Artist who is a friend of ours.

Christ it was who told us to look at the birds of the air and the flowers of the field, and to see in them reflections of the Father's love and care. But it was also he who told us to look inwards to where the image of God is stamped on our souls.

He made himself our Brother. He proved his love for us by living and dying for us. Then he left us his own Spirit to guide us into all truth. This is a mystery — one God in three persons, a God who is within us and yet beyond us. But above all it is a mystery of love. This is the mystery we celebrate today. It is not something we can ever hope to understand fully. It is something to believe and to live with love.

PRAYER OF THE FAITHFUL

Under the guidance of the Holy Spirit, let us pray to the Father as

Jesus urged us.   *R*. Father, hear us in your love.

For all Christians: that they may be tireless in their efforts at spreading the good news of God's love and care for all the human family. (Pause). ·Let us pray.

For all rulers: that God may grant them wisdom and love in their efforts at making the world a better place to live in for every one. (Pause).   Let us.pray.

For those who have no belief in God: that they may discover traces of his love in their hearts and of his greatness in the world. (Pause).   Let us pray.

That we may always know the loving presence of God in our lives, especially in life's blackest moments; that we may also find him and love him in other people. (Pause).   Let us pray.

For local needs.

Let us pray:

Father, source of all life, be our guide when we stray, our strength when we are weak, and our comforter when we grow discouraged. We ask this through your Son, our Lord Jesus Christ, who lives and reigns with you and the Holy Spirit, one God for ever and ever.

OUR FATHER

Until Jesus came people had thought of God only as, at best, a stranger and at worst, an enemy. But Jesus showed that he is a kind and loving Father. He taught us to pray to him in these words

COMMUNION REFLECTION

Isaac Newton was one of the greatest mathematicians and scientists who ever lived. Yet towards the end of his life he said of his achievements:

"I do not know what I appear to the world,
but to myself I appear to have been
like a little boy playing on the seashore
and diverting myself in now and then
finding a smoother pebble
or a prettier shell than ordinary,
whilst the great ocean of truth
lay all undiscovered before me".

Even when we think we understand the mystery of God,
we are still only beginning.
We are still only children playing on the shore.

But Jesus has lifted the veil on the mystery,
and so we know that our games have a meaning
and that our lives have a goal.

We have a Father who cares about us;
we have a Brother who died for us;
and we have a Spirit, a Comforter,
who will guide us to the shores of eternity.

Glory be to the Father,
and to the Son,
and to the Holy Spirit.

Sundays of the Year

SECOND SUNDAY OF THE YEAR
Encountering The Lord

INTRODUCTION AND CONFITEOR

"Speak, Lord, your servant is listening". We will hear these words in the first reading this morning. They remind us that we are here to listen to God. In the Gospel we will hear Jesus say to his first two disciples: "Come and see". They accepted his invitation and had a wonderful encounter with him after which their lives were never the same again. Here we too can encounter Christ, our Saviour. Let us reflect on this for a moment. (Pause).

Christ is the Lamb of God who takes away our sins. Let us confess them with humility and confidence.

I confess to almighty God . . . etc.

HEADINGS FOR READINGS

First Reading (1 Samuel 3:3-10, 19). This reading gives the story of the call of the boy Samuel to be a prophet. We see the persistence of that call and Samuel's ready response to it.

Second Reading (1 Cor 6:13-15, 17-20). Paul tells us that our bodies are temples of the Holy Spirit, and we must use them, not for sin, but for the glory of God.

Gospel (John 1:35-42). This gives John's account of the call of Andrew and his brother, Peter, and of their first encounter with Jesus.

HOMILY

Great events often begin very simply. Take spring for instance. How we love to see it arrive! Yet it arrives so quietly. One day we notice that the snowdrops are back. Then we know that spring is coming around the corner.

Thus it was with the arrival of Jesus on the public scene. The meeting between him and his future apostles happened in a very simple way. For some time his cousin John the Baptist had been telling the people that the long-awaited Messiah was close at hand. One day he was standing on the bank of the Jordan with two of his disciples, John and Andrew. It was just another day. There were no signs to be seen in the sky, or voices to be heard from heaven.

Everything was normal. Then a man passed by. There was nothing extraordinary about him either, at least not from the outside, for he was dressed just like themselves. Nor was there anything special about his background. In fact, quite the contrary. He was but a carpenter from a remote little village.

Yet on seeing him John the Baptist got all excited and said: "There he is! He's the man I was telling you about, the man who is to come after me". John and Andrew decided to follow the stranger. After a while he stopped, turned around, and said to them: "What do you want?" And they answered: "We just want to know where you live". And they went with him. It was four o'clock in the afternoon and they spent the rest of the day with him. No one knows what they talked about. What questions they asked him and what answers he gave. But one thing is certain. John and Andrew were greatly impressed by him, in fact they were completely won over by him. How do we know? The very next day they rushed off to bring their friends and meet him.

This is how St John describes the first meeting between Jesus and the nucleus of the group that became known as the Twelve Apostles. It all happened so simply, you might even say casually. But this is often how true encounters happen. You get on a train and find yourself sitting opposite a total stranger. You both have a long journey ahead of you. You are shy. Besides, you don't know if the stranger wishes to be left alone. Nevertheless, you begin to exchange a few words. By the end of the journey you are firm friends. It is as if you had known that person all your life. It bears out the truth of the saying: a stranger is a friend I have not yet met. You exchange addresses. The person came into your life so gently, and apparently accidentally, but once in, that person may well be there for life. It happened to myself.

This then was how the first meeting between Jesus and some of his future apostles took place. It was not just a meeting. It was an encounter, and there is a world of difference between the two. After a meeting people can still be strangers and go their separate ways. At a meeting people share ideas. They open their minds to one another, but mostly talk about trivialities. But in an encounter they open their hearts to one another. They pour out their most precious depths and secrets. Little wonder that after encounter there is a bond between them, a bond they want to remain.

Have we truly encountered Christ? This might seem a strange question to ask. After all, haven't most of us known him since our earliest years? Don't we pray to him? Don't we receive him in Communion? Yes, but this does not mean that an encounter of minds and hearts is necessarily taking place. People can sit side by side on a bus or train, and even engage in superficial conversation, and still they may never really meet each other; they may never truly encounter one another. So it could be between us and Christ. Yet, not to have encountered Christ as a Friend, a Brother, and a Saviour, is not to have discovered what Christianity is about. Christianity means enjoying a relationship of love with Christ.

What I have frequently to ask myself then is: do I let my prayers, my Communions, and other religious practices, bring me into real contact with Christ my Saviour? Do these provide not only an opportunity for me to speak to Christ but for Christ to speak to me: "Speak, Lord, your servant is listening".

Christ is for ever passing by. He is always available to those who are sincerely looking for him. But he never barges into our lives. People who love do not act like that. He says to us what he said to John and Andrew: "Come and see". If we accept his invitation he will reveal to us the mysteries of the kingdom of God.

Many people in the world today allow Christ to pass them by. Some simply fail to recognise him and have no one to point him out to them. As a consequence their lives are empty and meaningless, and their deepest longings remain unfulfilled. There are others who do recognise him but who do not want to get involved with him in case following him might demand a change of lifestyle. These settle for a distracted and superficial life. Then there are those who have a passing or nodding acquaintance with him. They make no serious effort to follow him or to seek a close relationship with him. They confine him to the fringes of their lives. What a pity! If only they realised what they are missing.

Most of us can look back on some encounter with another person that greatly influenced our lives. Can we say that we have had such an encounter with Christ? How can we encounter him? By making time available so that we can meet him, especially in daily prayer. Having encountered him there, we will be more open to encounter him in our brothers and sisters.

Of course it is not a once-and-for-all encounter that we are talking about, but a continual and a growing one.

PRAYER OF THE FAITHFUL

Let us pray to Christ our Brother who joins us on the road of life at this time, in this place, and on this day.　*R*. Lord, graciously hear us.

For the Church: that it may help people to encounter Christ as the one who will answer all their longings. (Pause).　Lord, hear us.

For our civil leaders: that they may experience the presence of Christ with them in the midst of all their worldly concerns. (Pause).　Lord, hear us.

For those to whom Christ is only a name: that they may get to know and encounter him in us his followers. (Pause). Lord, hear us.

That we may deepen our own relationship with Christ through daily prayer and the living out of his commandment of love. (Pause). Lord, hear us.

For local needs.

Let us pray:

Lord, you are our companion on the road of life. Do not go ahead of us, we may not follow; do not follow us, we may not lead; just walk beside us and be our friend. We make all our prayers to the Father, though you, Christ our Lord.

OUR FATHER

One day the disciples came to Jesus and said: "Lord, teach us how to pray". And he said: "When you pray, pray like this: Our Father . . ."

COMMUNION REFLECTION

There is a world of difference between a meeting
and an encounter.
People can live in the same house,
sit at the same kitchen table,
kneel in the same church pew,
they can exchange many words,
they may even give each other signs of love
and apparent tenderness,
and yet they may never meet in the real sense,
they may never really encounter one another.

An encounter is a strange and wonderful thing.
In an encounter people open their hearts to one another.
They become fully present to one another.
As a result life flows from one to the other
and people are transformed.

When you have once seen the glow of happiness
on the face of a loved one,
you know that a person can have no higher vocation
than to awaken that light on the faces surrounding him.

May we never allow Christ to pass us by.
May we not confine him to the margins of our lives.
May we rather invite him into our lives.

May he become our Friend,
our Brother,
and our Companion
on the road to the Father's Kingdom.

THIRD SUNDAY OF THE YEAR
The Bringer of Good News

INTRODUCTION AND CONFITEOR

Every time we pick up a newspaper, or turn on the radio or TV, we are confronted with bad news, much of it of a very distressing nature. It leaves us numb and helpless. We are in real danger of being swamped by bad news.

Christ came with good news — the good news of the Father's love, acceptance, and forgiveness, which is offered free to all those who desire it and seek it. Let us open our minds and hearts to let it in. (Pause).

You raise the dead to live in the spirit.   Lord, have mercy.

You bring pardon and peace to the sinner.   Christ, have mercy.

You bring light to those who live in darkness and in the shadow of death.   Lord, have mercy.

HEADINGS FOR READINGS

First Reading (Jonah 3:1-5, 10). This relates how the preaching of the reluctant Jonah meets with an immediate response in the pagan city of Nineveh.

Second Reading (1 Cor 7:29-31). Paul asks for an attitude of detachment from the dear, familiar things which tend to absorb us completely.

Gospel (Mark 1:14-20). Jesus begins to preach and he calls his first disciples.

HOMILY

In the book, *The Fall,* Albert Camus tells the story of a successful Paris lawyer called Jean Baptiste Clamence. Jean Baptiste is above reproach in his professional life. Never once has he accepted a bribe, or stooped to any kind of shady deal. He takes up the cause of the widow, the poor, and the defenceless, and he does so free of charge. He practises small acts of kindness, such as helping a blind person across a street, at every opportunity. He is a model citizen — responsible, high-minded, virtuous and respectable. He is very popular and in great demand.

But all the while he had been neglecting the most important thing, the substance, namely, "What kind of man am I?" He has a great need to feel superior to others. He takes immense pleasure and satisfaction in his own excellence. He owes nothing to anybody, but many people are indebted to him. He looks upon himself as something of a moral superman. Though of modest origins, at times he feels like the son of a king. The road ahead of him glitters with the lights of further successes and fame. He does not practise any religion. Then one evening something happens which causes the music to stop and the lights to go out on his life.

It is late and he is returning home along the banks of the Seine. On the bridge he passes a figure leaning over the railing and staring into the river. It is a young woman and she is dressed in black. He walks by her. However, he has gone only some fifty yards when he hears the sound of a body striking the water. He stops but does not turn around. Then he hears a cry which is repeated several times. It appears to be going downstream. Then it ceases. A terrible silence follows. He wants to run but he cannot. He is trembling from cold and shock. A great weakness steals over him. Then he goes away slowly. He tells no one.

The incident has a terrible effect on him. Like a thunderbolt it shatters the illusions of his own virtue and goodness. Why had he not been able to go to the rescue of the drowning girl? Suddenly he begins to see himself as he really is — a phoney, a play-actor, a man bursting with vanity, full of pride, anger, lust, and shrewd selfishness. Everything he does has one aim — to build up the castle of his own supposed goodness and excellence. Unable to take what he discovers about himself, he closes his law-office, leaves Paris, and throws himself into a world of alcohol and debauchery.

He ends up frequenting a bar in the fog-shrouded waterfront of Amsterdam. There he tells his story to anyone who will give him an ear. But it is all hopeless, for in his world there is no such thing as redemption. So Jean Baptiste spends his time looking back on that fateful night wishing that the girl might throw herself in again so that he could have the opportunity of saving her and himself. But, "It's too late now. It will always be too late". And that is how the story ends.

This is a story without redemption. There is no good news in it. Only the bad news of man's sinfulness and capacity for self-deception. There is no forgiveness in it either, no possibility of recovery. What might have provided Jean Baptiste with a unique moment of enlightenment and opportunity for conversion, turns out to be the gateway to damnation.

Today, thanks to the media, we are in danger of being drowned in bad news. It is interesting then to notice how Jesus begins his ministry by announcing good news. "The kingdom of God is at hand. Repent and believe the *good news*".

What is this good news? Essentially it is that forgiveness is available. Recovery is possible. One can find one's true self, even after the most disastrous fall or series of falls. In fact, the suggestion is that in order to do so some sort of a 'fall' is required. We can come back to the Father's house, where not judgement but welcome awaits us. The Good Shepherd has arrived. His stated aim is "to seek out and to save the sheep that are lost".

So Jesus has good news for the Jean Baptiste's of this world — for those who are not afraid to look at their own sinfulness. It has been said that Christianity begins with a sense of sin — with the sudden realisation that the life we have been living will not do. But Christ's message is not good news for the self-sufficient, the self-righteous, for those Pharisees who in their own eyes "are not like the rest of men". The hardest people of all to convert are the pious and the good because they do not see any need of conversion. When you experience your own need you are open to the good news, much the same as a man who feels ill is open to seek help from a doctor.

Many of us will be able to identify to some degree with Camus' lawyer. No matter what we may appear to others to be, deep down we know that we are not the people we should be. We have all had our 'falls'. But we are still loved by God, and loved unconditionally. His love, his mercy, his forgiveness are available to us through Christ. All we have to do is recognise our need and seek his help with humility and sincerity.

If the house I am building with my life is a false one, or if I am building it on false foundations, then the sooner it falls down the better. Then with God's help I can start to build the real thing.

PRAYER OF THE FAITHFUL

Let us pray to God the Father, who sent his Son to us with the Good News of his love and forgiveness. R. Lord, hear our prayer.

1. For the Church: that it may work tirelessly to bring the Good News of Christ's salvation to all people, but especially to the poor. (Pause). Let us pray to the Lord.

2. For those who make and enforce our laws: ~~that they may be firm but at the same time kind and fair.~~ (Pause). Let us pray to the Lord.

THAT THEY MAY RESPECT & DEFEND HUMAN LIFE - ESPECIALLY THE LIFE OF

For those who have fallen, and for those who have lost their way in life; that they may find understanding and love from the followers of Christ. (Pause). Let us pray to the Lord.

That we may never become complacent or self-righteous; that we may always hear the call of Christ to a deeper and a more authentic life. (Pause). Let us pray to the Lord.

For local needs.

Let us pray:

Lord, in your gentle mercy, guide our wayward hearts, for we know that left to ourselves we cannot do your will. We make our prayers through Christ our Lord.

COMMUNION REFLECTION

Jesus opened his ministry with the call:
"Repent and believe the Good News".

Repentance is often presented
as a harsh, sad, and totally negative thing,
as if it merely consisted
in feeling guilty about one's sins
and doing penance for them.
It is something far more positive.

It is discovering something wonderful about yourself:
that you have potentialities
which you didn't know you had;
that up to now you have been living in darkness,
whereas from now on you are determined
to live in the light.

It means acquiring a new vision,
taking a new direction,
setting yourself more worthwhile goals,
living by better values.
In a word — it means a new life.

Understood like this, repentance is exciting,
and it always leads to joy.
It means that we have heard the Good News
and embraced it.

THE DEFENCELESS UNBORN CHILD.

FOURTH SUNDAY OF THE YEAR
Speaking With Authority

INTRODUCTION AND CONFITEOR

When certain people begin to speak, we refuse to take them seriously. Why? Because for us their words carry no authority. When Christ spoke, all open-minded people listened. Why was this? Because he spoke with authority. His words had the ring of truth, and people knew he meant them. Do we listen to the words of Christ? What authority do our words carry? (Pause).

Lord, you speak words of truth to those who are in error.   Lord, have mercy.

You speak words of comfort to those who are sad or lonely.   Christ, have mercy.

You speak words of forgiveness to those who are in sin.   Lord, have mercy.

HEADINGS FOR READINGS

First Reading (Deut 18:15-20). Moses tells the people about the coming of a prophet into whose mouth God will put his own words.

Second Reading (1 Cor 7:32-35). Paul here urges those who are celibate to give their undivided attention to the Lord.

Gospel (Mark 1:21-28). Here we see the prophecy of Moses fulfilled in the teaching of Christ.

HOMILY

In a certain country fruit was the staple diet of the people. The whole growing and marketing operation was in the hands of a group of very influential men who formed the Abel Company. It was a long-established company and produced a great variety of fruit. And yet the people were dissatisfied. They were forever complaining about the poor quality of the fruit that was being offered to them.

What was wrong with it? Some of it was inferior. To tell this all you had to do was look at it. However, most of it looked okay. But when you sank your teeth into it you knew there was something missing. It was tasteless, and though it filled your stomach and took away your hunger for a while, it did not nourish you. No one had ever been known to grow fat on it. Finally, some of the fruit was absolutely inedible. It was rotten through and through. But once again this did not show up on the outside — at least not immediately.

The people felt they were getting a bad deal. They were being over-charged, yet they were undernourished. But complaining was useless. Though the merchants were for the most part hard-working, and their fruit was always available, yet it was obvious that they were interested mainly in the profits. The people felt trapped. They had no one to turn to, because the Abel Company enjoyed a complete monopoly.

Then one day a stranger by the name of Benson appeared in the marketplace of a small village. In front of him he pushed a cartload of fresh fruit. He set up his stall in the middle of the marketplace. His fruit looked good and was reasonably priced. At first the people were a bit apprehensive. But soon the word got around that his fruit was different — that it was both appetising and nourishing. By the end of the first week he could not meet the demands of the people and had to take on helpers.

The people not only liked the stranger's fruit. They at once liked the man himself. They liked his manner of doing things. He treated them not just as customers but as people. He had a kind word and a smile for everyone. He was warm and genuine and clearly not just out to make a fast buck for himself. He went out of his way to be kind to the beggars in the marketplace.

It was inevitable that Benson would come into conflict with the Abel Company men. He was cutting across their business. He was taking customers away from them. This aroused their jealousy and anger. They ordered him out of the marketplace. He left and went elsewhere. Everywhere he went the people flocked to him. But everywhere he went he was soon made to move on by the authorities. Finally the men of Abel Company decided to get rid of him. They paid some ruffians. Benson's body was found lying on a city dump. He had been bludgeoned to death.

However, by this time his helpers were in a position to carry on where he left off. They were greatly helped in this by the fact that he had awakened in the people such an appetite for good fruit that many of them refused to settle for anything else.

In this story the company stands for the religious establishment of Christ's day. The merchants are the scribes, the official teachers. The fruit stands for their teaching. Benson stands for Christ. His fruit is his teaching. The official teaching no longer satisfied the people. All the scribes did was lay down the law, thus crippling people with burdens, burdens they made no effort to lighten. It did not help that they themselves did not always practise what they preached.

Along came Christ. The people liked his teaching. He spoke with authority. What authority? you might well ask, for he had no official

position. There was a transparency about what he was saying. It had
the ring of truth. Yet he quoted no authority but his own. He spoke
from the heart. And most important of all — he backed up his words
with deeds.

Today we have a glut of words but many of them are rendered
worthless by insincerity or poisoned by falseness. All those in
positions of leadership and responsibility have a grave obligation to
offer people the wholesome fruit of the truth, not half-truths, much
less lies. Yet how few speak with real authority, in the sense that
people find it easy to believe what they say. Is there not a terrible
scepticism at present about the words of people in authority? Often
public figures appear to be merely voicing what the party tells them to
say. Not surprising then if people find their words often have a false
and empty ring about them. They lack credibility because people do
not believe that the speakers themselves really believe what they are
saying and certainly are not prepared to live according to their own
words.

The same danger faces the Church. Often it appears to be more
concerned with preserving its own traditions than with the truth. But
we are all involved in this. Daily we offer a diet of words to others, to
those with whom we live and work. How much authority do our
words carry? Do they nourish people or deceive them?

Do we find nourishment for our lives in the words of Christ which
we hear every Sunday? Have we developed a taste for the wholesome
fruit of Christ's truth, so much so that we refuse to settle for anything
else? How much are we parpared to risk on his words? Do we try to
offer some of the nourishment we find in Christ's words to others, not
by preaching to them, but by the way we treat them?

If we are living by anything other than the truth we are undernourished. "One word of truth outweighs the whole world". (Russian
proverb).

PRAYER OF THE FAITHFUL

Jesus spoke the words of the Father with an authority that made a
deep impression on his listeners. We pray that we may be able to
speak like him.   *R.* Lord, hear our prayer.

For the priests and ministers of the Church: that they may practise in
their own lives the values they preach to others. (Pause).   We pray
to the Lord.

For all who hold public office: that their deeds may match their
words and their promises. (Pause).   We pray to the Lord.

Words can lift people up to heaven or plunge them down to hell: let us pray for the victims of broken promises, especially for deserted wives and husbands. (Pause). We pray to the Lord.

Insincere words are as false and meaningless as smoke without fire: let us pray that we may always speak with sincerity to one another. (Pause). We pray to the Lord.

For local needs.

Let us pray:

Grant, O Lord, that what we have said with our lips, we may believe in our hearts, and practise in our lives. We ask this through Christ our Lord.

OUR FATHER

Were it not for Jesus we would not know how to address God properly, or what words to use when we pray to him. But he taught us how to pray.

SIGN OF PEACE

Lord Jesus Christ, you said to your apostles: 'I leave you peace, my peace I give you'. We find it hard to give peace to others because often we do not have it ourselves. Take pity on our weakness and grant us the peace and unity of your kingdom where you live for ever and ever.

COMMUNION REFLECTION

What was it about Christ that made him so different
from the official teachers of his day, the scribes?
It was the fact that he taught with personal authority.

No scribe ever expressed an opinion of his own.
He would always begin by quoting his authority.
He would buttress his statement with quotations
from the great legal masters of the past.
The last thing he would ever do
was give an independent judgement.

How different Jesus was!
When he spoke, he spoke as if he needed
no authority beyond himself.
He cited no authorities and quoted no experts.
He spoke with the finality of the voice of God.

For the people, to hear someone speak like that,
was like a cool breeze from the ocean
on a hot stifling day.

FIFTH SUNDAY OF THE YEAR
A Lonely Place

Most of us live very busy lives. We devote very little time to prayer and reflection on our lives. The result is that many of us live very restless and spiritually impoverished lives. Today's Gospel shows us how in the midst of his most pressing work Jesus took time out to pray and to restore his energies. We need to do the same. (Pause).

Let us confess our neglect of something so vital for us, and all our other sins:

I confess to almighty God . . . etc.

HEADINGS FOR READINGS

First Reading (Job 7:1-4, 6-7). Job is wrestling with the problem of why the innocent should suffer. As a result of his own sufferings he takes a rather pessimistic view of live.

Second Reading (1 Cor 9:16-19, 22-23). St Paul tells how he has made himself all things to all people in order to bring them the Good News of salvation.

Gospel (Mark 1:29-39). In the midst of all his activities of teaching and healing Christ finds it necessary to escape to a lonely place to pray.

HOMILY

For several years Tom was a sergeant in a provincial town. Because of his position he was one of the most important people in town. No one could afford to ignore him. No one would pass him in the street without saying hello. He was a good man and highly regarded. He did his job well and derived great fulfilment and satisfaction from it. But then he retired. Instead of being able at last to sit back and relax, he felt useless and his life lost all its meaning. Now he was a nobody. No one took much notice of him. Immediately he began to sink into oblivion. Having lived all his life in the sunlight of the public eye, he could not adjust to the shadows of obscurity. He went about with his head hung low. He rarely smiled. He died eighteen months after retiring. Up to that he had never been sick.

Here was a man who made the mistake of thinking that his

value as a person depended on his usefulness. He had become the job. Once the job was gone he collapsed. Yet a little reflection, a little standing back to get some perspective on his life, could have saved him.

Mary was the mother of four children. She was also working by day at a full-time job. Her spare time was also filled for she served on no less than three committees. A generous woman who liked helping others, she was always on the go. By the time she got home she was often too tired for anything but sleep. Everything was being done badly. Still she gloried in calling herself a liberated woman. Eventually she paid the price. She had a nervous breakdown and her world collapsed around her. It took her years to pull herself from the pit of depression that followed.

Here was a woman who desperately wanted to accomplish something. She wanted to be a success at all costs. In the process she lost herself. It's very easy for people to lose themselves in their jobs, even good jobs in which they provide a worthwhile service to others. The mistake they make is that they fail to take care of themselves as persons.

Now let us look again at the Gospel we have just read. In the middle of sentences that are packed with action — healing the sick, casting out devils, dealing with his impatient apostles, travelling about — we find these words: "Early in the morning, Jesus got up and left the house, and went off to *a lonely place* to pray".

Why? Because even he could not live a life of feverish activity and self-giving without from time to time standing back from it and seeking strength in solitude and prayer. Here lies the secret of his successful ministry. He knew that it cannot be all out-put and no in-put. "If you want a lamp to keep burning, you must keep on putting oil into it". (Mother Teresa). People who have no resources but their own are like tall trees with shallow roots. Such trees are very vulnerable when the storm strikes.

What did the lonely place do for Jesus? First and foremost it provided him with a breathing space and a chance to recover lost energy, physical, mental, and spiritual. Then it gave him a chance to pray. It helped him to keep clearly before his mind the main purpose of all his activity — to do, not his own will or to seek his own glory, but to do the will of his heavenly Father and to seek his glory only. But above all, it was during these hours of solitude that he maintained and fostered his intimate relationship with the Father. It was this, not his work, that was the most important thing in his life.

Whatever our role in life we too need a 'lonely place' in our lives. Often, however, we seem to be unable to disentangle ourselves from our work and our preoccupations. We have no shortage of excuses: 'There is so much to be done. If I don't do it no one else will. I don't like wasting time . . . etc.' Generous people are more likely to fall into the 'activity trap' than the selfish. But Helder Camara suggests that the real reason why we cannot leave our work and go apart to a lonely place in this: we are afraid of a "self-to-self encounter", which might shame us and wound our pride.

Yet how much we need it! Mothers are often so busy with the children and the housework that they have not a minute for themselves. Career-conscious men are always on the go. Many exhaust themselves in a multiplicity of pursuits, yet fail to take care of themselves. The result is that they fall a prey to childish attitudes and anxieties. With some, activity becomes a well-nigh incurable disease.

In our restless and often impoverished lives we should avail of every opportunity to withdraw, however briefly, from our everyday concerns — to reflect, to meditate on the past and the future, to draw up a balance sheet, to examine the world and ourselves. Merely to reflect, whether in grief or in joy, on the passage of time, on the transience of our lives and undertakings, is a kind of purification and a test as well. In quiet and stillness our projects lose their power over us, and we experience our true worth, which consists not in doing but in *being*. In stillness we grow like corn in the night. "The essential thing is not to lose oneself". (A. Camus). Certain kinds of work dry up the mind and heart of a human being, and suck the life out of him. Our only salvation lies in not allowing ourselves to become absorbed in the work.

In practice what are we talking about? Most people manage some morning or evening prayers. But often these consist of some over-familiar formula mumbled in haste while our thoughts are on other matters. But this is only like splashing water on our face while fully dressed. From time to time we need a proper bath. From time to time we need to seek out God and lay before him the totality of our lives and our struggles. This kind of prayer will always transform and fortify us. If we are convinced of its importance we will find a place and a time for it.

"I go to church every Sunday. A man needs this moment of stopping and paying some attention to himself". (Lech Walesa).

PRAYER OF THE FAITHFUL

Let us pray that we may be able to find a lonely, quiet place in our lives, where we can meet our heavenly Father — there to lay our lives before him and to feel loved and renewed. *R*. Lord, hear us in your love.

For all followers of Christ: that they may realise that without a lonely place to pray and reflect, their lives are in danger, like a candle in the wind. (Pause). We pray in faith.

For those in a position of trust and responsibility: that they may realise their need of God, and seek his guidance in all their decisions. (Pause). We pray in faith.

For all those who are immersed in activity: that they may realise that no work is more important than prayer; for without prayer work will sap their energy and leave them spiritually empty. (Pause). We pray in faith.

That we may realise that we can meet God anywhere and everywhere –— all we have to do is turn inwards and he is with us. (Pause). We pray in faith.

For local needs.

Let us pray:

Father, Jesus your Son taught us to pray by word and example. Help us to learn from him. We make all our prayers to you through the same Christ our Lord.

OUR FATHER

Jesus often went off to a lonely place to pray to his heavenly Father. What prayer did he make? He said: "When you pray to the Father, pray like this".

COMMUNION REFLECTION

The same Christ who prayed in lonely places said:
"When you pray, go into your room,
and pray to your Father in secret".

We should not imagine then that the lonely place
is necessarily a place far away,
or that by room he means four walls
that separate us physically from others.

The room is the room within ourselves.
It is the room of our innermost heart,
where our plans are hatched,
where our hopes reside,
where our true self is to be found.

This room is with us at all times.
We carry it around wherever we go.
We should make it a place where we can retreat,
a home where we find rest and spiritual recovery
when 'the world is too much with us'.

Then we will make an exciting discovery
that the inner room is not empty after all,
but is occupied by the God of love
who dwells in us all.

SIXTH SUNDAY OF THE YEAR
Rejection

Leprosy is a terrible disease, though it is almost unknown in the, western world. But it still concerns us for it is a symbol of sin. We are all tainted with the leprosy of sin. Christ wasn't afraid to reach out and touch lepers. He still reaches out to us, to heal in us the wounds of sin. Let us not be afraid to approach him. We need his healing touch. (Pause).

Lord, you raise the dead to life in the spirit.   Lord, have mercy.

You bring pardon and peace to us sinners.   Christ, have mercy.

You bring light to those who live in darkness and in the shadow of death.   Lord, have mercy.

HEADINGS FOR READINGS

First Reading (Leviticus 13:1-2, 45-46). This describes how lepers were considered ritually unclean and were compelled to live apart from the community.

Second Reading (1 Cor 10:31-11:1). St Paul urges us never to do anything offensive to anyone.

Gospel (Mark 1:40-45). This tells how Jesus cured a leper by touching him.

HOMILY

In a certain part of northern India a number of villages lie scattered among the mountains. It is a very backward area untouched by progress. Each year ten or twelve people leave these villages and make their way down to a place called Rishikesh. They are lepers and they have been turned out of their homes because of this. It is believed that leprosy is a punishment for some crime committed in a previous existence.

As soon as the first signs of leprosy appear, the patient must bid goodbye to his family and to the village in which he has grown up. He leaves behind his whole way of life, his trade (if he has one), and everything and everybody he has known and loved. His wife puts on the white dress of a widow. If he has sons they will accompany him down the mountainside but then they too will part from him in a farewell that is as final as death.

Imagine, if you can, how he feels. His body is physically rotting away. But deep inside him he is convinced he is rotten too, for he is a sinner. He is rejected by both God and man. He is unclean, cast off in case he should spread contamination. There is no doubt but that his greatest pain is caused by the feeling that he is rejected, abandoned by all. This makes him feel that he is worthless, that he is already dead. He is like an infected branch that has been lopped off a tree.

It was such a man as this who, in today's Gospel, came out of the shadows, who emerged from the pit of loneliness, rejection and worthlessness, to confront the one man he believed would not reject him, namely, Christ. The most important thing was not the fact that Christ cured him but the caring way in which he did so.

It is quite common today to help a person but, as it were, from a distance, that is, without getting deeply involved with the person. There is a tendency for doctors to give out pills instead of care and time. Yet to cure without care is like giving a gift with a cold heart. There is a tendency for parents to say to troublesome children: "Go and watch TV", instead of sitting down and trying to listen to them. There is a tendency for society to give handouts instead of tackling the root causes of deprivation. In all these cases we are saying in effect: keep your distance, don't touch me.

This was not the way Christ dealt with the leper. He allowed the man to approach him. A little dialogue took place. I feel sure it was longer than Mark indicates. Then he did the unthinkable. He reached out and touched him. Imagine how good that made the poor man feel. How honoured we feel if somebody important shakes hands with us or gives us a pat on the back, even though we are not suffering from leprosy with its resulting feelings of worthlessness.

No doubt Christ could have cured the man without touching him. But before curing his wounded body he had to cure his wounded spirit. He had to touch the wounds caused by rejection and cure them first. By touching he made him feel he was not worthless as society made him believe he was. He was worthwhile, even precious, to God and to him.

But we have no lepers among us, so you might ask: What is the relevance of all this for us? Well, we already saw that the worst suffering of the leper was caused, not by the leprosy itself, but by the consequences of it — being rejected by people. The relevance for us lies there — in the people we reject, whom we treat like 'lepers'.

We see them all around us in society. Old people abandoned by everybody. Young people from broken homes, unloved and unwanted. Handicapped people who are locked out of life's banquet. The travellers and down-and-outs. The unemployed and redundant who are thrown on life's scrap heap.

Nearer to home, the 'leper' is anyone I exclude or cut off, anyone I look down on or despise. That person may well be living under the same roof as me. I can reject in small but subtle ways — by the tone of my voice or even by a look I can convey to another person that I do not like him, in other words, that I reject him. But perhaps the worst form of rejection is indifference. As one disillusioned married person said: "I hope you never experience the humiliation of living with someone who is completely indifferent to you". Many people have so little self-awareness that they are not conscious of the ways in which they are rejecting others.

Rejection hurts beyond any other state or emotion. It leaves a wound that lasts. A child who is rejected is poisoned at the roots of his existence. Rejection makes people feel worthless and makes them want to rebel. To feel the whip of rejection causes an explosion of anger and resentment. But even pinpricks of rejection can accumulate with the same long-term effects.

If we find we are very rejecting towards others, it is a sure sign that all is not well within ourselves. Perhaps we don't fully accept ourselves? We can only do so if we have experienced acceptance. Do we believe that Christ accepts us just as we are? When we are okay within ourselves, we feel good about ourselves, and we have compassion for others and want to reach out to them.

Acceptance is the opposite to rejection. It makes the other realise that he is loved. Acceptance demands a deep, loving involvement with the other. If we want to be Christlike we must open ourselves to the people we are rejecting. Then we can become people who are able to bring peace and healing, rather than conflict and hurt.

About £1's worth of a certain modern drug can cure a person of leprosy. What does it take to cure a person of feelings of rejection? A little dose of the oldest drug of all — love. Everybody has a great capacity for love. The pity is that it often goes undiscovered and therefore unused.

PRAYER OF THE FAITHFUL

God gave us hearts, not of stone, but of flesh. Let us pray that he may deliver us from hardness of heart, and help us to accept others as he accepts us.   *R.* Lord, graciously hear us.

For the Christian community: that it may be warm and caring towards the rejects of society. (Pause).   Lord, hear us.

For the world and all humankind: that God may bind the human family in ties of love, friendship, and mutual acceptance. (Pause). Lord, hear us.

For all those who feel rejected and unwanted: that they may realise that even if people reject them God never does. (Pause). Lord, hear us.

That we may realise how the quality of our presence, of our looks and words, affects others, bringing them happiness or misery, life or death. (Pause). Lord, hear us.

For local needs.

Let us pray:

Lord Jesus, in the Gospel we see how, by your looks, words, and touches, you called forth life and hope and joy in wounded people. You can do the same for us, and you will help us to do the same for one another. We ask this of the Father, through you, Christ our Lord.

SIGN OF PEACE

Lord Jesus Christ, you reached out your hand and touched the leper so that you might make him feel loved and accepted. Help us to reach out and touch those we are rejecting, and so bring them love and acceptance, so that we may all enjoy the peace and unity of your kingdom where you live for ever and ever.

COMMUNION REFLECTION

Each of us to some extent
has felt the pain of rejection.
Rejection makes us feel that we are worthless.
It makes us want to shrivel up
or even openly rebel.
It is like a shower of hail
falling on tender young flowers.

Each of us longs to be accepted,
accepted for what we are.
When someone accepts us they give us
the feeling that we are worthwhile.
Acceptance means that we are free to be ourselves.
Even though there is need for growth and change
we are not being forced.

It is the love and acceptance of others

that makes me the unique person that I am.
When I am accepted only for work I do,
then I am not unique,
for someone else can do the same work
perhaps even better than I can.
But when I am accepted for what I am,
then I become unique and irreplaceable,
and I can blossom to my full potential.

This is how Christ accepts us.

SEVENTH SUNDAY OF THE YEAR
Forgiveness of Sins

INTRODUCTION AND CONFITEOR

At the heart of today's liturgy is the good news that God forgives the sins of his people. The first reading declared: "Your sins I will remember no more". And in the Gospel we find: "The Son of Man has authority on earth to forgive sins".

We all need this forgiveness. Let us call to mind our sins, perhaps one in particular. (Pause).

Lord, as far as the east is from the west, so far do you remove our sins.   Lord, have mercy.

Even if our sins were as red as blood, you would make them as white as snow.   Christ, have mercy.

With you, O Lord, there is mercy and forgiveness; for these we revere you.   Lord, have mercy.

HEADINGS FOR READINGS

First Reading (Isaiah 43:18-19, 21-22, 24-25). Isaiah tells the people that God is going to give them a fresh demonstration of his love and care. Their past sins will be blotted out.

Second Reading (2 Cor 1:18-22). St Paul declares himself to be a man of his word. He is conscious that he represents Christ, who is fidelity itself.

Gospel (Mark 2:1-12). Christ declares that he has authority to forgive sins, and proves it by curing a paralysed man.

HOMILY

A former SS officer was dying. Ever since the time of the Holocaust the things he had seen and taken part in had been tormenting his conscience. But faced with death an avalanche of guilt and remorse descended upon him. A dark, bottomless crevice of despair yawned beneath him, But then he began to wonder that maybe forgiveness was still possible. He desperately needed it and desired it. To whom could he turn for this forgiveness? Who could forgive him for his part in the Holocaust? Only a Jew could. It had to be a representative of the people who were its chief victims.

So he sent for a Jew, a man who had been a servant in his father's house, who had survived the camps. The Jew turned to the dying man and asked: "What do you want from me?" And the SS officer said: "Will you forgive me on behalf of the Jewish people for the crimes I took part in?" The Jew looked at him for several minutes without expression. Then he turned his back on him and walked away without saying a word. He refused to forgive him. And the SS officer died unforgiven. What a terrible way to die.

Forgiveness is a wonderful thing. It is a miracle. Had that Jew been able to forgive the SS officer he would have set him free from his past. He would have lifted an enormous load off his conscience. Through forgiveness what is broken is made whole again. The forgiven person is no longer paralysed by feelings of guilt. He is set free to walk in friendship with God and with the person he has offended. The more generous the person who forgives is, the more the sinner recognises his sin and the more he wants to repair the damage done by it. Forgiveness has to be unconditional or it is not forgiveness at all.

We should not be surprised to find forgiveness at the heart of Christ's ministry. However, the religious leaders were scandalised when Jesus said to the paralytic: "Your sins are forgiven". They were shocked at hearing him claim the power to forgive sins. How much more shocked would they have been if they had been present on Easter Sunday evening when Christ passed this power on to his apostles when he said: "Whose sins you shall forgive, they are forgiven; whose sins you shall retain, they are retained".

The power to forgive sins in his name is one of the greatest gifts Christ left to his Church. G. K. Chesterton when asked why he became a Catholic said: "Because I wanted to have my sins forgiven". As simple as that. God's forgiveness is available through the ministry of any priest, a man who himself bears the scars of sin and needs forgiveness. By sharing in the power of Christ every priest becomes a wounded healer. Yet it is not the priest who forgives, but Christ acting through him.

We no longer, therefore, have to carry around a load of guilt on our consciences. Guilt is useless. It is worse than that, for it keeps our heads buried and suffocating in our past. Forgiveness sets us free. Yet the frequency with which some people keep going back over their past sins (sins they have already confessed) makes it obvious that they do not fully trust God's forgiveness. It is as if, like the scribes, they too are shocked on hearing the words: "Your sins are forgiven", and do not believe them. For heaven's sake, having committed our sins to the mercy of God let us leave it at that. Let us not go back and keeping raking over the ashes. Rather, let us imitate the people in the Gospel, who on seeing what Christ had done for the paralytic, said: "We have never seen anything like this!", and they went away praising God.

Why did Jesus begin the cure of the paralytic with the forgiveness of his sins? I don't believe for one moment that Jesus was suggesting that the man was a greater sinner than any of the others in the room. He was simply stating that like everyone else he too was a sinner. But by beginning there he was saying that sin too is an illness, the worst illness of all, for it is an illness of the soul.

Sin is a form of paralysis and we are all afflicted with it. Each of us could give plenty of examples of it from our own lives. There are times we find it hard to settle our differences. There are people we find it hard to be kind to. There are important tasks we don't seem to be able to get done. There are obligations we fail to honour. Why? Because we suffer from a form of paralysis — paralysis of the will and the spirit.

Jean Vanier says: "Everybody is handicapped. It's just that the handicaps of some are more visible. In the case of others they are hidden. Think of their fears, their selfishness, their hardness of heart, their pride, their smugness, their inability to see or to listen".

Once our sins are forgiven we too have to do as the paralytic did -- we have to get up and walk. He was brought into the house but he walked out of it, carrying his own stretcher. To be forgiven is to be set free -- free to move forward again, able to shoulder our own burdens and responsibilities. The sacrament of forgiveness is not an impersonal laundering service. It is an encounter with Christ who draws us forward to walk ever more freely and fully in the ways of God. And having been set free from the chains that bind us, we will be only too happy to set free anybody who is still bound by the chains of guilt and who may be waiting to hear those words from us: "I forgive you, go in peace".

PRAYER OF THE FAITHFUL

Jesus came to bring us the good news of the Father's forgiveness. Let us pray that we may believe and live this good news. *R.* Lord, hear our prayer.

For all the disciples of Jesus: that having experienced his forgiveness in their own lives they may set an example for the world in forgiving those who offend them. (Pause). Let us pray to the Lord.

For all those in positions of power: that they may be gentle and merciful in the exercise of their authority. (Pause). Let us pray to the Lord.

For all those who are handicapped in body or mind; and for those who through sin are crippled in spirit: that the Lord may bring them hope. (Pause). Let us pray to the Lord.

The cripple, once cured, carried his own bed away. That we may be able to accept responsibility for our own sins, and carry our own burdens instead of placing them on others. (Pause). Let us pray to the Lord.

For local needs.

Let us pray:

Almighty and compassionate Father, as Jesus your Son brought us the good news of your forgiveness, help us never to doubt your forgiveness and constantly to avail ourselves of it. We ask this through the same Christ our Lord.

OUR FATHER

Let us ask our Father to forgive our sins, and to bring us to forgive those who sin against us.

COMMUNION REFLECTION

Forgiveness is the answer
to the child's dream of a miracle.
Through forgiveness
what is broken is made whole again,
what is soiled is made clean,
what is lost is found.

Nothing greater can happen to a human being
that that he or she is forgiven.
A person is no longer trapped in his past.
He is set free —
free to love again,
free to move forward again.

Forgiveness is unconditional
or it is not forgiveness at all.

Can one forgive oneself?
No. it doesn't work.
We have to be forgiven.
But we can only believe that this is possible
if we ourselves are able to forgive.

These words of Christ:
"Your sins are forgiven, go in peace",
are among the most wonderful in the Gospel.

EIGHTH SUNDAY OF THE YEAR
The New Wine

INTRODUCTION AND CONFITEOR

The teaching of Jesus was new and different and exciting. He himself compared it to new wine which cannot be contained in old wineskins. It thrilled the ordinary people. But the Pharisees did not like it because it showed up the inadequacy of their own teaching. Is the Gospel still new for me every time I hear it? Or has it become old and boring and dead, so that I switch off? (Pause).

One thing new in Christ's teaching was his idea of God as forgiving and merciful. Let us now turn to this God.

You, Lord, are compassion and love, slow to anger and rich in mercy.   Lord, have mercy.

You do not treat us according to our sins not repay us according to our faults.   Christ, have mercy.

As a father has compassion on his children, so you, Lord, have pity on those who revere you.   Lord, have mercy.

HEADINGS FOR READINGS

First Reading (Hosea 2:16-17, 21-22). God is calling his people back to their first fervour — back to the honeymoon period of their relationship with him at the time of the Exodus.

Second Reading (2 Cor 3:1-6). Paul is confident of the success of his work, because success comes from God. Of himself he can do nothing.

Gospel (Mark 2:18-22). This underlines the radical newness of the teaching of Christ.

HOMILY

There are two ideas in today's Gospel: joy and newness. Though they are obviously connected I want to concentrate on the second. The newness is conveyed in two similes: the garment and the wine.

Jesus was suggesting that the old garment (the old teaching) was no longer adequate. Nor was it any good putting on a few new patches. A completely new garment was called for. He also said that the old wineskins were no longer any use, for he had new wine to offer. New wine demands new wineskins.

The newness Christ spoke about obviously went beyond mere teaching, but perhaps in a short homily we might do well to concentrate on that aspect only.

Let us look at some examples of how Christ's teaching was new to the ears of his listeners. Indeed, not only was it new, it was revolutionary, so much so that it shocked the Pharisees, the religious professionals of the day. (In what follows two voices could be used).

Whom should you love and show concern for?
Your friends of course, say the Pharisees. Those who are good to you. Those who are deserving of your love.

No, says Jesus. When you give a party don't invite your friends who will invite you in return. Invite the poor — those from whom you can expect nothing in return. Then you will have your reward in heaven.

If you are offering a gift to God and suddenly you remember that you have offended someone, what should you do?
Go ahead and offer the gift of course, say the Pharisees. God comes first. Worship of him is the most important thing in life.

No, says Jesus. Leave your gift there. Drop everything and go and be reconciled with the person you have offended. The come back and offer your gift to God and it will be acceptable to him.

If someone treats you badly, how should you react?
Give him back the same kind of medicine, say the Pharisees. Teach him a lesson he'll never forget. Otherwise he'll just go on doing it and walk all over you.

No, says Jesus. Do not react. Do not return evil for evil. Pray for those who persecute you and who make life difficult for you.

Who is the greatest — the person who sits in the chair of honour at the top table, or the waiter?
The one at the top of the table of course, say the Pharisees.

No, says Jesus. The man who puts the needs of others before his own is the greatest in the kingdom of heaven.

Who puts in the most in the collection for the poor — the wealthy person who puts in £10 or the poor who puts in 10p?
The one who puts in £10 of course, say the Pharisees.

No, says Jesus, but the one who puts in 10p. Surely we should judge a sacrifice, not by the amount, but by the cost.

What is God like and how does he deal with us?
He's just and gives us what we deserve, say the Pharisees. If we keep his laws he will reward us. If we break them he will punish us.

No, says Jesus. God is loving and treats everybody with compassion. There is joy in heaven when even one sinner comes back to him.

Who is my neighbour?
Anyone who is from my tribe, or class, or race, or nation, say the Pharisees.

No, says Jesus. My neighbour is any one who needs my help, regardless of class, or creed, or race, or nation.

Who is the person blessed by God?
The one who has an abundance of goods of this earth and who has made a success of his life, say the Pharisees.

No, says Jesus. The one who is truly blessed by God is the person who knows that no matter how much he owns he is always poor before God, and who therefore puts all his trust in God and not in money.

Who is the fortunate one?
The man who enjoys the honour and esteem of his contemporaries, say the Pharisees.

No, says Jesus, but the one who practises honesty, and truth, and justice in all his dealings. If he makes enemies, and if people try to discredit him, let him rejoice. He is in good company. That is how all true prophets have been treated.

We could go on, but I think the point has been made. The teaching of Jesus was refreshingly new. Yet it was profoundly disturbing for those who clung to the old ways and the old values. Thomas Merton said that the Gospel should come to us as brand-new or not at all. Unless we hear this 'newness' then it ceases to be news. And if it is not news it is not the Gospel. The Gospel is the announcement of something absolutely new, everlastingly new, not a message that was once new but is now two thousand years old. We so easily make a fossil of the Gospel.

Can we say that we have heard the Gospel in this way? That even once we were shocked, or at least disturbed, by it? The teaching of Christ is different. It goes against practically everything we hear from so many other sources today. If even goes against our own natural inclinations.

However, it is only when we live according to the teaching of Christ that the new wine begins to flow for us. And that new wine is still being offered to us — this very day we can taste it and feel intoxicated by it.

PRAYER OF THE FAITHFUL

Let us pray to the Father who sent his Son into our world with the good news of salvation.   *R.* Lord, graciously hear us.

For the Church: that through its preaching people may hear the Gospel in all its freshness and purity. (Pause).   Lord, hear us.

For our government leaders: that they may find inspiration in the Gospel to work for a more just and a more human society. (Pause).   Lord, hear us.

For those who have heard the words of the Gospel but whose lives remain untouched by them. (Pause).   Lord, hear us.

That we may realise that we will never understand the words of Christ, nor will they change our lives, until we try to do them. (Pause).   Lord, hear us.

For local needs.

Let us pray:

Heavenly Father, open our ears so that we can hear the Gospel of your Son; guide our minds so that we may understand it; and strengthen our wills so that we may live it. We ask this through the same Christ our Lord.

COMMUNION REFLECTION

Jesus spoke about new clothes and new wineskins,
in a word — new times.
He said that those who wanted to belong to these times
would have to put aside the old garment
and put on a new one;
they would have to cast aside the old wineskin
and get themselves a new one.

You we know that he was not really talking about new clothes
but about new attitudes, new standards, new people;
for he condemned the scribes and the Pharisees
who went around in fine robes
but whose minds and hearts were full of decay.

The great American writer, Thoreau,
surely reflected the mind of Christ when he said:

"Beware of those enterprises that require new clothes
and not rather a new wearer of clothes.
Perhaps we should never procure a new suit,
however ragged or dirty the old one,
until we have so conducted ourselves
that we feel like new men in the old,
and that therefore to retain it
would be like trying to keep new wine
in old wineskins".

NINTH SUNDAY OF THE YEAR
The Sabbath Day

INTRODUCTION AND CONFITEOR

The Sabbath is *the Lord's Day*. It reminds us that God must have the first place in our lives. But it is also *Our Day*. It is a gift from God, a day in which we can take care of the most important things in life. On this day we bring our tattered, fragmented lives to God and ask him to mend them. (Pause).

Let us bring him our sins, asking him to pardon them, and to heal the wounds they cause in our lives.

I confess to almighty God . . . etc.

HEADINGS FOR READINGS

First Reading (Deut 5:12-15). The sabbath is not just a day of rest, but a reminder to the people of their deliverance from slavery in Egypt.

Second Reading (2 Cor 4:6-11). Though the ministers of the Gospel may be heavily burdened with tribulations, nevertheless the life of Jesus flows from them to others.

Gospel (Mark 2:23-3:6). Jesus states that the sabbath was made for man, not man for the sabbath.

HOMILY

In his travels from his small planet the Little Prince (cf. *The Little Prince* by Antoine de Saint-Exupery) meets different people at various stopping-off points. In one tiny planet he is fascinated by a Lamplighter he meets. He is very conscientious and does his job with the regularity of a clock. What fascinates the Little Prince is that apart from the Lamplighter the planet has no inhabitants. He asks the man why he lights the lamp so faithfully each evening and extinguishes it each morning. The answer he gets is: "Orders are orders". In other words he no longer knows why. He is functioning like a machine.

The Little Prince reflects on this absurd situation, and suddenly it dawns on him what a beautiful occupation is that of the Lamplighter. Each evening he causes a new star to shine in the dark heavens. To bring a little light into the universe is surely a splendid and noble occupation. But the Lamplighter fails to see this beauty.

"I follow a terrible profession", he moans. "In the old days things were reasonable. I lit the lamp in the evening and had the rest of the night for sleep. I put it out in the morning and had the rest of the day for relaxation. In those days the planet turned slowly, now it turns faster and faster".

"And the orders haven't changed?" asked the little Prince. "That is the tragedy", replied the Lamplighter. "Even though from year to year the planet has turned more rapidly, the orders have remained the same. It's got so bad that now the planet makes a complete revolution every half-hour so that I get no rest night or day".

Though the Little Prince liked the Lamplighter, and admired the fidelity with which he carried out his task, nevertheless he felt deeply sorry for him. Why? Because he saw that he was completely trapped, being forced to obey orders without knowing where they came from or why they were issued. He had no time for himself. He was for ever on the go. He no longer saw any meaning in what he was doing. His once lovely job had degenerated into a dull, repetitive, and monotonous chore. But what concerned him most was the effect all this had on the Lamplighter himself. He was old, disillusioned, drained of life by the whole business. His 'inner light' had long since gone out.

Many of us could identify with the Lamplighter. Our world too has changed. It has become very impersonal. People who work for big companies do not really know who they are working for. They are not appreciated at a personal level. They are mere cogs in a machine. If they died they would never be missed. Someone else would be slotted in and the machine would grind on without as much as a splutter. Often the work is dull and repetitive. And of course, as everyone knows, the pace of life is getting faster and faster. People are unable to slow things down. It is all one mad scramble. People cannot find time to relax, much less to reflect on their lives. We pay a big price for all this. "We live too fast and too coarsely, just as we eat too fast, and do not know the true flavour of our food", so said Thoreau, writing over a century ago. Is there no hope then? There is. we need to take time out. We need to be able to stand back and look at what we're doing and where we're going. Above all, we need a chance to look at ourselves, and take care of the 'spirit'. This is where the Sabbath or Sunday comes in. And this is the revolutionary aspect of today's Gospel. Christ says that the Sabbath was made for us, not us for the Sabbath.

However, I'm afraid that, for many, Sunday means very little, apart from "getting Mass in". It is possible to obey the commandment to "Keep holy the Sabbath day" without really knowing why. What is meant to be a day of joy, and of freedom to be ourselves, has become a day of fun, and of running from self. For some Sunday can even be a depressing experience. When the rush of the busy week is over, and the clock stops, so to speak, people suddenly come face to face with the emptiness of their lives. Unable to face this, they rush to do other things, and so the merry-go-round continues.

The Sabbath is a gift from God. On this day our whole value system is upended. During the week we are enslaved to things, to work, to profit-making. On this day we are free, free to care for the seeds of eternity planted in our souls. On this day the productivity mentality is abolished. We may not be able to shut the world out entirely. We still have to cook, to mind the kids, etc. but we can slow things down. We can try to look at where our lives are going, and to remind ourselves that we belong to the Lord, not to Mammon.

Understood like this the Sabbath is a beautiful thing. "What are three score years and ten hurriedly and coarsely lived compared to moments of divine leisure in which your life coincides with the life of the universe?" (Thoreau). It would be a pity if we took this day for granted, if it became just like any other day. For Christians this day has a communal aspect. This is the day we join the People of God and are reminded that life is a pilgrimage to the Father's Kingdom. We listen to the Word of God, which is "a lamp for our steps and a light for our path". And we receive the Eucharist, which is the food of our journey. Christ, our Brother who rose from the dead on this day, has gone ahead of us. He invites us to follow.

PRAYER OF THE FAITHFUL

Let us pray to God for a better and a richer understanding of the Sabbath, the Lord's day and ours too.   *R.* Lord, hear our prayer.

That Christians may see the Sabbath as a day of freedom: freedom from sin and wrong-doing, and from the pursuit of money and material success. (Pause).   We pray to the Lord.

For all those in charge of civil affairs: that they may fulfil their responsibilities worthily and well. (Pause). We pray to the Lord.

For those for whom this day has no meaning, being either a day of boredom and illness, or of dissipation and frivolity. (Pause). We pray to the Lord.

That we may see the Sabbath as an opportunity, not only to give more attention to God, but also to share more of ourselves with those we love (Pause). We pray to the Lord.

For local needs.

Let us pray:

Father, for the Jews the Sabbath was a day when they celebrated their deliverance from the slavery of Egypt; for the early Christians it was a day they celebrated your Son's resurrection from the grave. May our celebration of it be a sign that we are no longer slaves but your children. We ask this through Christ our Lord.

OUR FATHER

We've been busy with our private little wars, watching each other from separate shores; we lose our way, and we need to ask God to teach us to say . . .

COMMUNION REFLECTION

Six days a week we work under strain,
beset with worries, enmeshed in anxieties,
slaves to material things.
But on the Sabbath we turn our attention
to the things of the spirit.

The Sabbath gives us a sacred place,
a reserved space:
for inwardness and reorientation,
for experience of the spirit,
for meaning and values to live by.

Here we are given time:
to be thankful,
to be joyful,
to be free,
to look where we are going in life,
and, if needs be, to correct our compass;
time to be with one another and with the Lord.

On this day Christ broke the chains of death
and rose in triumph from the grave.
It provides us with a window into eternity.
It is a place of refreshment, light, and peace;
a halting place
on the road that leads to the Father's Kingdom.

Thank you, Lord, for the gift of the Sabbath.

TENTH SUNDAY OF THE YEAR
The Divided Kingdom

INTRODUCTION AND CONFITEOR

One of the things that brings many a good project to a bad end is
when cracks and divisions appear. In other words — when people fall
out. As today's Gospel puts it: "Any kingdom that is divided against
itself cannot stand".

We are all divided within ourselves. Each of us is pulled towards
good and evil at the same time. (Pause).

Let us ask God in his love and mercy to heal this inner division
which is caused by our sinfulness.

You were sent to heal the contrite of heart.　Lord, have mercy.

You came to call us sinners to repentance.　Christ, have mercy.

You plead for us now at the right hand of your Father.　Lord, have
mercy.

HEADINGS FOR READINGS

First Reading (Genesis 3:9-15). Adam and Eve were tempted and
fell. This reading deals with the tragic consequences of that fall.

Second Reading (2 Cor 4:13-5:1). In the midst of his trials Paul
looks to the world to come in which God will provide us with a
permanent dwelling place instead of a temporary tent.

Gospel (Mark 3:20-35). In this passage we see how Jesus was
misunderstood by his family and slandered by the scribes, yet he was
accepted by the ordinary people.

HOMILY

Once upon a time there was a king who placed great trust in his
servants and treated them very well. However, instead of repaying

him with faithful service, the servants neglected their duties and sought to grab as much as they could for themselves. When the king heard this he went to meet them. But the servants, fearing punishment, fled from the place and went to live in a nearby forest. The king could have dispatched a detachment of soldiers to hunt them down but he did not.

Years passed. The king thought often about his disloyal servants. He felt sorry for them, living in fear and isolation in the woods. He dearly wanted his kingdom to be a place of unity and peace for all his people. So he hit upon a plan of action.

Meanwhile, things had not been going well for the rebellious servants. Life was a constant struggle. To make matters worse they frequently fought among themselves. But what pained them most of all was their sense of separation from their king. One day one of their children wandered off and got lost in the forest. They had given up hope of finding the child alive when a young man dressed in working clothes came out of the trees leading the lost child by the hand. They were over-joyed, especially the child's parents.

"Who are you?" they asked the stranger.

"I'm just a woodcutter", he answered.

"Where do you live?"

"Oh, nowhere in particular".

"Would you like to stay with us?"

"I'd be glad to".

And he stayed with them and became their friend and adviser. They soon began to realise that he was no ordinary man. There was something special about him. He often spoke about the king. He spoke as if he was a personal friend of his. He spoke about him as a forgiving and merciful man.

"You're not really a woodcutter, are you?" they asked him one day.

And he replied: "I can cut wood as well as any man, but I've something more important to do".

"And what is that?"

"I want to make you friends once more with the king".

"Who are you then, an envoy of his?"

"More than that. I'm the king's son. It was he who sent me to you".

It will come as no surprise that they were unable to keep this astounding piece of news to themselves. It soon reached the royal palace. On hearing it the prince's mother and members of the royal household grew alarmed for his safety. They did not like the idea of the prince keeping company with disloyal servants of the king. So they sought for a way to rescue him. The official seers of the realm took a different view. They refused to believe the story. They accused him of being an imposter, a spy planted by enemies of the king.

But the servants continued to believe in him. Ashamed of what they had done to their king, they said: "Is there any chance he would take us back as servants?"

"It all depends on you", answered the prince.

"What do you mean?" they asked.

"Are you willing in future to do the king's will?"

"Most certainly", they replied. "We're ready to do anything to get back on good terms with our king".

"Well then, I've got great news for you", the prince went on. "Not only is the king ready to accept you back as servants. He is willing to accept you back as his sons and daughters".

"Son and daughters? But do we not need royal blood for that?"

"No, all you need is a royal spirit — a spirit of obedience, love, and trust".

On hearing this they danced for joy. And all this time the prince's family were saying that he was mad. And the seers of the land were saying that he was an agent of the enemy.

There you have the theme of today's readings. The first reading told how Adam and Eve disobeyed God, felt ashamed, and hid from him. Ever since there has been a rift between God and man. That is until Christ came among us. He came not only to restore us to God's friendship but to offer us the possibility of becoming his sons and daughters.

It was to outcasts and sinners that he first brought the Good News. These accepted it like manna from heaven and flocked around him. His family thought he was mad and feared for his safety. The scribes accused him of working not for God, but for Satan. But Jesus was undeterred by this misunderstanding and opposition. He continued to preach the Good News to those who were willing to listen.

We are the rebellious servants. But if we become willing to do God's will in our lives, then Jesus becomes our Brother and God becomes our Father. Then we will feel no need to hide from God or to be ashamed of our former sins.

Sin is a rebellion against God. It divides each one of us in two — part of us is pulling with God and part of us is pulling against him. Sin also divides us from each other, because essentially sin is a refusal to love. It means that we always put our own needs before those of our neighbour.

But there is a unifying force at work among us and within us — the love of Christ. He will heal the division within us and help us obey the Father in love. He will also help us to reach out to our neighbour. And so the divisions will gradually be overcome. And the Kingdom of God will be seen to have come among us.

PRAYER OF THE FAITHFUL

Let us pray to our Father that his Kingdom may come among us
— the Kingdom for which Jesus gave his life.   *R*. Lord, graciously
hear us.

For the Church: that it may be a sign of unity and an instrument of
reconciliation in a world riddled with divisions. (Pause).   Lord, hear
us.

For all the human family: that the Spirit of God may heal its divisions
and bind it together in ties of mutual respect and care.
(Pause).   Lord, hear us.

For all those who suffer because of divided families or divided
countries: that they may not lose heart or hope. (Pause).   Lord, hear
us.

That each of us may strive to live up to our dignity as sons and
daughters of our Father, and so be a source of unity among our
friends and neighbours. (Pause).   Lord, hear us.

For local needs.

Let us pray:

Father, help us to do your will in our lives, to do it freely and out of
love, so that we can enter into intimacy with you. We ask this
through Christ our Lord.

SIGN OF PEACE

Lord Jesus Christ, you said to your apostles: 'I leave you peace,
my peace I give you'. We find it hard to give peace to others because
often we don't have it ourselves. Take pity of our weakness, and
grant us the peace and unity of your kingdom where you live for ever
and ever.

COMMUNION REFLECTION

"No kingdom that is divided within itself can stand",
said Jesus.
I myself am a divided kingdom.
I am divided within myself.

"The good which I want to do,
I don't do;
the evil which I want to avoid,
I find myself doing".
This is how St. Paul puts it.

There exists within me forces
that will do their utmost to drag me down,
so that my life is like a field in which
wheat and weeds grow side by side,
struggling for supremacy.

Who will save me from myself?
Who will keep my kingdom from falling down?
Only Jesus, who overpowered Satan,
will heal the division within me,
and help me to take complete possession
of my own house.

Then I shall be free, united, and at peace.
Perhaps I shall never gain the complete victory in this life.
Enough that I keep up the fight,
and that final victory is achieved
in the life that is to come.

ELEVENTH SUNDAY OF THE YEAR
Small Beginnings

INTRODUCTION AND CONFITEOR

Everybody knows that if you plant an acorn in the ground, given time, it will grow into an oak tree. Yet nobody knows how. And how extraordinary that a huge oak should have such humble origins. Jesus says this is how it is with the reign of God in our lives and in our world. It begins in a small way, but given time, it grows into something great.

Is this growth happening in my life? Am I growing into a more loving, compassionate, Christlike person? (Pause).

I have to make the effort. But then I must trust that God's grace will take over.

You make the just to flourish like the palm tree and to grow like a cedar of Lebanon.   Lord, have mercy.

You plant them in the house of the Lord, to flourish in the courts of our God.   Christ, have mercy.

You make them bear fruit even when they are old; they will still be green and full of sap.   Lord, have mercy.

HEADINGS FOR READINGS

First Reading (Ezekiel 17:22-24). The prophet foretells the downfall of Jerusalem. At the same time he tells of a restoration that will be brought about by a member of the chosen people (namely, the Messiah), who will set up a universal kingdom.

Second Reading (2 Cor 5:6-10). St Paul says that his priority at all times is to please the Lord. Hence he has no fears of appearing before him.

Gospel (Mark 4:26-34). This contains two parables about the slow but steady growth of the Kingdom of God from insignificant beginnings. It is God who brings about this growth.

HOMILY

Even though the blacks in the USA gained their emancipation in 1864 it was not until 1964 that an Act was passed giving them the same civil rights as whites. In between they were the victims of terrible discrimination, especially in some of the southern states. To take an example: Montgomery, Alabama, 1955.

Although 70% of the passengers using the city bus lines were black, they were treated very much as inferiors. The first seats on all buses were kept for whites. Even if they were empty and the rear ones crowded, blacks would have to stand at the back in case some more whites might get on the bus. And if the front seats were taken and more whites got on the bus, black people seated in the rear were forced to get up and give them their seats.

Blacks had to pay their fares at the front of the bus, get off, and walk to the rear door to board again. Sometimes the bus would drive off without them even though they had paid their fares. This would happen to elderly people and even to pregnant women, and was a great joke among the drivers, all of whom were white. But a single incident brought this whole shabby business to an end.

On December 1, 1955, a 42-year-old woman boarded a bus to go home after a long day working and shopping. She found a seat at the start of the black section. At the next stop some whites got on and the driver ordered her to get up and give her seat to a white man. This meant that she would have to stand all the way home. Mrs. Parks said later that she was not in a revolutionary state of mind and she had not planned to act as she did. "I was just plain tired and my feet hurt". So she sat there and refused to get up. The driver called a policeman. Mrs. Parks was arrested and put in jail, though later she was released on bail.

But what she had done was like a spark in a forest that hasn't seen rain for a whole year. Word quickly spread. The blacks suddenly saw that the whole system was grossly unfair and decided to do something about it. A meeting was called and Martin Luther King was asked to address it. The outcome was that they made one basic demand: that passengers be seated on a first-come first-served basis. To achieve this end a boycott of the buses was planned to begin on December 4th. But would the people support it?

They did. People walked to work. Those who had cars ferried fellow workers to their jobs. It was an extraordinary scene. Everywhere the sidewalks were crammed with people walking to work, and the buses went by empty but for whites. The boycott dragged on all that winter, and through the spring and summer of 1956. Meanwhile the leaders of the movement were all arrested. Martin Luther King's home was bombed. The people dreaded facing a second winter walking to work. But they were spared the hardship. For on Nov. 13 the Supreme Court of the United States declared that Alabama's segregation laws were unconstitutional.

Victory was achieved and an unjust situation put right because on one particular day one woman decided to act. It all began with one small act. As the proverb says: a journey of a thousand miles begins with one step. And Mrs Parks herself had no idea of what she was starting on that fateful day in 1955.

In today's Gospel Jesus speaks of God's Kingdom in a similar terms. He says that it is like a mustard seed which a man plants in his garden. Even though it is tiny, given time it will grow into a large shrub in whose branches the birds of the air will find food and shelter. What is he teaching us?

Maybe it could be put like this: How God depends on us and how we depend on him. If we want to change something in our own lives or in the world around us we must make a start somewhere. That start will necessarily be very small, and may appear to be totally insignificant and useless in the circumstances.

Once we take our first step in what we believe to be a just cause, we must trust that God will help us to go forward as surely as he makes a seed grow once we have taken the trouble to plant it. We must go forward even though we do not know where it will lead us. We must persevere in spite of delays and obstacles. We must trust in God.

This is a valuable and consoling lesson if we want God to reign in our lives. If there is some area of my life where he does not now reign, when am I going to take the first step to change this situation? If there is some unjust situation in the world around me, then maybe I can be the one to take the first step to correct it. Then others will follow and God will help us to see it through.

For God's kingdom to come — a kingdom of justice, love, and peace — each of us has a part to play, but it is God who gives the increase. A individuals we may feel that we haven't much to contribute. Yet to plant even one seed of truth, or justice, or peace. is a worthwhile thing. And we can leave it to God to bring forth the harvest and perhaps others to reap it. Jesus began his great work by calling a handful of fishermen.

"We can do no great things — only small things with great love" (Mother Teresa).

PRAYER OF THE FAITHFUL

Let us pray for the growth of God's Kingdom on earth — a Kingdom of justice, love, and peace for all of his children.   *R*. Lord. hear us in your love.

For the Church: that Christ may sustain it in its task of being a transforming leaven in the modern world. (Pause).   We pray in faith.

For the world and its leaders: that they may further the Kingdom of God by promoting harmony and justice among peoples. (Pause).   We pray in faith.

For all those who are victims of unjust situations: that God may sustain them in their struggle to achieve their human rights. (Pause).   We pray in faith.

As a forest cannot be green unless the individual trees are green. we pray that we may realise that each of us has a part to play in making the Kingdom of God a reality in the lives of people. (Pause).   We pray in faith.

For local needs.

Let us pray:

God our Father, you are the same yesterday, today and for ever: help us to have confidence in your unchanging love for us. so that when things are difficult we may have the strength to persevere in goodness. We make our prayers through Christ our Lord.

COMMUNION REFLECTION

A soldier, recuperating from a war injury, looks out the hospital window.

It was springtime and the trees and shrubs
were filling up with leaves and blossoms.
He reflected on their simple beauty.

As he looked at them he noticed
how birds of every description

moved freely in and out among them —
robins, and sparrows, and wrens,
blackbirds, and thrushes, and wagtails.

Here they held their various branch meetings.
They shared the shelter and the fruit,
and they still managed to live at peace with one another.
From here their music went forth
to fill the world with its joyous sound.
If they can do this, why can't we?

Suddenly the words of Christ came alive for him:
"The Kingdom of Heaven is like a tree
in whose branches all the birds of the sky
can find a home".

And a deep longing filled his soul.
He longed to belong to such a Kingdom,
to open his arms and embrace all his brothers and sisters.
And the bitterness caused by his injury
suddenly flowed away from him,
and he was healed
and at peace with himself and the world.

TWELFTH SUNDAY OF THE YEAR
Storm on the Lake

INTRODUCTION AND CONFITEOR

We all encounter storms of one kind or another during the course of our lives — troubles, disappointments, quarrels, set-backs, accidents, illness . . .

Every storm severely tests our faith in God. Though we turn to God in the midst of the storm at the same time we often doubt him. (Pause).

Today's Gospel shows Christ present with his disciples in the midst of the storm. He is also present with us in our storms. Let us ask forgiveness for our sins, especially our lack of faith and trust in God.

I confess to almighty God . . . etc.

HEADINGS FOR READINGS

First Reading (Job 38:1, 8-11). God alone is able to exercise control over the sea. In this way we see God's care for the human family.

Second Reading (2 Cor 5:14-17). Christ died so that we might live a Christ-centered life, not a self-centered life.

Gospel (Mark 4:35-41). When the apostles witness Jesus calming the sea they are dumbfounded and ask who this man can be, who is able to do a work of God.

HOMILY

Group Captain Leonard Cheshire, one of the most respected Catholics in the world today, tells how at the end of the war (a war in which he distinguished himself) when he retired from the RAF he was very confused about what he wanted to do with his life. He felt terrible about the war, a war that had claimed a staggering fifty-five million lives. He desperately wanted to do something to make sure that such a thing could never happen again. Eventually he decided to dedicate his life to working for the disabled.

The first man to be sent to him was a man called Arthur. Arthur had been a minder of pigs but was now dying of cancer and had only a few months to live. Cheshire felt totally inadequate when it came to caring for such a man. He had little ability with words. Consequently there was not much that he could say that might be of benefit to Arthur. So he fell back on the only things he knew he could offer him, namely, companionship and availability.

During those last months of Arthur's life a great bond of friendship developed between them. The big house had no bells, not even electricity. Arthur was in great pain. The long nights were the loneliest time of all. When he got very ill Cheshire took to putting a mattress outside the door of Arthur's bedroom and sleeping there. He had given Arthur a little hand bell. He was to ring it whenever he needed help. He should not hesitate to ring it several times during the course of the one night. Cheshire would not mind having his sleep disrupted.

This was enormously reassuring to Arthur. Knowing that help was available, that someone cared about him, that nothing else mattered in the house at that particular moment but himself and his need — that made the world of difference to him, even though it did not take away his pain and was powerless to hold back the advance of death.

Arthur was a simple man yet he died a death of great dignity. When he first came to the home Cheshire had no idea that he was a Catholic. But he had long given up the practice of his faith. However, during his last three months he had steadily regained his faith, acquiring in the process a serenity and a sense of purpose that made

him an altogether different person from the one he had been up to
that time. It was in fact through him that Cheshire first heard of the
Catholic teaching and faith, and as a result eventually became a
Catholic himself. He felt there was no greater gift Arthur could have
given him and he remained deeply grateful to him.

Let us now turn to the Gospel of today's Mass. The apostles were
crossing the lake to escape from the crowds. Jesus, worn out from
work, was asleep in the stern. Now they can enjoy a well-earned
break. No such luck! The fact that the Master is aboard their little
boat does not prevent a wicked storm from blowing up. The apostles
strive to cope with it on their own but it proves too much for them.
They awaken the Master and he speaks to the wind and there comes
a great calm.

Ah, we might say, if only it were like that in real life! If only the
Lord would intervene when we are caught in the middle of some
storm, and with a simple command, restore calm to our troubled
lives! Well, let us take a closer look to see if we can grasp what this
story is really saying to us.

We too encounter various kinds of 'storms' — bad situations of
one kind or another which disrupt our lives and sometimes even
threaten to sink us. But this should not surprise us. The mere fact that
we are trying to follow Christ is no guarantee that we will be spared
the storms. Christ never promised his followers that their lives would
be like a Mediterranean cruise. Rather he hinted that they would have
to pass through many stormy waters. Therefore, when the storm
strikes us, we must not feel that God has abandoned us, much less
that he is punishing us for our sins.

In some of these storms we may feel that we can no longer cope on
our own. Our own resources are clearly not enough. The waves of
anger, fear, pain, and despair rise up and threaten to engulf us. It is
then that we must believe that Christ is with us and that his help is
available to us — like Cheshire's was to Arthur. If our faith is strong
we will know that Christ is sleeping at our door, that all we have to do
is awaken him with the bell-ringing of our prayer. With his help we
will survive any storm. Our fears will subside, and peace and calm
will return to our troubled hearts.

And if, like Arthur, we should be faced with death, and there is
no escape (which sooner or later is the case with everyone), then is it
not immensely consoling that we have the Captain beside us who will
help us to negotiate the dark and threatening waters of death? Every
priest has seen this happening. Meanwhile, however, let us make sure
that Christ is a familiar travelling companion on the great voyage of
life.

Christ doesn't save his friends from the storm, but what he does is
be present with them in the middle of it, helping them to come

through it. He also asks each of his followers to do the same. To do what Cheshire did. To make ourselves available to the person who is caught in the middle of the storm. We will have no magic words to offer, none except our presence and our availability. But these are precious things. These are the things that calm the storm — not magic words, but a loving, supportive, and calming presence.

PRAYER OF THE FAITHFUL

Let us pray to God our Father that with his help we may be able to weather the various storms which threaten our lives and our world.   *R.* Lord, hear our prayer.

For the Church, the barque of Peter: that it may not lose heart when storms of dissension or persecution blow up and threaten to sink it. (Pause).   Let us pray to the Lord.

For world leaders: that they may spare no effort to bring peace to those troubled spots of the world where the storms of war are wrecking lives and homes. (Pause).   Let us pray to the Lord.

For families which are threatened by continual fighting; and for homes threatened by unemployment, hardship, and poverty. (Pause).   Let us pray to the Lord.

That we may be able to overcome our impatience, anger, and resentments, which upset our lives and the lives of those who are close to us. (Pause).   Let us pray to the Lord.

For local needs.

Let us pray:

Heavenly Father, in the midst of life's storms let us be certain that Christ your Son is with us. Let us hear again his voice saying: 'Peace, be still!' so that we can find peace again within our souls and with one another. We ask this through the same Christ our Lord.

SIGN OF PEACE

Lord Jesus Christ, when a storm blew up and threatened to sink the disciples' boat, you said: 'Why are you frightened, men of little faith?' Then you spoke to the wind and the sea, and there came a great calm. Calm the storms our anger causes to blow up among us, so that we may enjoy the peace and unity of your kingdom where you live for ever and ever.

COMMUNION REFLECTION

One minute our lives are free and easy.

Next minute we are cast down.
All it takes is a piece of bad news
or some disappointment,
and suddenly for us the whole world
becomes dark and sombre.
Waves of discouragement, fear, and despair
rise up all around us,
threatening to engulf us.

In such moments
who will save us from drowning and help us
to keep the barque of our lives on course?

Christ our Brother will.
He who is our companion
on the voyage to the eternal shore.
All we have to do is awaken ourselves
to a sense of his presence,
and call out to him in our distress,
as the apostles did.
Then we will hear his gentle voice saying to us:
"Fear not, for I am with you".

And the waves of fear will subside,
and the sun of hope will shine for us again.

THIRTEENTH SUNDAY OF THE YEAR
Making Contact

INTRODUCTION AND CONFITEOR

We hear in today's Gospel how a sick woman had the most
amazing faith in Christ. She believed all she had to do was touch the
hem of his robe and she would be well. And just as soon as she made
contact with him, power flowed out from him and healed her. Here
we can draw close to Christ, very close, depending on the depth and
intensity of our faith. And we too need his healing touch in our lives.
(Pause).

Lord, you lift up the broken-hearted.   Lord, have mercy.

You bind up the wounds of those in anguish and despair.   Christ,
have mercy.

You bring pardon and peace to those who repent of their sins. Lord, have mercy.

HEADINGS FOR READINGS

First Reading (Wisdom 1:13-15; 2:23-24). God did not make us to destroy us. He made us to enjoy a blessed immortality.

Second Reading (2 Cor 8:7-9, 13-15). St Paul here is appealing to the Corinthians to contribute to a collection for the poor in the Church at Jerusalem.

Gospel (Mark 5:21-43). This contains two separate miracles of Jesus: the cure of a woman with a haemorrhage, and the raising of the daughter of Jairus. Both are signs of God's power, restoring life and health through Jesus.

HOMILY

I was desperately anxious for a cup of tea, so I went to the electric kettle. Noticing that there was hardly any water in it, I disconnected the lead and filled the kettle with fresh water from the tap. Then I reconnected the kettle to the lead, plugged it into the socket in the wall and went away.

I came back a few minutes later with a pleasant sense of expectation. The kettle should just about be coming to the boil by now. I already saw myself with that cup of tea in my hand. But what did I find? When I looked towards the kettle I saw that it hadn't the slightest sign of boiling. I heard no sound from it either. I touched it gingerly with my hand. It was stone cold. What could be wrong? I wondered. A blown fuse perhaps? That would take some time to locate and to replace. But then in a flash I saw my mistake. In my hurry I had forgotten to switch on the power in the socket.

I could have waited until doomsday for that kettle to boil and I would have waited in vain. The power was available in the socket but it could not flow into the kettle's elements because the connection had not been made.

We read in the Gospels that power went out from Jesua and healed many people. We think especially of that long-suffering woman we met in today's Gospel. She was determined to meet Jesus. She had pushed and elbowed her way through the crowds to do so. Her friends had told her she was wasting her time. If doctors had been unable to halt her flow of blood, what could a wandering preacher do for her? But she had the most fantastic faith in Jesus and in his power to cure. "One touch and I'll be cured", she said. "Even if I can only touch the hem of his robe, I'll be well".

And so it turned out. As soon as she got within arm's length of him she reached out and touched the hem of his robe. The connection was made. Immediately healing power flowed from Christ to her and she was cured.

And yet we read in the same Gospels how there were some people for whom Jesus could do nothing. His fellow villagers from Nazareth for instance. When he visited them he could do no cures among them. It was the same with the Scribes and Pharisees. Why was this? Whose fault was it?

These people could see him. They could hear what he was saying. No doubt they touched him. Yet nothing happened. There was no response for them. They were like that kettle — stone cold. Why? They were not switched on to his power. They either refused to believe in his power, or they did not think they needed it. One way or another, nothing happened between him and them. Though they were physically close to him there was no connection. The fault was entirely theirs.

Christ was unable to reach them. He was unable to get through to them. They never warmed to him. His power was available to them, power which could have transformed their lives, but they could not or would not connect with it. And we know that it was not his way to force himself on anyone. He waited for three years and still could not connect with some of these people. The choice was theirs.

And the choice is ours too. Though we can no longer make physical contact with Christ, nevertheless his power is available to us too, just as surely as it was to that woman and to the parents of that little girl. But we too can be switched off. And probably for the same reasons as the villagers of Nazareth. We do not have enough faith in him and in his power. Or we do not really believe we need his healing touch. Or maybe it is that we are afraid to make real contact with him because of the changes it might force us to make in our lives?

But for one reason or another it can happen that we remain largely unaffected, untouched. True, we have superficial contact with Christ. We are here in church and maybe at the sacraments. But perhaps we are merely going through the motions. Nothing much happens. We remain as cold and hard and unaffected as ever. "Right from my childhood I have believed that 'touching Christ' can heal, but it is useless to touch unless you have faith". (Catherine de Hueck Doherty).

What a pity if this should happen since Christ wants to touch us so that we can be healed and raised to life. We all really do need his healing touch in some way. People can be wounded, and deeply wounded, but it never appears on the outside. They are wounded inside. They carry invisible wounds ... feelings of rejection, of worthlessness, of loneliness, of bitterness, of hostility ... We tend to hide our wounds and pretend, like the Pharisees, that all is well with us. A hidden wound cannot be healed. If we believed in Christ's love for us, why should we want to hide our wounds from him?

Then Jesus calls us to be healing towards one another. Our lives are continually touching those of other people. We might therefore ask ourselves: what goes out from us through our words, our deeds, our relationships — hurting or healing?

For the Gospel to come alive we must live it. Here is an opportunity to give it a try. Every Christian ought to be a channel of Christ's healing power. As St. Francis put it: "Where there is hatred let me bring love; where there is injury let me bring pardon . . ."

Christ knew at once when the woman had touched him? How? Because every cure took something from him. Every cure cost him something. Every cure will also cost us, but if we keep close to Christ then power will be continually restored to us.

PRAYER OF THE FAITHFUL

Let us pray earnestly for God's healing for our wounds and the wounds of all his children. *R*. Lord, hear our prayer.

For the Church: that it may continue Christ's healing work by caring for all those who are sick in body, mind, or spirit. (Pause). Let us pray to the Lord.

For doctors and nurses and all those who care for the sick: that they may do so with patience, skill, and care. (Pause). Let us pray to the Lord.

For those who have no one to care for them, no one to touch their wounds, no one to introduce them to Christ their Saviour. (Pause). Let us pray to the Lord.

That we may be aware of the power we have to heal the wounds of others: a kind word can heal a wounded heart; a kind deed can repair the damage done by rejection. (Pause). Let us pray to the Lord.

For local needs.

Let us pray:

Heavenly Father, you sent your Son to heal all our wounds of body, mind, and spirit. Help us to have more faith in his healing power and in your love for us. We ask this through the same Christ our Lord.

OUR FATHER

Let us pray to God our Father, who cares about all his sons and daughters, especially the little ones and the wounded ones.

SIGN OF PEACE

Lord Jesus Christ, we live in a world that is deeply wounded by divisions and war. Help us to extend the hand of peace to one another, so that these wounds may be healed in us, and together we may enjoy the peace and unity of your kingdom where you live for ever and ever.

COMMUNION REFLECTION

Power went out from Jesus and cured that woman.
He felt it happen.
You might well ask how this was possible
with all those people pressing in on him?
The reason is simple.
Each cure took something out of him.
Each act of caring costs.

We could all do a little healing
if only we allowed ourselves
to become instruments of Christ.
With a little sympathy
we could heal a wounded heart.
With a little care
we could ease a troubled mind.
With a little of our time
we could ease the pain of loneliness for someone.

Each act of caring would cost us something.
But if we keep up our contact with the Master,
then power will continually be restored to us.
And all the time we are thinking of others,
we ourselves are being made whole and well.
We are being raised from the grave of selfishness
and healed of our hardness and coldness of heart.

FOURTEENTH SUNDAY OF THE YEAR
Rejecting the Messenger

INTRODUCTION AND CONFITEOR

Jesus had made a big impact in other towns and villages, yet when he came to his native village his own people rejected him. Why? They felt they knew all about him, and that there he had nothing to offer them. The same Jesus comes to visit us during his Eucharist. We have a chance to listen to him and to receive him into our hearts and into our lives. (Pause).

Lord Jesus, you come to reconcile us with one another and with our heavenly Father.   Lord, have mercy.

Lord Jesus, you heal in us the wounds of sin and division.   Christ, have mercy.

Lord Jesus, you intercede for us now at the right hand of your Father.   Lord, have mercy.

HEADINGS AND READINGS

First Reading (Ezekiel 2:2-5). God will not allow his chosen people to remain in ignorance of their disobedience. He sends them a prophet to call them to change their ways.

Second Reading (2 Cor 12:7-10). In the midst of temptations and difficulties of every kind Paul does not reply on his own resources but on the grace of God.

Gospel (Mark 6:1-6). True to the proverb that no prophet is honoured by his own people, Christ is rejected by the people of Nazareth.

HOMILY

What is the one thing we all need to hear, at least from time to time? The truth. Though we need to hear it, rare is the person who welcomes it, particularly when it is unpleasant.

It is hard enough to hear the truth when it is told to us by a friend. But it has no chance on earth if it comes to us from an enemy. Woe betide that person! If we reject the messenger we will automatically reject the message. We've all had this experience. Just as soon as a certain person begins to talk (say on TV) we either switch off or immediately go on the defensive or on the attack.

Once upon a time a travelling circus was staying on the outskirts of a village. One evening, shortly before show time, a fire broke out. The manager sent the clown, who was already dressed up for his act, into the nearby village for help. There was a danger too that the fire would spread across the fields of dry stubble and burn the village itself.

The clown hurried into the village. He asked the people to come out as quickly as possible to the blazing circus. But the people only laughed at him. They thought it was a brilliant piece of advertising on the part of the management. "What a clever stunt to get the people to go to the circus", they said. They even applauded the clown and nearly broke their sides laughing at his attempts to look serious and worried. He tried his best to make them understand that it was no trick, that there really was a fire. But the harder he tried the more they laughed. Finally the fire did reach the village and burned it to a cinder. Basically the reason why they did not listen to him was that they looked upon him as a clown. This made it virtually impossible for them to examine the truth or otherwise of what he was saying to them.

Something similar happened to Jesus when he returned to his native village. Because they could not accept him, neither could they accept his message. He was telling them only what he had told others: of the need to change, to repent, to be converted, if they wanted to enjoy the fruits of the Kingdom of God, a Kingdom he claimed had come with himself.

But his message never had a chance because they rejected the messenger. They knew too much about him. Who did he think he was anyway? After all, was he not just one of themselves? And here he was putting on airs and presuming to tell them what they should do! And so they were left in a terrible darkness. They thought that the mere fact that they belonged to the Chosen People was in itself a passport to the Kingdom, irrespective of the kind of lives they lived.

When it comes to accepting news that is unpleasant, however true and necessary it may be, none of us are any different. We all find it painful.

If some prophet or other comes along and says to certain parents: "You are working too hard. You are out of the house far too much. You have no home life for yourselves or for the children". Or: "You're not really loving your children. You're spoiling them. You're paying too much attention to them. You always defend them even when they are wrong". Or: "You're far too materialistic. You are not passing on any spiritual values to your children. You never pray with them". Or if he were to say to a man in an important position: "You drink far too much". Or to a woman who considers herself a very religious person: "Your religion is only skin-deep. Your worship of God is mere lip-service. No one would ever suspect from the way you live that you were a follower of Christ. Would you listen to the prophet who dared tell them such things as these? Would they not immediately want to make excuses and to defend themselves.

And what if the prophet were to turn on our character? If he said: "You are full of blatant prejudices. You always have to be right. You're a bore. You are a most conceited person. You always put yourself first . . ." How would we take to that kind of news? Would we not want to attack the messenger?

The fact is that none of us have any particular appetite for the truth. Hence we run the risk of living our entire lives ignorant of what everyone close to us knows and is probably talking about. We ought to pray for the courage to listen to the truth even though it is painful and comes as a blow to our pride. One of the signs of God's care for his people was that he kept on sending them prophets who would call them back to the right path. He does the same for us. He does not leave us in the darkness of error or wrong-doing. He sends us messengers, mostly those near us. Who else could it be?

We should also pray for the courage to be able to speak the truth when and where necessary. To set a person on the right road is a great thing. But there is a way of doing this. It must be done with love and concern for the person. The secret is to be totally honest and totally kind at the same time.

The truth Christ said will set us free. Which of us would like to spend our lives chained to lies and falsehood? But if we keep on rejecting God's messengers, how do we expect to escape such a fate?

PRAYER OF THE FAITHFUL

Let us pray to God, that unlike the people of Nazareth, we may be open to his message no matter how it comes to us. *R.* Lord, hear our prayer.

For Christians: that they may be able to speak Christ's truth to the world with courage and love, even though they too may frequently be rejected as he was. (Pause). Let us pray to the Lord.

For all temporal leaders: that they may be open to God's guidance, so that they may secure peace and freedom for all those entrusted to them. (Pause). Let us pray to the Lord.

For all those who live in the darkness of error or prejudice: that they may receive the truth with humility. (Pause). Let us pray to the Lord.

That we may be able to recognise the good in the people with whom we work and live, and be influenced by that rather than by their human weaknesses and imperfections. (Pause). Let us pray to the Lord. *Lourdes* *Holiday*.

For local needs.

Let us pray:

Father of all truth, through the grace of your Son, deliver us from the cowardice that shrinks from new truth; from the laziness that is content with only half of the truth; and from the arrogance that thinks it knows it all. We ask this through the same Christ our Lord.

COMMUNION REFLECTION

None of us likes to hear the truth especially when it hurts
Who likes to be told that he is on the wrong track?
Who wants to hear that things in his garden
are far from rosy?

We shy away from these things.
The reason is obvious.
The truth hurts and none of us likes being hurt.

Consequently we can take the truth
only in small doses.
Few people are prepared to tell us the truth.
They do not want to upset or hurt us.

And yet the truth is the only thing that will save us,
the only thing that will set us free,
the only thing that will let light into our darkness.

But there is an art in telling it.
That art consists in being
totally honest and totally kind at the same time.

The person who out of love for us tells us the truth,
knowing that it is going to hurt,
and at the risk of losing our friendship,
is a true friend.

FIFTEENTH SUNDAY OF THE YEAR
Working For Christ

INTRODUCTION AND CONFITEOR

The apostles were very ordinary men. In no sense could they be called specialists. Yet Christ involved them in his own work of teaching and healing.

Christ wants us to be part of his work too. Each of us is responsible for a small corner of the world where it is up to us to make the influence of Christ felt. But often we leave Christ's work to others to do. (Pause). Let us ask him to forgive our sins — what we have done and what we have failed to do.

I confess to almighty God ... etc.

HEADINGS AND READINGS

First Reading (Amos 7:12-15). Here we see how that great champion of justice. Amos, is faithful to the task God gave him, even though he is rejected by those to whom he is sent.

Second Reading (Ephesians 1:3-14) (Shorter form recommended). This is a hymn of thanksgiving to God for the great spiritual gifts he had given us through Christ.

Gospel (Mark 6:7-13). The time has come for Jesus to involve the twelve apostles in his own work. Accordingly, he sends them out in twos as his representatives.

HOMILY

The Korean war was raging. A little village came under heavy artillery fire. In the village stood a Catholic church. Outside the church, mounted on a pedestal, there was a fine statue of Christ. However, when the smoke of battle cleared away the statue had disappeared. It had been blown off its pedestal and lay in fragments on the ground.

A group of American soldiers helped the priest to dig out and collect up the bits and pieces. Carefully they helped him to put the statue together again. They found all the pieces except the hands. They offered to have the statue flown back to America and have hands made for it. But he refused.

"I have a better idea", he said. "Let's leave it as it is without hands. And let us write on the pedestal for all passersby to see the words: FRIEND, LEND ME YOUR HANDS. In that way we may get them to see that Christ now has no hands but ours with which to raise up the fallen. He has no feet but ours to seek out the lost. He has no ears but ours to listen to the lonely. He has no tongue but ours to speak words of sympathy, of comfort, and of encouragement to those weighed down by sorrow, pain, and failure".

I think this little incident brings out very well the message of today's Gospel. It is a very important Gospel even though we might not think so. We might easily get the impression that it is all about the apostles and has no relevance for us.

Jesus involved the apostles in his work. He sent them out in twos into all the surrounding villages. In that way he shared his divine mission with them. He gave them his own authority and power. He knew well that they would make mistakes. This is not surprising considering they were very ordinary men. Amos, whom we met in the first reading, was a simple shepherd. Yet God called him and sent him to preach a message of repentance to his people. Most of the apostles were fishermen. Yet Jesus did not hesitate to share his work with them. More surprising still. The day came when he entrusted his entire work to them.

Today many people in authority have a fear of involving people in a work, especially so-called ordinary people. Hence people are left with a feeling of worthlessness, a feeling that they have nothing to contribute. Yet it is good for people to be involved, not only in a scheme to help other people, but more especially in a scheme to help themselves. It makes them responsible. It helps them grow. It builds up a community spirit.

Of course often people just do not want to be involved. It is too demanding. Far easier to leave it to the experts, the professionals. And today this practice of leaving it to the professionals is all too common. All healing is left to doctors and nurses. As if there were no wounds of the mind and heart that ordinary people could help to heal. All teaching, even that of handing on the faith to small children, is often left entirely in the hands of teachers. As if parents were not the first and most important teachers and evangelisers of their own children. All the work for the poor and the disadvantaged is left to the Government or the Vincent de Paul Society. As if the rest of us were blind and helpless.

This suits us. It frees us from any feeling of responsibility. We do not have to do anything. We can leave it to someone else — the social worker, the priest, the nurse . . . We shut our hearts and go by, immersed in our own often selfish concerns.

Of course we need experts for specialised jobs. But the non-specialist too has a lot to contribute and often has a warmer heart. The sick, the lonely, the unloved, stand not so much in need of medicine as companionship — someone who will listen to them. The old need someone who will spend some time with them. The young need someone who will show an interest in them. This is work we all can do. It does not call for any expertise — only a caring heart. In no sense could the apostles be called experts. Yet we saw how Christ did not hesitate to involve them in his work.

If that be so, then as surely as the apostles I am doing the work of Christ, if we may so put it, depends not so much on our intelligence especially the little ones and the wounded ones. Our usefulness to Christ, if we may so put it, depends not so much on our imtelligence as on our willingness and generosity.

"When you have once seen the glow of happiness on the face of a beloved person, you know that a man can have no other vocation than to awaken that light on the faces surrounding him". (Albert Camus).

PRAYER OF THE FAITHFUL

Let us pray that the faith we profess with our words may be borne out by our deeds.   *R*. Lord, graciously hear us.

For all the baptized: that they may realise that Christ has made them his co-workers in building the Kingdom of God on earth. (Pause).   Lord, hear us.

For all those in positions of leadership: that they may learn the art of involving others in their work. (Pause).   Lord, hear us.

For missionaries, working to spread the Gospel; and for all those who are suffering for their belief: that God may sustain their efforts and their hope. (Pause).   Lord, hear us.

That we may realise that we show our love for Christ and for our fellowman in a most practical way by doing our ordinary work well. (Pause).   Lord, hear us.

For local needs.

Let us pray:

Lord, may everything we do begin with your inspiration, continue with your help, and reach perfection under your guidance. We ask this through our Lord Jesus Christ, your Son, who lives and reigns with you and the Holy Spirit, one God, for ever and ever.

COMMUNION REFLECTION

To do the work of Christ
is not a complicated thing.
It is really quite simple.

It means to be faithful in little things,
for to be faithful in little things is a big thing.

It means to do one's task,
no matter how humble it may be,
not only thoroughly but joyfully.

It means to make oneself available,
yet never to seek the limelight.

It means to make oneself useful,
without seeking to push oneself.

It means to strive to remain calm
amid the hustle and bustle of life.

It means to carry one's own burden,
without, as far as possible, becoming a burden on others.

In a word it means to be at one's post,
helpful and faithful, loyal and constant.

As Mother Teresa says:
"We can do no great things —
only little things with great love.
You can do what I can't do.
I can do what you can't do.
Together we can do something beautiful for God".

SIXTEENTH SUNDAY OF THE YEAR
Sheep Without A Shepherd

INTRODUCTION AND CONFITEOR

In today's Gospel we see how Christ cared about people as a good shepherd cares for his sheep. How do we know? Because he put himself out for them.

Every Christian ought to be a person who cares about others. We sometimes tell people that we care about them yet we fail to prove it by our deeds. (Pause).

A caring Christ — this is the kind of Christ we encounter here in the Eucharist. Let us trust him and come to him with confidence.

You, O Lord, are our shepherd, there is nothing we shall want. Lord, have mercy.

You guide us along the right path; you are true to your name. Christ, have mercy.

In your house, O Lord, we shall dwell for ever and ever. Lord, have mercy.

HEADINGS FOR READINGS

First Reading (Jeremiah 23:1-6). In this reading the shepherds who neglected the flock are severely indicted by God. At the same time God promises to send shepherds who will care about his sheep.

Second Reading (Ephesians 2:13-18). By his death Christ broke down the wall that divided Jews from gentiles, and he united all peoples as children of the one Father.

Gospel (Mark 6:30-34). In this Gospel we see the care of Christ for his apostles as well as his compassion for the people who were "like sheep without a shepherd".

HOMILY

Mother Teresa talks a lot about poverty, and she should know about it for she has spent most of her life working for the destitute. But her definition of poverty is different. Material poverty is the only poverty most people are aware of. But Mother Teresa says that there is a worse form of poverty than that. It is to be lonely, unloved, and unwanted. Thus it is possible to be materially well-off, and yet be among the poorest of the poor.

She gives an example of what she means. She tells how one day she visited an old people's home. It was well run — orderly, clean, and neat. The food was good. The staff was trained, highly efficient, and on the whole treated the old people with no little care. An ideal place then in which to end one's days? Not so.

As she moved among the old people she noticed that not a single one of them smiled. She noticed something else. They kept on looking towards the door. She asked one of the nurses why this was so. The nurse replied: "They are looking for someone to come to visit them. But no one ever comes. It's the same every day". "No one ever comes!" The phrase haunted Mother Teresa. It was then she became convinced that these were suffering a great poverty. They had been abandoned by their families and friends and put away in this home.

We come to today's Gospel. The apostles had just returned from their first experience of missionary work. They were tired and needed a rest. Christ knew this and showed his concern for them by inviting them to go off with him to a quiet place on the far side of the lake. But it did not work out like that. The people saw them getting into the boat and followed them.

You might have expected Christ to tell the people to go home so that the apostles could get a well-earned rest. Besides, had he not done enough for them already? But no. He took a look at them and saw that they were leaderless — like a flock of sheep without a shepherd. He knew well the attitude of the official teachers to people such as them. They despised them for not keeping to the letter of the law like they did. So they simply abandoned them — gave them up as hopeless. They wrote them off like the people in the home were written off. Naturally the people felt it. This is why they flocked to Jesus. They saw that he was different.

The Gospel says that Jesus looked at them, saw their plight, and had pity on them. We sometimes see people in great need and our first reaction is to judge them. To say that it is their own fault. Or perhaps we do genuinely feel sorry for them. But it ends there. We turn our backs and walk away. We do not want to get involved. Not so Jesus. He felt sorry for them and immediately decided to do something for them.

First he taught them at length, that is, he gave them food for their minds. Then, seeing that they were hungry, he fed them with bread and fish. (Cf. the passage that follows). In doing these things he did something more important. He showed them that he cared about them. He made them feel that they were worthwhile. "The corporal works of mercy should be done with great love, gentleness, under-standing   compassion and delicacy. Efficiency alone is not enough". (Catherine de Hueck Doherty).

We are all in need. At times our minds are confused, our hearts restless, and our souls empty. Above all we need love. At heart we all yearn to love and to be loved. We need not just to be admired but to be loved. There is a great hunger at the centre of our being for someone who will understand us and accept us, with all our lostness (to coin a phrase). Hence we all need the care of Christ, the Good Shepherd.

Today there are lots of people in our world who are like sheep without a shepherd. Such people are very vulnerable. Those who are unable to think for themselves are very vulnerable and can so easily be led astray. But the most vulnerable of all are those who are unloved and unwanted. Those who have no goal or aim in life, and for whom life is therefore meaningless. We think especially of certain young people who have known no love at home and who have little possibility of worthwhile employment. Such people will soon end up locked away in prison unless someone takes an interest in them. The Christian community should be alert to them and their needs.

Those who really encountered Christ, especially the apostles, had an anchor in their lives. That anchor was the care and concern of the Good Shepherd. This is the kind of Christ we too believe in. Have we ourselves allowed Christ to show his love to us? Have we heard him asking us to show some of that love we have experienced from him to others who are less fortunate than we are?

PRAYER OF THE FAITHFUL

Let us pray to the Father who cared about us so much that he sent his Son to be our shepherd and friend.   *R*. Lord, hear us in your love.

For the Christian community: that it may never doubt the love and care of Christ the Good Shepherd, and that it may listen to his voice. (Pause).   We pray in faith.

For the whole human family: that God may fill its leaders with a strong and unselfish love so that they may work for the progress of all peoples. (Pause).   We pray in faith.

For all those who are lost, and lonely, and depressed, and who feel that nobody cares about them: that they may experience the love of Christ the Good Shepherd. (Pause).   We pray in faith.

Each of us have within us the gift to care and to be compassionate: that we may use this gift in the many opportunities that come our way each day. (Pause).   We pray in faith.

For local needs.

Let us pray:

Heavenly Father, in Christ your Son we experience your love and care for us. Help us to care about one another and so imitate the Good Shepherd, who lives and reigns with you and the Holy Spirit, one God, for ever and ever.

SIGN OF PEACE

Lord Jesus Christ, you said to your disciples: 'Come to me, all you who labour and are overburdened, and I will give you rest. Learn from me, for I am gentle and humble of heart, and so you will find rest for your souls'. Lord, we come to you so that you may teach us gentleness and humility of heart, so that we may enjoy the peace and unity of your kingdom where you live for ever and ever.

COMMUNION REFLECTION

Christ looked at the people; and seeing
that they were like sheep without a shepherd,
he took pity on them.

Lord, look upon us and take pity on us,
for at times we too are like sheep.
Save us from a blind following of the herd.
Help us to follow you,
  even if it means leaving the crowd
  and walking a lonely path.

Lead us from death to life,
from error to truth,
from despair to hope,
from fear to trust,
from hate to love,
from war to peace.

Help us to listen to your voice,
to trust you and to follow you.
You carry all our hopes and dreams.
You alone can give us
what we hunger and thirst for — our heavenly Father's love
and eternal life in his Kingdom.

SEVENTEENTH SUNDAY OF THE YEAR
Hunger

Seeing that the people were hungry Christ fed them, and did so with generosity. Most of us have experienced momentary hunger, but not long-term hunger. But there are many people in the world who are dying of hunger and malnutrition at this very moment. They are our brothers and sisters. Do we feel any active solidarity with them? (Pause).   The Father wishes all his children to have food so that they can live. Let us turn to him as people who hunger for his love and blessings.

The eyes of all creatures look to you O Lord, and you give them their food in due time. Lord, have mercy.

Lord, you are just in all your ways, and loving in all your deeds.   Christ, have mercy.

Lord, you are close to all who call on you, to all who call on you from their hearts.   Lord, have mercy.

HEADINGS FOR READINGS

First Reading (2 Kings 4:42-44). The prophet Elisha miraculously provides abundant food for a hundred men. The miracle is a sign of God's concern for his people.

Second Reading (Ephesians 4:1-6). St Paul pleads with the Ephesians to live a life in keeping with the Gospel. He stresses the need for unity and harmony.

Gospel (John 6:1-15). Like Elisha Jesus feeds the people miraculously. However, the people misunderstand the meaning of this event.

HOMILY

Not many of us have experienced real hunger. Hours of it maybe, but hardly days of it. If we have not experienced real hunger then we should at least listen to those who have. Solzhenitsyn, the exiled Russian writer, experienced a lot of it during his years in the camps. He describes what it does to a human being.

He says that hunger rules the world. It rules every human being, that is, unless he is already dead. It forces an otherwise honest man to become a thief. It makes the most unselfish person look towards his neighbour to see if his ration is bigger than his own. Hunger darkens the mind so much so that it refuses to dwell on anything else but food, food, food. Severe hunger turns a person into an insomniac. Even when one does manage to fall asleep food is still present, for even one's dreams are concerned with it. After prolonged hunger food becomes virtually useless for a person's stomach has been turned into a one-way pipe system and everything emerges from it in exactly the same state as it entered. He says: "If you were to ask a wartime camp inmate what his highest, supreme, and totally unattainable ambition was, he would reply without a second's hesitation: 'To eat just once a bellyful of black bread — and then I could die happy'."

Another former Russian camp inmate says: "When you are starving day after day, week after week, you reach a stage where you can't think of anything else except food. You gladly eat grass and chew on an old belt. When you're being marched off in formation to a work site, the mere sight of a turnip in the ground or a piece of carrion will make you break ranks, no longer caring if the guards shoot you down".

That's what hunger means. That's what hunger does. First, then, a man needs food or nothing else is of the slightest value to him. Without food no life at all, much less a higher form of life, is possible. Little wonder that the great Mahatma Gandhi once said: "To a starving people the only form in which God can dare appear is in the form of food".

In today's Gospel we see how the people had followed Jesus to a lonely place. So anxious were they to hear what he had to say that they had forgotten to bring food with them — except one little boy. So naturally they got hungry. And what did Jesus do? He gave them the only thing that mattered to them at that moment. He gave them food, and plenty of it. How happy that young lad must have been that he had given his all to Jesus when he saw what he did with it.

Our problem in the developed world is not that we have too little food but too much, and too much food is almost as dangerous as too little. So the main preoccupation of many people has become how to cut down on their food. But this leaves people preoccupied with themselves — which is the death of love.

We waste so much food today. This is criminal, for we live in a world where at least a third of the people are hungry at any given moment. But the problem has become much more serious, especially in Europe. Christians in Europe must be profoundly disturbed over what to do with our surplus food. The EEC has mountains of it — apples, butter, meat, grain, skimmed milk . . . It is estimated that the butter alone if put into supermarket-sized packets would reach half way to the moon. And how expensive these mountains are to maintain.

It's hard to know what we can do. But in a way I feel that the stock-piling of surplus food is as great a scandal as the stockpiling of nuclear weapons. Yet it is accepted as normal. Martin Luther King had a simple answer. "We can store our surplus food free of charge in the shrivelled stomachs of the millions of God's children who go to bed hungry at night." But the chances of that happening are pretty remote. The member countries can't even agree on cheap butter sales to their own countrymen at Christmas.

So what can we do about the hungry in the world? Let us return to Solzhenitsyn. In order not to forget his camp experience and the benefits he derived from his years there, each year on the anniversary of his arrest he organises what he calls a "Zek's Day". (Zek means a camp prisoner). In what does this consist? In the morning he cuts off 650 grams (slightly less than 1½ lbs.) of bread. He then puts two lumps of sugar in a cup and pours water on them. That is his breakfast. For lunch he gets some broth and a ladleful of thin mush. And he says: "How quickly I get back to my old form. By the end of the day I am already licking the bowl and licking up the crumbs to put in my mouth. All the old sensations come back to me".

Maybe we could do something like that? Have a day every year in which we fast in solidarity with the hungry of the world. And what money we spare we could give to some organisation that is working for the relief of hunger. "You have to fast for those who are hungry. It's a question of atonement. You can't eat too much when so many people are hungry". (Catherine de Hueck Doherty).

In describing the things on which his followers would be judged, Christ put at the top of the list: "I was hungry and you did or did not feed me". We can't multiply the food like Christ could. But then we do not have to. All we have to do is share it, or the money to buy it. Christ continues to ask us the question he asked Philip: "Where can we buy bread for these people to eat?"

PRAYER OF THE FAITHFUL

In this Gospel we see the Lord's concern for the hungry and the needy, and his generosity in helping them. As he looks to his followers to carry on this work, we pray that we may not fail.   *R*. Lord, hear our prayer.

For Christians: that they may imitate the generosity of that young boy and not hesitate to share what they have with those who are less fortunate than themselves. (Pause).   We pray to the Lord.

For all Government leaders: that at least some of the vast amounts of money being spent on weapons of death and destruction may instead be used to feed the hungry of the world. (Pause).   We pray to the Lord.

For the hungry of the world: that their hunger may be satisfied through the generosity of the well-off. (Pause).   We pray to the Lord.

For local needs.

Let us pray:

Those things that we pray for, good Lord, give us grace to labour for. Through Jesus Christ our Lord.

OUR FATHER

We are hungry beings who must eat in order to stay alive. Let us pray to God our Father for the daily nourishment we need for our souls and bodies.

COMMUNION REFLECTION

Mother Teresa tells how once in India
she came across a family
that hadn't eaten for days.
It was a Hindu family.
So she took a small quantity of rice.
and gave it to that family
What happened surprised her.

Before she knew where she was
the mother of the family
had divided the rice into two halves.
Then she took half of it to the family next door,
which happened to a Moslem family.

Seeing this she turned to the mother and asked:
"How much will you have left over?
Are there not enough of yourselves?"
And the women replied simply:
"But they haven't eaten for days either".

"That", says Mother Teresa, "takes greatness".
Her greatness consisted in being able
to look beyond her own need.

EIGHTEENTH SUNDAY OF THE YEAR
The Further Hunger

We cannot have the joys of a new world without abandoning the comforts of the old world. Instead of going forward towards the Promised Land the Jews continued to hanker after the "fleshpots of Egypt". After having fed the people with ordinary bread Jesus offered them something far better — "the bread of eternal life", but they didn't want to know. We ourselves are reluctant to go beyond material things. Yet what God offers us is much better. (Pause). We ask God to pardon our foolishness and lack of courage.

I confess to almighty God . . . etc.

HEADINGS FOR READINGS

First Reading (Exodus 16:2-4, 12-15). God feeds his people in the desert by sending them manna and quails. This became the classic example of his care for his people.

Second Reading (Ephesians 4:17, 20-24). Paul urges the Ephesians to turn aside from the aimless life they lived before they heard the Gospel, and to live lives of goodness, holiness, and truth.

Gospel (John 6:24-35). Jesus declares that he himself is the true bread from heaven of which the manna provided by Moses was but a pale image.

HOMILY

Peter was forty years old and was a school principal. He was highly qualified and doing a good job. He had a happy marriage and enjoyed a generous portion of the so-called 'good things of life'. We are dealing then, not with a failure, but with a success. Yet this was the man who one day came to the Master asking if he could talk to him. (What follows would be more effective if done as a dialogue. If this is done, then the material could perhaps be developed just a little).

"There is something missing in my life and I don't know what it is", Peter began. "I feel an emptiness inside me. When I started out I believed that if I achieved what I have achieved I would be radiantly happy. But it hasn't worked out like that. There is still something missing in my life, but I don't know what it is".

"You are a lucky man", the Master replied. "Lucky? How can you say such a thing? I feel so unhappy inside myself", said Peter. "You are lucky because you are being called to something deeper", the Master answered. "Something deeper? What do you mean?" "Well, from a material point of view your life has been very successful. You have achieved all the goals you have set yourself. As a result you have slipped into a rut, a rut of contentment, and that is not good. Contentment — the total satisfaction of one's material desires — kills off all spiritual striving. The bread of material things can never satisfy the heart of man".

"What must I do then?" "You must resist the temptation to rush out and try to fill the inner vacuum with more of those things which so far have left you dissatisfied. What you are really experiencing is hunger". "Hunger?" said Peter. "I don't understand. I have a freezer full of prime meat, and a garden full of vegetables". "You are experiencing spiritual hunger", said the Master. "To nourish man is not the same as to fatten cattle. Man is a creature not with one hunger but with a hundred hungers. After he had eaten his fill of bread life is still only beginning". "Speak to me about our hungers", Peter pleaded.

"Not all our hungers should be satisfied", the Master replied. "Some of them are false and must be resisted. However, I will limit myself to our genuine hungers, the ones which must be satisfied if we are to be properly nourished as human beings and children of God.

"We hunger for a feeling of importance. Nobody wants to be nobody. We all want to matter, if only to one person. We hunger for acceptance. If I am not accepted it becomes almost impossible for me to realise myself.

"We hunger for relationships. Without them we are at the mercy of every wind that blows — like a lone tree on a hilltop. We hunger for motivation. Without it we are like a sail boat without the wind.

"We hunger for faith — for a set of positive beliefs to guide us. Otherwise we are like the crew of a ship adrift on the high sea, without chart or compass or port of destination.

"We hunger for hope. To give up hope is like going on spiritual hunger strike. We hunger, of course, for love. If this was fully satisfied then most of our other hungers would disappear".

The Master paused, then added: "There is one further hunger, a deeper one, one that underlies all our other hungers, including that of love". "And what is that?" asked Peter eagerly. "It is the hunger for the bread of eternal life. In other words, the hunger for God. To experience this hunger is a blessing, not a misfortune. It keeps the little stream of your life moving forward towards the sea, and saves it from running into a stagnant swamp. We are talking about the hunger of the heart and of the spirit. Only God can satisfy this hunger".

God led the Israelites into the desert so that freed from the ties of material things they might experience their utter need of him, and so get close to him. Many of them, however, could not get beyond their need for ordinary bread, a need which God catered for generously. That was all they wanted. They could not see anything else, or rise to anything higher, and so they perished in the desert.

Jesus gave the people who followed him into the desert as much food as they needed. (Cf. last Sunday's Gospel). In today's Gospel he offers them something more wonderful still, a new 'manna' from heaven — the bread of eternal life (himself). To 'eat' this bread would involve believing in him, entrusting their lives to him, and following him as their sure guide to the Kingdom of God. But once again many of them cannot get beyond the material. They are unable to face the further hunger — the hunger of the human heart and the human spirit. They do not even understand what he is talking about, and eventually turn their backs on him.

We must all know by now (even children) that material things will never satisfy the hunger the heavenly Father has put in our hearts. But have we experienced even a little of this inner hunger — the hunger of the heart, the hunger for God? Lucky for us if we have. Christ will satisfy this hunger. No one else but he offered the "bread of eternal life".

"People don't know what they are striving for. They exhaust themselves in the senseless pursuit of material things and die without realising their spiritual greatness". (Solzhenitsyn).

PRAYER OF THE FAITHFUL

God alone can give us the bread of eternal life. Let us pray that we may hunger for this bread so that we may enjoy even now a taste of the new life Christ promised his followers.   *R*. Lord, graciously hear us.

For all Christians: that Christ may awaken in them a hunger for the bread of eternal life, and that they may never settle for anything less. (Pause).   Lord, hear us.

For the world we live in: that God may guide the human family during its earthly pilgrimage, enabling all his children to travel in faith, hope, and love. (Pause). Lord, hear us.

For those who are going through the desert right now, the desert of hardship, trial, and pain; that God may give them the bread of endurance. (Pause).   Lord, hear us.

That we may be able to let go all undue attachment to comfort, ease, the worldly success, which make us the slaves of all things material. (Pause). Lord, hear us.

For local needs.

Let us pray:

Heavenly Father, you heard the prayers of your chosen people in their wanderings through the desert. Hear our prayers now as we journey towards the eternal life promised us by your Son. We ask this through the same our Lord Jesus Christ, who lives and reigns with you and the Holy Spirit, one God, for ever and ever.

COMMUNION REFLECTION

You cannot satisfy the satisfied,
or fill those who are already full,
or meet the needs of those who have no needs.

Jesus said:
"Blessed are the hungry,
for they shall get their fill".

It is a happy day then when we can admit
that we are poor and vulnerable,
weak and wounded and in need of nourishment.

For it is in our emptiness that we are filled.
It is in our confusions that we are guided.
It is in our weakness that we are strengthened.
It is in our sins that we are forgiven.
It is in our hunger that we are fed.

Lord, we turn to you for that food
which endures to eternal life,
which you alone can give us,
and which alone can satisfy all our hungers
and all our longings,
and which will sustain us
as we journey through this life,
which at times can become as bare as a desert,
until we reach at last the promised land of heaven.

NINETEENTH SUNDAY OF THE YEAR
An Angel Of Mercy

INTRODUCTION AND CONFITEOR

For some people life at times becomes so full of failure and disappointment that they just do not want to live any more. It is comforting to know that even the saints knew such moments. In today's first reading we see the great prophet Elijah experiencing such a moment. But God sends him help and he is able to continue. In our bleak moments. do we trust in God's help? (Pause).

You hear us, Lord, when out of the depths we cry to you.   Lord, have mercy.

With you is found forgiveness; for this we revere you.   Christ, have mercy.

With you, O Lord, there is mercy and fullness of redemption. Lord, have mercy.

HEADINGS FOR READINGS

First Reading (1 Kings 19:4-8). Elijah is a broken and dispirited man. But when he is at his lowest an angel gives him food and drink. Sustained by these he reaches the mountain of God.

Second Reading (Ephesians 4:30-5:2). St Paul urges the Ephesians to be kind and forgiving towards one another as God was towards them.

Gospel (John 6:41-51). Jesus is the new 'manna' from heaven. We must eat this food if we wish to have eternal life.

HOMILY

Mary and Kathy shared a flat on top of a three-storey building. Kathy was struck down by pneumonia and suffered a complete collapse of spirit. She gave up hope, and believed she was doomed to die. She even refused to take food or drink.

The doctor came. When he left, Mary went into Kathy's bedroom. She found her lying in bed looking out the window. And in a low voice she was counting backwards: "Ten . . . nine . . . eight . . . seven . . ." Mary looked out the window to see what her friend was counting. Outside there was a dreary yard. The only thing to be seen was the brick wall of the house next door. An old ivy plant grew on the wall. The cold wind had already stripped it of most of its leaves. "What are you counting?" she asked. "The leaves on the ivy plant", Kathy answered. "A few days ago there were hundreds of them on it. Now there are only a few left. I believe I will die when the last leaf falls".

Having tried in vain to talk this nonsense out of her head, Mary went to look for help. In the basement flat there lived an old artist by the name of Benson. As an artist he was a total failure. Now he drank to excess but still talked about the masterpiece he would one day paint. Mary went and told him about her friend's condition. "Leave her to me", Benson said, who in spite of his condition still had a soft heart. When Mary went back to Kathy's room she found her asleep. Before pulling the curtain across she looked out the window. A cold wind was blowing and a steady rain was falling.

Next morning when she entered Kathy's room she found her awake and staring hard at the drawn curtain. "Pull it over", Kathy shispered. Mary obeyed. To her surprise, after the beating rain and fierce gusts of wins that had lasted all night long, there was still one leaf left on the ivy. It was a mixture of green and yellow in colour. "It's the last one", said Kathy sadly. "But it will surely fall today and I will die at the same time". The day wore on and still the lone leaf clung to the branch. With the coming on of night the north wind was again let loose, and the rain beat against the window panes.

At the first sign of dawn on the second morning Kathy again gave orders for the curtain to be pulled back. The ivy leaf was still there! She looked at it in silence for some time. Then she said: "I've been wrong. I've been selfish. Something has made that leaf stay there to show me how wrong I was. Please bring me a little soup".

It was the beginning of her recovery. On the third day the doctor declared her out of danger. He was in a hurry as he said he had a chronic case on his hands. It was Mr. Benson. He had caught pneumonia and was dying.

That afternoon Mary entered Kathy's room to find her sitting up in bed knitting. "Kathy", she began slowly, "I've something to tell you". "What is it?" Kathy enquired. "Mr Benson died this morning. He had been sick only two days. Two days ago the caretaker found him in his room in great pain. His clothes were soaked through. They couldn't imagine where he had been the previous night. But then they found a lantern, still lighting and some scattered brushes, and a palette with green and yellow paint on it. And look — look out the window at the last lear. Did you never ask yourself why it never moved with the wind? Benson painted it there the night the last leaf fell". By painting that leaf — such a small thing — Benson saved the girl from despair. But it cost him his life.

In the first reading of today's Mass we met the man who is generally regarded to be the greatest of all the Old Testament prophets — Elijah. But we meet him here when he is in the depths of despair. A wicked queen (Jezebel) is hunting him down to kill him. So what does he do? He flees into the desert. There a terrible anguish comes over him. He feels he has taken all he can take. He just wants to die, so he asks God to take his life away. But instead of doing so God sends an angel to him with food and water. Strengthened by these the prophet arises and makes his way to the mountain of God (Horeb). There he encounters God and is enabled to resume his mission.

Who was this kind angel who saved his life? I believe it was a human 'angel'. More than likely the prophet's own servant whom he had left a short distance away. The same kind of 'angel' that had saved the dying girl Kathy.

In some ways it is a consolation for us to think that a great man of God like Elijah could feel like that. That he could be down, broken, and crushed. Many people go through a period like that. It is only the care of some human angel that helps them go through it. This is the normal way in which God's care is mediated to us. We too may get the glorious privilege of being that kind of mininstering angel to someone in despair. By our love we can help them pull through it, through small acts, insignificant in themselves.

Ultimately the 'angel' God sent to us is none other then his Son Jesus. It is he who stays by our side when we are down and crushed and unable to carry on. He gives us, not ordinary bread, but the "bread of life". In the strength of this bread he will walk all the way to the Mountain of God, namely, eternal life.

How much do we trust him? How much do we hunger for the bread only he can give? If a poor broken-down man like Benson could care so much, surely Christ will care a lot more?

PRAYER OF THE FAITHFUL

We are brothers and sisters of the Lord, journeying on the road of life — the road that leads to the Father's Kingdom. We pray for what we need so that we may reach our destination.   *R*. Lord, hear us in your love.

For all the followers of Jesus: that they may always believe that he is with them at every step of their journey. (Pause).   We pray in faith.

For all of God's children: that amid all the distractions of life they may never forget the meaning of it all. (Pause).   We pray in faith.

For those who right now are going through a difficult period: that the Lord will support them and help them carry on. (Pause).   We pray in faith.

That we may be grateful for the angels of mercy who care for us when we are in distress; that we may care for others in their need. (Pause).   We pray in faith.

For local needs.

Let us pray:

Heavenly Father, in Christ you not only gave us the hope of eternal life, but you made him the bread of our journey there. Strengthen our belief in him, so that with his help to sustain us, we may make steady progress towards your Kingdom. We ask this through the same Christ our Lord.

COMMUNION REFLECTION

Like a fruit tree we all know our seasons.
In spring the tree is full of buds and blossoms.
So at times our lives are full
of hope and promise.

In summer the tree is full of leaves.
Our lives at times are like that.
They are full of joy and contentment.

In autumn the tree becomes a feast of colour
and is full of ripe fruit.
At times our lives are like that —
full of meaning and achievement.

But in winter the tree is stripped bare.
So winter can hit our lives.
We are in the grip of a pain and depression
that robs us of everything,
even of the will to live.

It is on that day we need the visit
of an angel such as Mr. Benson.
However, if in the height of my summer
I failed to see my neighbour's winter,
what right have I to expect such an angel?

The marvellous thing about Mr. Benson was this:
in the midst of his own winter
he created spring for another person.

TWENTIETH SUNDAY OF THE YEAR
Partaking Of The Banquet

INTRODUCTION AND CONFITEOR

The Eucharist which we are about to celebrate is a banquet given
by the heavenly Father. The central guest is Christ his Son. Why are
we here? Because we are worthy? No, but because we have been
invited by Christ, our Brother, and we have accepted his invitation.
We begin by calling to mind our sins. (Pause).   We confess them to
God and to one another.

I confess to almighty God . . . etc.

HEADINGS FOR READINGS

First Reading (Proverbs 9:1-6). This reading contains an exhortation to us to turn aside from the ways of foolishness, and invites us to walk in the ways of wisdom.

Second Reading (Ephesians 5:15-20). The wise Christian will make the most of the present time, being alert to the will of God, and shaping conduct accordingly.

Gospel (John 6:51-58). This contains Christ's great promise of eternal life to those who eat his body and drink his blood (in the Eucharist).

HOMILY

The theme is the Eucharist, more specifically, Holy Communion. In most of our churches large numbers of people leave early. The main reason seems to be that they do not receive. Others stay to the end but also do not receive. This homily is geared especially to those who come to Mass yet do not partake of the "bread of eternal life". How can we convince them of what they are missing?

Suppose you have been invited to a public function, say the opening of a new school. You are a parent with a child in the school. You live in the local parish. Several hundred people gather in the school hall. Up front are special chairs reserved for honoured guests and 'big noises' in the community.

Somebody important, a member of parliament or a minister, has been invited to perform the opening ceremony. There are speeches. Then comes the opening ceremony itself. There is much clapping and rejoicing. They what usually happens? The 'top brass' and honoured guests are taken off to some inner room for food and drinks.

As for you and many others — the party is over. You have not been invited to the inner room. You are left out. You feel disappointed, to put it mildly. The main speaker talked about the school being 'your school'. It is, but only in the sense that without your children there would be no school.

Inside in the inner room there is much talk and laughter. The drink is flowing. The food is being passed around. But you have been excluded. You are good enough to be asked to attend the preliminaries — the speech part, but not the real thing which is now taking place in the inner room. You are made to feel that when the chips are down you do not really count. Most hurtful of all — you feel ignored. You were given no choice. Nobody came near you and gave you the feeling that you really did matter, much less that you were the most important person there.

Here we are celebrating the banquet Christ left his followers, the banquet that is meant to give them life and keep them united. In this banquet Christ becomes the very bread of our lives. The first part of the banquet consists to a large extent of 'speeches' (the readings and the homily which together constitute the Liturgy of the Word). This is a very important part and should not be played down. Yet, in a sense, we are still dealing with the preliminaries. The central part is yet to come. In the central part (the Liturgy of the Eucharist) we are invited to eat the Body and drink the Blood of Christ, to partake of what he himself called "the bread of eternal life".

Unlike the opening ceremony we describe above, here all are invited. "Take and eat . . . Take and drink". And it is Christ himself who invites us. No one is excluded. Yet what happens? By their own choice some do not partake. To go to Mass and not receive is like visiting a friend on Christmas Day and walking out just as the family sit down to the Christmas dinner (having been invited of course!).

No doubt people who do not receive have what they consider good reasons for not doing so. They probably feel that they are unworthy. The answer to this is: nobody is worthy. We receive first of all because we have been invited by Christ; and secondly because we cannot survive without the bread Christ offers us.

Mother Teresa says: "In the Eucharist I receive the spiritual food which sustains me in all my labours. Without it I could not get through one single day or hour of my life".

We may fee that we are in sin. If that is the case then there is another sacrament (the Sacrament of Forgiveness) in which I can meet the forgiving Christ, and put that right. As for what we might call 'ordinary sins' which, according to Scripture, even the just man falls into seven times every day, well we get a chance to confess them at the start of the Mass. So they should not keep us from Communion.

Listen again to the immortal words of Christ: "Anyone who eats my flesh and drinks my blood has eternal life, and I will raise him up on the last day". What an incredible promise.

I will always be unworthy of it. But Christ, who made himself my Brother, invites me. Here he comes to me as if I was the only one in the world at that moment, the only one that mattered to him. He comes to me because he cares about me, because I am important to him. What then have I to be afraid of?

PRAYER OF THE FAITHFUL

Jesus is the living bread that has come down from heaven. We pray that we may partake of this bread at his invitation. *R*. Lord, hear our prayer.

For the Church: that the eucharistic banquet may be a sign and a source of unity for all its members. (Pause).   We pray to the Lord.

For all humankind: that all peoples may come to know and to welcome Christ as the one who alone can give them the bread of eternal life. (Pause).   We pray to the Lord.

For our lapsed brothers and sisters: that they may hear the gentle voice of Christ, the Good Shepherd, calling them back to be part of the flock he nourishes. (Pause).   We pray to the Lord.

That we may receive Jesus in Communion with faith and humility, and so deepen our love for him and for our brothers and sisters. (Pause).   We pray to the Lord.

For local needs.

Let us pray:

Father, your Son Jesus has made himself the very bread of our lives. Grant that by listening to him and receiving him we may grow in wisdom and favour with you and all people. We ask this through the same Christ our Lord.

SIGN OF PEACE

   Lord Jesus Christ, you said to your disciples: 'If you are bringing your offering to the altar, and there you remember that your brother has something against you, leave your offering there before the altar, go and be reconciled with your brother first, and then come back and present you offering'. By this you wanted us to know that we cannot be reconciled with God if we are not reconciled with one another. Lord, help us to seek reconciliation with one another, so that we may enjoy the peace and unity of your kingdom where you live for ever and ever.

COMMUNION REFLECTION

Above all in Communion we draw close to Christ.
And having received him here
we bring him out with us into life.
We can, therefore, make our own the lovely prayer:

Christ be near at either hand,
Christ behind, before me stand.
Christ with me where e'er I go,
Christ around, above, below.

Christ be in my heart and mind,
Christ within my soul enshrined.

Christ control my wayward heart,
Christ abide and ne'er depart.

Christ my life and only way,
Christ my lantern night and day.
Christ be my unchanging friend,
Guide and Shepherd to the end.

TWENTY-FIRST SUNDAY OF THE YEAR
Freedom of Choice

INTRODUCTION AND CONFITEOR

Before his death Joshua said to the people: "Choose today whether you want to follow the Lord or false gods". And Jesus said to his apostles: "Will you also leave me?" In other words the people were given a choice. God, it has been said, is the greatest democrat of all. He forces no one to obey him. He leaves us free. We often abuse our freedom. We choose evil instead of good. (Pause). We ask the pardon and mercy of Christ.

You were sent to heal the contrite of heart.   Lord, have mercy.

You came to call us sinners to repentance.   Christ, have mercy.

You plead for us now at the right hand of the Father.   Lord, have mercy.

HEADINGS FOR READINGS

First Reading (Joshua 24:1-2, 15-18). Joshua tells the people that now that they have arrived in the Promised Land they have a vital decision to make — to serve the one true God or to serve idols.

Second Reading (Ephesians 5:21-32). St Paul uses the image of a marriage relationship to express the bond of love that exists between Christ and the Church.

Gospel (John 6:60-69). Many of Jesus' disciples leave him because they cannot accept his teaching. Jesus then confronts his apostles with same choice: "Will you also leave me?"

HOMILY

In recent years we have seen the appearance of a large number of cults, and between now and the end of the century we are likely to see a lot more. One of the most disturbing things about them is the hold they get on those who join them. Once in, there is hardly any getting out. Many are puzzled at how easily people can sell themselves and their freedom down the drain. Let us look at one example.

Pastor Jim Jones gathered followers around him in California. When things got difficult there he took them down to Guyana. There his People's Temple settled in what was called Jonestown. In 1978 the world was shocked when Jones involved some of them in one of the most bizarre cases of mass suicide ever seen. The journey that was to lead to the Promised Land became a journey to nowhere. To understand how this could happen we have to look at a number of things.

First we look at Jones himself. Here you had a man who could have done with help himself. He always had to be Number One. He lusted for power. He had to have people under him whose lives he could control. He sought only his own glory. His native followers believed he possessed the nine gifts of the Holy Spirit.

Next we look at the kind of people he attracted to himself. We are dealing with a collection of socially maimed and inadequate people, many of them delinquent and unable to fend for themselves. The kind of people Jones gathered around him were like migratory birds in search of a suitable climate. Jones offered them such a climate.

Then we have to look at the methods he used. His followers lived under a reign of terror. Armed guards patrolled the perimeters. No one could escape. Only the most trusted were allowed to leave, and this for the most urgent reasons. By February of 1978 half of them were suffering from diarrhoea and fever as a result of overwork and malnutrition. On top of all this they had to put up with Jones' harangues. He would preach to them over the public address system for an average of six hours a day. His voice followed them into the fields and to their beds. Letters were censored. No telephone calls were allowed. They were encouraged to spy on one another and to report any word or act that smelled of rebellion. Anyone who broke the rules was severely punished. Thus, through a combination of fear, guilt, poor diet, overwork and indoctrination, Jones gained almost complete control over the minds and bodies of his unhappy followers.

How different was Christ's approach! Let us look at some vital differences between him and the false messiahs.

(1) In the cults we have the personal glorification of the leader. We saw how Jones was always Number One. Mr. Moon (of the Moonies) claims he will succeed where Christ failed.

Christ never sought glory for himself. He referred everything to his heavenly Father whose will he came to do. When he cured the leper he said to him: "Make sure you do not tell anyone". (Mk 1:44). He refused honours. After he had fed the people in the desert they wanted to make him king, but he refused. Rather, he made himself the servant of all. at the last supper he washed the feet of his disciples, something that was normally done by a slave.

(2) Through a combination of inducements and indoctrination the new recruits to the cults become little better than a fly caught in a spider's web. Their freedom is almost completely taken away.

Christ never took away people's freedom. We have a splendid example of this in today's Gospel. The people, unable to accept his teaching, were leaving him in droves. He let them go. Then he turned to his twelve intimate followers and gave them the same choice: "Will you also go?" They stayed, but the choice was entirely theirs. Neither did he encourage excessive dependence on himself. Thus when the man from Gerasene (from whom he had driven out the devils) wanted to stay with him, Jesus said: "Go home and tell your own people what great things the Lord has done for you". (Mk 5:19).

(3) The false messiahs usually promise their followers an earthly paradise in some shape or form. It becomes a form of inducement.

Christ made no such promise to his followers. In fact quite the contrary. He told them that they would suffer persecution if they followed him. To one man who said: "I will follow you wherever you go", he replied: "The Son of Man has nowhere to lay his head". (Lk 9:57-58). True, he did promise eternal life — but only to those prepared to do the will of the Father.

(4) When Jones saw that the ship was sinking he made sure that the crew would go down with it.

Christ, the Good Shepherd, laid down his life to save the lives of his sheep. In the garden at the moment of his arrest he asked that his apostles be allowed to go free.

What is destroyed in the cults is a person's freedom of choice. But this is the greatest thing we have. It is our greatest dignity, and to use it well is the greatest challenge of our lives. Freedom is not something we are born with. In fact we are born totally dependent on others. Freedom is something we grow into. The only thing that has moral value and that helps us to grow is what is done freely. What is done through fear or coercion is of no value and in no way enhances the doer.

If we follow Christ we will always be free. And here is a strange thing. We are free not when we do whatever we please. We are free only when we do what is right. We are like an instrument that is being played properly. In other words, we are free when like Christ, the perfectly free one, we do the will of God.

PRAYER OF THE FAITHFUL

Let us pray to God for the grace to be able to live as his free sons and daughters, and not as slaves of error or evil.   *R*. Lord, hear our prayer.

For all the followers of Jesus: that they may realise that they are truly free only when they do the will of God in their lives. (Pause)   We pray to the Lord.

For all God's children: that they may value the gift of freedom: that they may not abuse it or throw it away. (Pause).   We pray to the Lord.

For all those who have become slaves of wrong-doing, or who are caught up in a web of lies and deceit: that God may set them free. (Pause).   We pray to the Lord.

That we may have the courage to accept responsibility for our own lives, especially for our mistakes and sins. (Pause).   We pray to the Lord.

For local needs.

Let us pray:

Heavenly Father, help us to follow Christ your Son, who by doing your will at all times traced out for us the way to live in freedom and dignity on this earth. We make our prayers through the same Christ our Lord.

COMMUNION REFLECTION

"Lord, you alone have the words of eternal life".
So answered Peter.
The words of Jesus truly brought life to people.

"Go in peace, your sins are forgiven".
With these words he set sinners free.
"Fear not, it is I".
With these words he calmed the fears
of his apostles when they thought they were lost.

"Launch out into the deep
and let down the net for a catch".
With these words he challenged Peter
to try again after a long night of failure.
"This day you will be with me in Paradise".
With these words he brought light
into the dark world of a condemned man.

Jesus truly had the words of life.
Yet many of his followers
refused to believe in him and left him.

We live in a world that is full
of contradictory voices and false prophets.
May we not be led astray.
Jesus alone can give us eternal life,
if like Peter we stay with him
even when many forsake him.

TWENTY-SECOND SUNDAY OF THE YEAR
Lip Service Or Service Of The Heart

INTRODUCTION AND CONFITEOR

The Pharisees were mainly concerned with externals, so that their worship of God became a matter of outward show. They gave God the service of their lips, but their hearts were far from him. The danger faces us all — mere externalism. We are about to begin our great weekly act of worship. Are we going to worship our Father with our hearts or with our lips only? (Pause). Let us open our hearts to God and confess our sins with confidence in his love for us.

I confess to almighty God . . . etc.

HEADINGS FOR READINGS

First Reading (Deut 4:1-2, 6-8) Moses once again urges the people to be faithful to God's law. It is not a burden to be endured, but a source of life and wisdom.

Second Reading (James 1:17-18, 21-22, 27). St James says that it is not enough to listen to the word of God. We must put it into practice. He gives some concrete examples of what he means.

Gospel (Mark 7:1-8, 14-15- 21-23). This passage contains a clash between Christ and the Pharisees. Christ tells them they have substituted their own law for the law of God, with the result that their worship of God has become mere lip-service.

HOMILY

I picked up the phone and called a friend of mine. I needed his advice about some practical matter on which he is an expert. As I waited for the message to reach the other end I was a little apprehensive. What if the line was engaged? What if my friend wasn't in?

Then I heard it ring. After what appeared an eternity I hear a 'click', and heaved a sigh of relief. I waited for his breezy 'hello' but it never came. I said 'Hello'. Nothing. I repeated it twice. Still nothing. Just as I was about to replace the receiver and ring again, in case that in my hurry I had got a wrong number, I heard his voice. "Oh good!" I said to myself. "Thank God he's in!"

Alas, as he started to talk I soon noticed that there was something wrong. It was not his usual tone of voice. It was a special one, cold and formal. In fact I had some difficulty in recognising it.

"This is a recorded message", the voice began. "Mr B. is out at present and will not be in until late tonight. However, if you wish to leave a message, you may do so after you hear . . ." In other words I was dealing with an answering machine, not a human being.

As I replaced the receiver I was very disappointed. I felt let down by my friend. Why was he not there? I asked myself. Where had he gone, anyway? He should be there. He had no right to do this to me! Even though I knew it was unworthy of me and unfair to my friend, nevertheless, I could not prevent such sentiments from arising within me.

I felt frustrated. The business in hand could not wait. And he was the only one I could trust to give me the information I needed. But he was not there! Yet, thanks to the marvels of modern technology, his voice was there. But what use was his voice when it was he I needed?

Long before such gadgets as answering machines were invented people were able to do that — to be present in voice only. Nowhere is this seen so clearly as in the case of worship. Christ said of the Pharisees: "These people honour God with their lips, but their heart is far from him".

People can be present in church in voice only, and so their worship of God becomes mere lip-service. And to make matters worse, very often it is not even their ordinary voice. It is a phoney voice, a special one they put on for Sundays, a solemn and serious one. Such people are no better than answering machines. The most important element is missing — the heart. The fact that they are there physically makes matters worse, not better, for it introduces an element of deceit. Such worshippers are like a stake holding up a fence. Okay, it is there. It is doing its duty, so to speak. But the vital element is missing. There is no inner assent.

This applies to other areas besides worship. It applies to any meeting or gathering of people. But it is most likely to manifest itself at public functions and on formal occasions. People are there, yet it is not their true self that is there. It is an artificial self, a dressed up likeness.

To meet such a person is to meet a shadow. You talk to him but you do not communicate. You are face to face with him, yet you never really meet him (or her). You are left with an empty feeling. The presence of such a person is like that of a December sun that dawns and sets without even defrosting the land.

How different real presence is! The heart is in it, and the words that are spoken flow from there. For our words to ring true, they must be spoken from the heart. If they come only from the lips, they will have a hollow sound. And while they may be clever, they will not convince or inspire.

Take the word of forgiveness for instance. If it does not come from the heart, of what use is it? It will not set the offender free. And the word of peace. If it is not spoken from the heart, can it bring peace? Of course not. And the word of welcome. You may open the door of your house to me with kind words, but unless you make room for me in your heart I am still a stranger to you. It is only with the heart that we can speak rightly. And a presence without the heart is like a fireplace without a fire.

What is the quality of my presence here on a Sunday? How much of my heart is in what I say? And when I leave here, do I try to put the Word of God into practice in my life? No one but myself can answer these questions.

PRAYERS OF THE FAITHFUL

Let us pray to God our Father that our religion may be sincere, that it may be a matter of the heart, for that is the only worship that truly honours him.   *R.* Lord, hear our prayer.

For the Christian community: that it may realise that unless its worship comes from the heart it is false and empty, mere lip-service. (Pause).   Let us pray to the Lord.

For all men and women of good will: that they may realise that unless their goodness is an inner thing it is only a sham, for to show outwardly what is not inside is to live a lie. (Pause).   Let us pray to the Lord.

For those who worship no gods but those of money, pleasure, power, or fame: that they may realise that these false gods will eventually betray them. (Pause).   Let us pray to the Lord.

That we may be saved from the folly of thinking that it is more important to have clean fingernails than a clean mind and a clean heart. (Pause).   Let us pray to the Lord.

For local needs.

Let us pray:

Heavenly Father, knowing that you value purity of heart above all
else, we pray you to create within us a heart full of love for you and
for others. Through Jesus Christ our Lord.

OUR FATHER

Let us pray to our heavenly Father using the prayer Jesus taught
us. Let our prayer come not just from our lips but from our hearts.

SIGN OF PEACE

Lord Jesus Christ, you said to your apostles: 'Peace I leave with
you, my peace I give you'. Cleanse our hearts of all rancour, spites,
jealousies, and divisions, so that together we may enjoy the peace and
unity of your kingdom where you live for ever and ever.

COMMUNION REFLECTION

It is the heart that matters:

It is not clean fingernails,
or clean teeth, or a clean skin,
that makes a person clean
in the sight of God.
To be truly clean is to be clean of heart.

For the heart is what I am deep down.
It is the real me.
And while we are all capable of deception,
a corrupt heart will sooner or later
show itself in the face.
At the same time, a clean heart,
like a clean mountain lake,
shines in the face.

Jesus looked at the Pharisees
and said to them:
"These men are no better than white-washed tombs:
they are clean on the outside,
but inside they are full of corruption".
But he looked at Nathanael and said:
"Here is a true Israelite,
a man in whom there is no trace of deceit".

In other words, here was a transparent person.
Here was a man who was clean of heart,
and therefore clean all over.

TWENTY-THIRD SUNDAY OF THE YEAR
The Deaf Hear And The Dumb Speak

INTRODUCTION AND CONFITEOR

In today's Gospel we hear the story of how Jesus cured a man who was deaf and who had an impediment in his speech. You might say this has no relevance for us, but it has. There are so many important things we are not able to hear, so many important things we are not able to say. This is what sin does. (Pause). Let us ask Christ to cure our blindness, deafness, and dumbness.

Lord, you open the eyes of those who are blind to the heavenly Father's care for them. Lord, have mercy.

You open the ears of those who are deaf to his voice. Christ, have mercy.

You loose the tongues of the dumb so that they can praise the heavenly Father. Lord, have mercy.

HEADINGS FOR READINGS

First Reading (Isaiah 35:4-7). The prophet urges those who are losing heart to take courage, for God is coming to vindicate and save his people.

Second Reading (James 2:1-5). Class distinction should have no place among Christians.

Gospel (Mark 7:31-37). This tells how Jesus cured a gentile man who was deaf and who also had an impediment in his speech.

HOMILY

Aim: to put some 'flesh' on the story so that we may discover its relevance for our own lives.

My name is James. As you know I was completely deaf. When you are deaf you are deprived of so much that others take for granted. You cannot hear the laughter of children, or the singing of the birds, or the bleating of young lambs, or the sound of the wind in the trees, or the roar of the surf. You cannot hear the voices of your friends. You cannot hear words of comfort and encouragement, or words of hope and advice. Few people bother to try to communicate with the deaf. They find it too tedious. They haven't the time or the patience or the skills. They nod and pass you by. It makes you feel terribly isolated and cut off.

When on top of that you are practically dumb, as I was, it adds to your sense of deprivation and serves to cut you off even more. You cannot explain yourself, no matter how strong your feelings may be. You may be full of fears and anxieties but you have to keep them bottled up inside you. There may be a secret you long to share with someone. You cannot share it. At one time I used to try but I would get embarrassed. Insensitive people would laugh at my stammerings. So I gave up trying.

I was never given any opportunity to contribute anything to the community. Consequently I felt useless and in the way. People even hesitated to touch me, some people, that is. When you are handicapped you are different. And when you are different people are afraid of you. Furthermore, I was led to believe that my afflictions were a punishment from God, for what exactly I never knew. But what it meant was that I was cursed by God. Imagine how that made me feel.

I was brimming over with self-pity. I craved for compassion. I ended up, however, with the conviction that there was no single person who either understood or pitied me. That was until the day I learned about Jesus. He was a Jew and I was a Gentile, but I did not let this deter me from seeking his help.

What an experience! The first thing he did was take me aside from the crowd. Thus he made me feel that I was important to him. That in fact at that moment nothing or nobody else mattered to him but me. He gave me his undivided attention. At the same time he saved me from the curiosity of gawkers.

He did not speak to me as it would have been a waste of words. He did something far more important — he touched me. He knew that this was the only way to really communicate with me. It was in the quality of his touch that his compassion came through to me. There was nothing rough or hurried about his touch. It was tender, and patient, and loving.

He put his fingers into my ears. Then he did something unthinkable. He put his finger into his mouth, took some healing spittle from it, and put some of it on my tongue. Next he raised his eyes to heaven to show me that it was from God that help was to come. I was told afterwards that he then gave a great sigh. In this way he showed that he was entering into my pain and anguish, and sharing them with me. Only then did he speak. He said: "Be opened!" And suddenly my ears were opened and I began to hear. In the same moment my speech became normal. I was cured!

I can no more describe how I felt afterwards that I could describe how I felt before. He told me not to broadcast what he had done for me. But how could I keep quiet about it? I felt that the finger of God had touched me. To say that I became a new man would be an understatement.

At first I talked incessantly. There was so much bottled up inside me — so many suppressed feelings, so many secrets that I had never been able to share with anyone. I could not pass anyone in the street without at least saying "Hello'. I could not remain silent in the presence of someone in pain if I felt that a word would help. I could not bear to see an injustice done to an innocent person without crying out against it. Whenever I heard what I knew to be a lie I would shout out the truth.

But quite soon I realised that I was over-talking. I was not listening. In that way I was hurting people. So I made a special point of trying really to listen to people. I did not find it easy. To listen to another person you simply have to stop talking. And you have to open, not just your ears, but your heart as well. I listened avidly too to the joyous sounds of nature which had been previously denied to me.

I discovered some interesting things during those early months after my cure. I discovered how few people really listen. I discovered too that everybody has certain impediments that prevent them from making full use of the gift of speech — shyness, insensitivity, apathy . . . Otherwise why do they remain silent when a word might comfort another. Why are they unable to share what is hurting them?

Why am I telling you all this? It is to save you from the fate of those who have ears but cannot hear, and tongues but cannot speak. What I discovered from my experience is this: the greatest tragedy is not to be born deaf or dumb, but to have ears and yet fail to hear; and to have tongues and yet fail to speak. I believe these are the people we should really pity.

Hearing and speech are gifts from God, great gifts. But without a heart that is able to feel compassion, we will never be able to make full use of them. The man who touched my ears and my tongue also touched my heart. It was that above all that made me new. That was the real miracle.

PRAYER OF THE FAITHFUL

Christ made the deaf hear, and the dumb speak. May he touch our ears to receive his word, and touch our mouths to proclaim his faith, to the praise and glory of God the Father. Let us pray. *R*. Lord, hear our prayer.

For all those who call themselves Christians: that they may hear the words of Christ, and speak them with courage and confidence. (Pause). We pray to the Lord.

For the world: that all peoples may listen with good will to the message of the Gospel, and that they may speak words of peace and friendship to one another. (Pause).   We pray to the Lord.

For those who are physically deaf, that they may meet with understanding; for those who are spiritually deaf, that they may wake up to what they are missing and seek to remedy it. (Pause).   We pray to the Lord.

That we may be patient listeners, and kind speakers, so that we may become instruments of the compassion of Christ. (Pause).   We pray to the Lord.

For local needs.

Let us pray:

Father, help us to listen patiently, to speak kindly, to see truly, and to act rightly. We ask this through Christ our Lord.

COMMUNION REFLECTION

Entry from a college student's journal *

"If I had only a short time to live,
I would immediately contact all the people
I had never really loved.
I'd make sure that they knew
I really loved them.

Then I would play all the records
that meant most to me,
and I would sing all my favourite songs.
And oh, I would dance.
I would dance all night.

I would look at the blue skies
and feel the warm sunshine.
I would tell the moon and the stars
how lovely and beautiful they are.

I would say goodbye
to all the little things I own:
my clothes, my books, my 'stuff'.

Then I would thank God
for the great gift of life,
and die in his arms."

* From *You* by Mark Link SJ © 1976 Argus Communications, a division of DLM, Inc., Allen, TX 75002, U.S.A.

TWENTY-FOURTH SUNDAY OF THE YEAR
Being True To Oneself

INTRODUCTION AND CONFITEOR

We are all very much influenced by what others think and say about us. We all like to be well-thought of by others. There is a danger here. We might make popularity the goal of our lives. And we might forget the only thing that matters — the reality of who and what I am. (Pause). No matter what others may think of me, God thinks well of me, because I am his child. Each of us can say that. Therefore, let us ask his pardon for our sins, especially those of pride and vanity.

I confess to almighty God . . . etc.

HEADINGS FOR READINGS

First Reading (Isaiah 50:5-9). This passage talks about the sufferings of the just man whose task it is to teach people the ways of God. He is sustained in all his trials by the firm belief that God is with him.

Second Reading (James 2:14-18). This contains a very important message, namely, that faith without good works is dead.

Gospel (Mark 8:27-35). Even though Peter declared his belief in Jesus as the Messiah, he had no idea what that implied.

HOMILY

G. K. Chesterton has a story about a much-loved and wealthy philanthropist. He was very popular. The main reason for his popularity was his unfailing good humour. Anyone who, feeling depressed, went to see him, would come away feeling better. Hardly anybody ever stopped to ask how the man managed to be always happy. They just assumed that he was a member of that rare band of people — born optimists.

But then one day the man was found dead in mysterious circumstances. Naturally foul play was immediately suspected. Suspicion fell on a number of people. However, the case completely baffled the police. Eventually it fell to Fr Browne, Chesterton's unlikely detective, to solve the case. His verdict — the man committed suicide.

Those who knew him were shocked. At first they simply refused to accept Fr. Browne's verdict. They could not conceive how such a

happy man could commit suicide. But then the truth slowly emerged
— there was a serious side to the funny man. Inside himself, the man
who made others laugh was a deeply pessimistic and constantly
depressed man. But he could never tell anyone how he really felt.
With so many people depending on him for their happiness, the man
felt it would not be fair to own up. Besides, it would shatter his public
image. He lived on that.

Here you had a man who was playing a role. In fact, he had
become the role. Hence he was never able to be just himself. He had
constantly to live up to people's expectations, in return for their
attention and esteem. Finally, he realised that his whole life was false.
It was based in a lie. The strain of trying to maintain the public image
became so great that he could no longer cope with it. And seeing no
possibility of rectifying matters, he took the shortest route out,
suicide.

This is an extreme case, but it has important implications for us all.
Everybody likes to be well-thought of. Hence people try to carve out
for themselves a favourable image in the eyes of others. They tend to
say and to do only those things which help to build up that image. It
is what others think of them and expect of them that matters, not
what they think of themselves and expect of themselves.

Such people need praise and flattery like plants need air and water.
Acclaim affects them like a wedding feast. Criticism affects them like
a bereavement. They will do anything to maintain the image others
have of them (provided, of course, it is favourable), even when they
know that the inner reality is far different. One man gets a reputation
for being a 'hard' man, though at heart he may be a 'softie'. Another
gets the name of being a 'comic', while inside himself he is actually
very serious. Yet another appears to be out-going and full of
confidence, whereas inside he is shy and insecure. Such people cannot
tell anyone or let anyone see how they really feel inside themselves.
They have too much to lose. It might bring them toppling from the
pedestal on which others have put them or on which they may have
put themselves. They would also lose their following.

If we look again at today's Gospel we see how little attention Jesus
paid to what other people thought of him. They got it so wrong
anyway. They had such crazy ideas about who he was and what he
was about. Some were convinced that he was John the Baptist come
back to life. Others thought he was Elijah or one of the other Old
Testament prophets. What nonsense! People will believe anything.

Only Peter knew who he really was, namely, the Messiah. But even
he did not get it completely right. Peter obviously believed the
popular ideas about the Messiah — that he would be a great politician
who, like a new David, would once again establish Israel as a great
military power. But Jesus had no intention of living up to the popular

expectations. Had he done so, no doubt he would have carried most of the people with him, and he would have enjoyed immense popularity, fame, and acclaim. But he would not have been true to himself, and he would have betrayed the mission his Father had given him.

We cannot but admire the single-mindedness of Christ. Nothing will deter him. Nobody, not even Peter, will stand in his way and sway him from doing what has to be done, even though he knows he will disappoint a lot of people and that it will lead to trouble, sacrifice, and an ignominious death. He is not swayed by what people think, or want, or expect. He is true to himself and to God his Father.

This involves a certain 'losing of life' — that is, it means dying to a false self built upon the esteem of others who lure us into playing a false role. But it also leads to a 'saving of life' — that is, the finding of one's true self in doing what has to be done.

Many people go through their entire lives wearing masks. But one thing is sure — we cannot enter into eternal life wearing a mask. "Before they die, people who have worn masks during their lives will cry out: 'Why did I use this mask instead of being myself? Why did I not reveal what should have been revealed? Why did I hide what should never have been hidden — my true self?' " (Catherine de Hueck Doherty).

In a sense the only thing that matters in life is to be true to ourselves. Any other path is a false trail and will not end in growth or happiness, or fulfilment. After death we shall enter into true life. Then we will really be ourselves, instead of forever wearing masks to hide our real faces. But we do not have to wait until then.

PRAYER OF THE FAITHFUL

We are all children of the heavenly Father. Therefore we have a tremendous dignity. We have no need, then, to pretend. Let us pray that we may live up to our dignity.   *R.* Lord, graciously hear us.

For all the baptized: that they may strive to learn what is pleasing to God and to do it with all their strength. (Pause).   Lord, hear us.

For all government leaders: that they may strive to create such conditions of life as to enable all of God's children to live in freedom and dignity. (Pause)   Lord, hear us.

For all those who have never found themselves, especially prisoners and down-and-outs: that they may not lose respect for themselves. (Pause).   Lord, hear us.

That each of us may be happy to be the unique people that God made us to be, and that we may never be content until we have realised the best that is in us. (Pause).   Lord, hear us.

For local needs.

Let us pray:

Father, source of all that is good, you know our weakness. May we reach out with joy to grasp your hand and walk more readily in your ways. We ask this through your Son our Lord Jesus Christ, who lives and reigns with you and the Holy Spirit, one God, for ever and ever.

COMMUNION REFLECTION

"Faith without good works is dead".
So says the apostle St James in one
of the most important sayings of the New Testament.

A watch that has a gold chain
but which does not tell the time
is worthless.

A fruit tree which in spring
is full of blossoms and leaves,
but when autumn comes has no fruit,
is false and is only taking up space.

It is the same with faith.
A faith that does not lead to works of love —
such as kindness, compassion, forgiveness —
is false and useless and dead.

Mother Teresa puts it like this:
"If we believe, we will love.
If we love, we will serve".

It is as simple as that.

TWENTY-FIFTH SUNDAY OF THE YEAR
Who Is The Greatest?

INTRODUCTION AND CONFITEOR

Mohammad Ali used to ask: "Who is the greatest?" And the answer he used to give was: "I am!" In today's Gospel we find the apostles arguing over the same question. Jesus was not pleased with them. He did not want to see jealousy and false ambition among them. He wanted them to live in peace and harmony.

By the way we act we too often put ourselves first. Thus we

antagonise others and hurt them, causing unrest among those we live with. (Pause). Let us ask pardon for our sins and let us seek the grace to live like Jesus.

Lord, you said: "Blessed are the gentle, for they will inherit the earth". Lord, have mercy.

You said: "Blessed are the merciful, for they will have mercy shown them". Christ, have mercy.

You said: "Blessed are the peacemakers, they will be called the children of God". Lord, have mercy.

HEADINGS FOR READINGS

First Reading (Wisdom 2:12, 17-20). This tells how the godless plot to do away with the just man, the man of God, because his blameless life has become a reproach to them.

Second Reading (James 3:16-4:3). Jealousy, ambition, and self-seeking lead to disharmony and fighting. Gentleness, reasonableness, and mercy lead to peace.

Gospel (Mark 9:30-37). The Master had been telling his apostles that he must soon suffer bitter humiliation and death, but they have not grasped what he was saying. Instead they get involved in petty squabbling over who is the greatest among them.

HOMILY

Let me introduce you to two people you have never met before. Naturally the first thing you will want to know is their names. They are Patrick Murphy and Timmy O'Connor. The next thing you will want to know is what they do for a living. Let's start with the first of them.

Patrick Murphy is a doctor. Ah, I can sense that you feel we are not dealing with an ordinary man. We are dealing with somebody special — a doctor! It's surely the dream of all parents to have a son or a daughter a doctor. Who would not wish it? Look at what it implies. The brains it takes to cope with the long years of study. The dedication and perseverance required to see it through. And once the magic qualification has been acquired, look at the fruits that begin to flow.

Patrick Murphy is a man of status, a respected man, a leader in the local community. He is no longer just Patrick Murphy. He is Doctor Murphy. He is, of course, financially secure. He has a fine car and a splendid house in a select area. Many people are dependent on him. If he goes away he will immediately be missed, and somebody will have

to fill in for him. He need not worry about being made redundant.
People have a habit of getting sick.

Now let us turn our attention to Timmy O'Connor. I know Timmy
very well. I used to meet him every day for we worked together for
ten years. He is the father of nine children. At present he is very
worried about one of them. She has something wrong with her heart.
He lives in a corporation housing estate. Immediately you enter his
house you can sense that you are in a real home. You can sense a
togetherness, a sharing a concern for one another. One night when
both parents were out I arrived with a box of chocolates. I gave them
to the oldest girl. The first thing she did was go upstairs and give
some to the little ones who had already gone to bed. From whom did
she learn this? From Timmy and his wife, of course. There is no car
parked outside, only Timmy's bike leaning against the railings.

Timmy is a most obliging chap. He will always lend you a hand.
without even having to be asked. He is always in good humour —
well, almost always. He is the life and soul of every party. He has a
lovely knack of always being himself, no matter what the nature of
the company. Yet he has no great education. I doubt very much if he
even got as far as the Intermediate Certificate. But he knows how to
be a good husband and a good father. He is not only a fine man to
know. He is an excellent friend, and true friends are rare. What does
he do? It's not important. But if you must know — he is a school
porter.

In the case of Patrick Murphy I have defined him almost exclusiv-
ely in terms of the job he does and the perks that go with it. This is
something we do all the time instinctively. I did not tell you very
much about Patrick Murphy the man, the human being. I told you
quite a bit about Patrick Murphy the doctor and a little of what that
implies in terms of status, salary, and standard of living. But in the
case of Timmy O'Connor, I concentrated on Timmy the man, the
human being, the father, the husband, the friend. I talked about the
kind of man he is. The job came a very poor second.

**How often we get it the other way round. We put the job a person
does first in importance. The kind of person comes second. This of
course is to put the cart before the horse. Which is more important: the
job or the person?**

Turning to today's Gospel, we see that this was exactly the
mistake the apostles made. For them it was the job, the position, that
was important. In their eyes the greatest among them was obviously
the one who had the highest position — the one who was next to the
Master. Hence each wants to get that top job, for the lowest reasons.
They are victims of jealousy and selfish ambition. They obviously still
thought that Christ would set up an earthly kingdom, a kingdom of
power and glory.

But Christ put them right on that. His kingdom is not about seeking honour and glory for onself. It is about serving others. If they are prepared to serve others, then by all means they can have the top places. But they will not be sitting on high chairs and soft seats, with others bowing and scraping before them. They are more likely to be down on their knees with a basin of water in one hand and a towel in the other washing the feet of 'the little ones'. If they are ready for that kind of life then they are welcome to the top jobs. The choice is theirs.

It is not what we do that matters — being a doctor, or a carpenter, or a bus driver . . . It's the kind of doctor, the kind of carpenter, the kind of bus driver I am that counts. It is not *what I do* (what rank or status I hold), but *what I am* that is of most importance. We can judge the kind of people we are by one thing — our readiness to put the needs of others (especially the little ones from whom we have nothing to expect) before our own.

Christ not only urged us to do this. He gave us an example. He gave his very life for others. No one can go higher than that. He is the greatest.

PRAYER OF THE FAITHFUL

Let us pray that we may see greatness in terms of serving others after the example of Christ. *R*. Lord, hear our prayer.

For the pope and the bishops: that they may give an example of humble and loving service to all their brothers and sisters in the Church. (Pause). Let us pray to the Lord.

For all those in positions of authority: that they may put the needs of others before personal gain and ambition. (Pause). Let us pray to the Lord.

For all the little ones, those who are on the bottom rung of the ladder and who spend their lives doing menial jobs for others: that they may realise that they are close to Christ and important in his eyes. (Pause). Let us pray to the Lord.

That each of us may be constantly on our guard against selfishness and false ambition, so that we may be open to God and to others. (Pause). Let us pray to the Lord.

For local needs. — FOR ALL THOSE WHO WORK FOR

Let us pray: PRO-LIFE & FOR THE PROTECTION OF THE UNBORN

Lord, grant that what we have said with out lips, we may believe with our hearts, and practise with our lives. We make all our prayers to the Father through you, Christ our Lord.

SIGN OF PEACE

Lord Jesus Christ, you said to your disciples: 'Blessed are the peacemakers, they will be called the children of God.' We are better at making war than at making peace. Help us to put an end to jealousy and fighting, so that we may enjoy the peace and unity of your kingdom where you live for ever and ever.

COMMUNION REFLECTION

So often we take the service of others
completely for granted.
It is only when the bus does not arrive,
or the paper, or the light,
or when the refuse is not collected,
that we realise what others do for us.

One day a woman laid the table
for her husband and children.
She put flowers on it,
but on each plate, instead of putting food,
she put some hay.

"What's this? Hay to eat?" they cried.
"Oh no, I'm bringing the food soon", she said,
"But let me just say one thing:
for years I have cooked for you all,
trying to vary the food —
rice one day, soup the next,
a chop, a casserole, and so on.
But none of you ever tell me if you like it.
In heaven's name say something.
I am not a stone.
I cannot carry on day in day out
without encouragement and recognition".

TWENTY-SIXTH SUNDAY OF THE YEAR
A Stumbling Block Or A Stepping Stone

INTRODUCTION AND CONFITEOR

Modern life has brought us closer to one another than ever before. We influence one another in all sorts of ways. God wants us to be, not stumbling blocks, but stepping stones for one another.

(Pause). Unfortunately we fail. Let us ask pardon for the harm we do and the good we fail to do to our brothers and sisters.

I confess to almighty God . . . etc.

HEADINGS FOR READINGS

First Reading (Numbers 11:25-29). Up to this the gift of prophecy had been given only to Moses. Now many others are given it. Joshua resents this, but Moses welcomes it.

Second Reading (James 5:1-6). This contains a strong condemnation of wealth, especially when it is obtained through the exploitation of the weak.

Gospel (Mark 9:38-43, 47-48). Anyone who is not against us is with us. But woe to those who would scandalise the little ones.

HOMILY

The world has become a lot smaller. Today people live closer to each other than ever before. Hence they depend on each other, they need each other, to an extent they did not in the past. Therefore the influence they have on each other is greater.

The Christian must at all times be aware that the way he lives affects the lives of those around him for better or for worse. Whether I like it or not I am a stumbling block in my brother's path, or I am a stepping stone to him on the road to salvation. This is very important for all kinds of people: for young people vis-a-vis one another; for married people vis-a-fis their marriage partners; for parents vis-a-vis their children; for employers vis-a-vis their employees; for neighbours vis-a-vis one another; and so on.

Here are some of examples of the way we can be a scandal to another person.

You are a scandal to me when you are unkind or unjust in the way you treat me. You make me feel small. You damage my self-confidence.

You are a scandal to me when you fail to understand my weakness, faults, mistakes, and sins, and write me off as a result of them. When you condemn me you make me feel that I am evil.

You are a scandal to me when you humiliate me because I do not live up to your expectations. You hurt my pride and damage my self-image.

You are a scandal to me when you discourage me, keep me down, or hold me back. When you grab the limelight I am forced to retreat to the shadows and made to feel inferior.

You are a scandal to me when you refuse to accept me, when you exclude me, or ignore me. You make me feel a stranger and an outsider.

You are a scandal to me when you load me with unjust criticism and sour me with your own cynicism. You tear down my ideals, destroy my dreams, and act as a blight on my hopes.

You are a scandal to me when, God forbid, you exploit me by paying me poor wages (cf. Second Reading). You make me into a slave so that you can live like a lord. You impoverish me so as to enrich yourself.

If you do any of these things to me you are a darkness to me. You are an obstacle in my path. In a word that sums it all up — you are a SCANDAL to me in the road to self-development, and you make it difficult for me to reach the Kingdom of God. That is a very serious matter.

But you can also be a stepping stone for me, an example, a help on the road to salvation. I will give you some examples of how this can be.

You are a stepping stone to me when you support me in moments of weakness and doubt.

You are a stepping stone to me when you give me a belief in myself, when you boost my self-confidence. You see something in me that I am not able to see in myself.

You are a stepping stone to me when I am feeling inadequate and you help me to discover the special talents God has given me.

You are a stepping stone to me when you challenge me, make demands on me, are hard on me, not to hurt me, but to help me grow and to develop my potential.

You are a stepping stone to me when you accept me, though others reject me.

You are a stepping stone to me when you refuse to join the mob and throw the stone of accusation and judgement at me when I sin.

You are a stepping stone to me when you forgive me. You liberate me from my past, and I am free to move forward again.

You are a stepping stone to me when you understand me and listen to me. One who understands me is nearer to me than my own brother or sister.

You are a stepping stone to me when you refuse to exploit my weakness or to take advantage of my mistakes.

If you have done any one of these things for me, how can I tell you what you mean to me? You are a light to me in my darkness.

You are a signpost to me in my moments of doubt. You are a bridge over troubled waters. You are all this and much more. You are an example to me. You are a friend.

Jesus said if you gave me as much as a cup of cold water, you would be rewarded for it. But you have done much more than that. You have led me to your own well and shared it with me.

PRAYER OF THE FAITHFUL

Let us pray to the Lord that he will help us at all times to be a stepping stone and not a stumbling block to others.   R. Lord, graciously hear us.

For Christians: that they may be a light to others and never a source of darkness, a helping hand and not an obstruction. (Pause).   Lord, hear us.

For all employers: that they may never exploit their employees; rather that they may treat them in such a way as to further their dignity and self-respect. (Pause).   Lord, hear us.

For all those who have been victims of exploitation or scandal: that they may overcome the obstacles that have been placed in their path. (Pause).   Lord, hear us.

That we may never destroy the vision of others, or make a mockery of their ideals, or pour cold water on their efforts. (Pause).   Lord, hear us.

For local needs.

Let us pray:

Heavenly Father, we are weak and each of us is poisoned by sin. We ask the grace that we may never drag our brothers or sisters down; rather let our hands be the hands by which you lead them along the path of eternal life. We ask this through Christ our Lord.

SIGN OF PEACE

Lord Jesus Christ, you said to your disciples: 'A new commandment I give you: Love one another, as I have loved you. All people will know that you are disciples of mine if you love one another'. Lord, when we do not love one another we become a scandal to unbelievers. Touch our hearts so that we may be able to love, so that we may enjoy the peace and unity of your kingdom where you live for ever and ever.

COMMUNION REFLECTION

"Woe to the person
who leads the little ones astray
It were better
that a millstone were tied around his neck
and that he were drowned in the depths of the sea".

What would Christ say of today's abortionists
who terminate the lives of the little ones
even before they see the light of day?

Or of today's drug pushers
who wreck the lives of the young?
Or of those who corrupt the young,
pouring slops over their souls?

If you saw a young tree vandalised
you would be angry
because of what that tree could have become.
Christ saw a marvellous potential
in every child (and in every person).
He did not want to see that potential ruined.

A writer, looking at a little child
in a railway carriage, said:
"This is a life full of beautiful promise.
Little princes in legends are no different from this.
Protected, sheltered, cultivated,
what could this child not become?"

TWENTY-SEVENTH SUNDAY OF THE YEAR
What God Has Joined

INTRODUCTION AND CONFITEOR

The readings of today's Mass talk about the bond of love that
marriage creates between a man and a woman, a bond that God does
not wish to see broken. We come to this Eucharist as isolated
individuals. But the Eucharist, properly understood and celebrated,
creates a bond of love between us. Christ does not wish to see this
bond broken. But unfortunately, through our selfishness and
isolationism, we often do break it. (Pause). Let us ask Christ to
forgive us, for he is full of gentleness and compassion.

Lord, you were sent to heal the contrite of heart.   Lord, have mercy.

You came to call sinners to repentance.   Christ, have mercy.

You plead for your disciples at the right hand of your Father.   Lord,
have mercy.

HEADINGS FOR READINGS

First Reading (Genesis 2:18-24). God made man and woman for
each other. The bond of marriage means they are no longer two but
one.

Second Reading (Hebrews 2:9-11). By entering fully into human life, by experiencing the bitterness of death, Christ became a brother and a saviour to all people.

Gospel (Mark 10:2-16). (Shorter form recommended). Christ teaches that the marriage bond comes from God and that it is permanent and indissoluble.

HOMILY

I remember when Eileen and Joe got married. It was a good many years ago. I knew them well and used to visit them a lot during the early years of their marriage. In those days their house was poorly furnished, only one room was carpeted. They had a black and white TV set, but no car or washing machine. But it did not seem to bother them. They never seemed to have a disagreement, much less a serious row. It was obvious that they were really in love. You could tell this from the time they had for one another. Wherever I met them they were always together. The phrase: "What God has joined . . ." seemed so apt. The thought of separation was absurd.

Yet, for all that, they reminded me of two climbers who had set out on a long and difficult climb, and who were still only at the first stage. The going was relatively easy. The summit was clearly visible and very attractive. There were no real problems. Their individual skills, powers of endurance, and loyalty to each other — these had not yet been put to the test.

I went away for a number of years. When I got back I renewed my friendship with Eileen and Joe. You did not have to be clever as Kojak to see that changes had taken place in the intervening years. There was a car in the garage. A washing machine purred away in the kitchen. A colour TV glowed in the living room. Wall-to-wall carpets graced the house. Three bouncing children filled it with tears and laughter.

Something seemed to have changed in their relationship too. To me an outsider, the most obvious change was this. The old spontaneity, the old sparkle, was no longer evident. They still talked a lot to each other but now problems dominated their conversation. The problems mostly related to their children — how to keep them fed and clothed, what schools to send thtm to, the state of their health, and so on. Joe was now doing a lot of overtime and Eileen had joined a keep-fit club. This meant that they saw less of each other. Even when they went out they rarely went out together. Joe went to his golf, Eileen to her bingo. "What God has joined . . ." Are they still joined in God? The answer does not seem as clear-cut as before. The things that hold them together, such as concern for their children, seem to have so little to do with love!

The two climbers have reached the second stage. The going has got really tough. The way is very steep. The summit is lost in the mists. Now the strengths and weaknesses of each partner become clear and are daily subjected to a thorough examination. Faults show up like cracks in a new wall. Each is often so engrossed in watching his or her step that there is little time to consider the partner. Now only a piece of rope keeps them linked together. Yet that piece of rope is the difference between life and death. Faith and trust in each other are more necessary than ever. If Joe does not play his part, Eileen is put under double pressure. And vice versa. What God has joined could so easily be snapped. It is frail, human, and insecure.

The third stage is still ahead of Eileen and Joe. Will they finish what they started? Only God knows. When two people decide to get married they agree to link their lives together. They forge a bond of love with one another. This must be done in complete freedom and, as far as is possible, knowing what is entailed. God then seals and blesses this bond. God made us for love — to give it and to receive it.

However, the ability to love is not something that happens to the couple on their wedding day with all the other gifts. No, love is something that has to be learned. The real journey married couples have to make, and not just them but single people as well, is the journey from selfishness to love. Nothing is a greater challenge to love, nothing provides a greater opportunity for growth in it, than marriage.

The kind of relationship marriage entails is a very demanding one and calls for a lot of maturity. Gold fish in a bowl get along easily. But bring two human beings together and you soon have problems. When two people get married they bring to it their strengths and weaknesses, loves and hates, hurts and wounds, hopes and fears. This is the reality. But they also have a great potential for growth. This growth begins when they accept each other as they are — two imperfect and vulnerable human beings. Then the difficulties they encounter can become opportunities for growth. If these are really bad then they should not be too proud to go and look for help, and help is available. There is more depth to a relationship that has weathered some storms. Love has to be tested in order to grow and to prove itself.

What of those for whom the bond has snapped? Well, they should not feel failures. It takes two to make a marriage. Above all, they should not feel that God has abandoned them. And we hope that they will find support and love in the Christian community.

PRAYER OF THE FAITHFUL

Let us pray for all of God's people, but especially for married people, that the bonds of love Christ created among us may grow stronger.   *R.* Lord, hear us in your love.

For the Christian community: that it may be a sign and a source of unity for a fragmented world. (Pause).   We pray in faith.

For all married people: that the bond which drew them together, and which God blessed on their wedding day, may enrich them and prove to be truly unbreakable. (Pause).   We pray in faith.

For marriages that are under stress, and for those that have broken down: that Christ may heal the wounds that result. (Pause).   We pray in faith.

For single and widowed people: that they may find love and support within the Christian community. (Pause).   We pray in faith.

For local needs.

Let us pray:

O God, strengthen the bonds that exist between us. We do not ask that these bonds never be tested. All we ask is for the grace to be faithful. We make our prayers through your Son, our Lord Jesus Christ, who lives and reigns with you and the Holy Spirit, one God, for ever and ever.

OUR FATHER

United by the bond that Christ creates between us, we pray to our heavenly Father as he taught us.

SIGN OF PEACE

Lord Jesus Christ, the night before you died, you prayed for your disciples in these words: 'Father, may they be one as we are one'. May we be one in mind and heart, so that we may enjoy the peace and unity of your kingdom where you live for ever and ever.

COMMUNION REFLECTION

There are three possible levels
of communication between a husband and wife.

The first is really no communication at all.
Though they are physically close,
their minds and hearts never meet.
They are like shells on a shore.

The second is a superficial level.
They make polite

but meaningless noises to each other.
They never talk about their feelings,
and rarely give each other signs of affection.

The third is real communication.
They are not afraid to show each other
that they are full of fears and anxieties,
that they are deeply wounded by sin and selfishness.
It is only when we reveal our wounds
to someone who accepts us
that healing can happen and we can grow.

Love is something we have to learn.
The road from egoism to love
is a long and sometimes hard one.
But it is immensely rewarding.

A marriage without love
is like a summer without the sun.

Lord, teach us how to love.

TWENTY-EIGHTH SUNDAY OF THE YEAR
It Is Dangerous To Be Rich

INTRODUCTION AND CONFITEOR

A rich young man of excellent character came to Christ wanting to
live a better life. But when Christ told him that if he wished to become
a disciple of his he would have to give up his wealth, he went away
sad. None of us follow Christ as closely as we should. There is
something preventing us from doing so. That something is probably
different for each one of us. I wonder what it is? (Pause).   Let us ask
pardon for our lack of courage and generosity.

Lord we have sinned against you.   Lord, have mercy.

Lord show us your mercy and your love. And grant us your
salvation.

HEADINGS AND READINGS

First Reading (Wisdom 7:7-11). This is a passage in praise of
wisdom. Wisdom is more precious than gold, or silver, or health, or
beauty.

Second Reading (Hebrews 4:12-13). God's word is a source of true wisdom for us. It will help us to live as God wants us to live.

Gospel (Mark 10:17-30). (Shorter term recommended). We are presented with the case of a good young man who refuses to follow Christ because he is unwilling to give up his wealth.

HOMILY

Note: According to Matt 19:20 the man was young, and according to Luke 18:18 he was a member of an aristocratic family.

The man came *running* to Jesus. Why running? It seems to suggest that it was a decision he made on the spur of the moment. He had not really stopped to think out where his action might lead to. Rather typical of the young — and not so young!

Why did he come? Many a young man in his position would have been more than happy with his lot. Was it that, again like many a young person, he was still questioning. His heart had not yet been hardened by riches and comforts. Woe to us when we grow contented, when we become smug and satisfied with ourselves, when we no longer are open to the call of a better life!

His question: "What must I *do* to gain eternal life?" Again, like so many young people, he longed for action. He realised that it is deeds that count. This would have endeared him to the heart of Jesus. As we grew older, however, we tend to take an easier approach: we opt for words.

Jesus begins by getting the man to look at 'where he has come from', as they say. The young man has firm ground under his feet. Without fear of contradiction he can say: "I have kept all the commandments: I haven't killed anyone. I haven't stolen from anyone or cheated anyone. I haven't committed adultery. I haven't dishonoured my father or my mother . . ."

Here undoubtedly was a sheltered and pampered young man. Yet for all that, he was a good-living, decent, and respectable fellow. A young man any parent could be proud of. A model? Yes — up to a point. When we examine his claims to greatness they are less than convincing. He has not killed anyone — the vast majority of people could say the same. He has not robbed or cheated anyone — but what need was there to do so? He had everything he wanted or the money with which to buy it. He has not committed adultery — but he was probably still single. So he had honoured his parents — but that was no big deal. They had given him so much, and he stood to inherit their fortune.

In a nutshell, what the young man was saying was this: "I haven't done anyone any harm". It is surprising how many people think this is the highest criterion of virtue. But is it? Is it not like a fruit tree that

says: "I don't produce any poisonous fruit". But does it produce any
good fruit? That surely is the question.

No doubt the young man prided himself on his goodness. It would
be surprising if he did not. Many people pride themselves on their
goodness, as if they had achieved it solely through their own efforts.
Whereas the truth may be that they are good only because their
stomachs are full. If you were to deprive them of their food, or of
their comforts, or privileges, even for a short time, strange things
would be revealed.

We are dealing with a respectable young man. No doubt about
that. He has no blot on his copybook. A good man. But an
outstanding young man? A young man who has been through the
mill and proved himself? No. He simply has not been tested. But he is
about to be tested — to the very marrow of his bones.

Jesus looked at him with love and admiration. He saw great
potential in him. Then he offered him a new vision of goodness. This
consisted, not so much in avoiding things, as in doing things — such
as helping the poor. He even suggested that he was in a privileged
position. Because of his great wealth he had a lot to offer.

Christ says: "If you want to do something really worthwhile, if
you want to practise real goodness, sell what you have. Give it to the
poor. Then come back and follow me, and you will have treasure in
heaven. *If you want to* — the choice is yours".

Helping the poor sounds very attractive as long as it does not cost
us too much. As long as it does not mean becoming poor ourselves. If
it only means giving a little of our spare time or spare cash, that is
okay. As for treasure in heaven — very nice, but at the moment most
of us would prefer treasure on earth.

What a hold possessions have on the human heart! How easily
they can become our god. How they can take over our lives,
absorbing our time, energy, and attention, so that we become
enslaved to them. The young man could not give them up. So he went
away *sad*. Why was he sad? Because the vision Jesus had offered him
had stirred something in his generous young heart. However, the
price was too high. So instead of joy he opted for sadness. If that was
not folly? If that was not a very high price to pay for holding onto his
riches? So he returns to his old life, his old comforts and securities.
No doubt he will continue to dream about doing something really
worthwhile with his life. However, there is a world of difference
between dreaming and acting. In time, even the dream will fade. It is
interesting that Christ let him go. He did not run after him and offer to
fix it for him.

If we came to Christ, and if we let him look into our hearts and
into our lives, and if we ask him what we must do in order to be his
true followers, what would he say? No doubt the answer would be

different for each of us. With a little bit of honest self-examination we could come up with the answer ourselves. Like the young man we too sometimes dream of a better and a more authentic Christian life. We dream — but are we prepared to act? The rewards in terms of joy, meaning, and fulfilment, even in this life, for those who follow Christ whole-heartedly are tremendous — in spite of trials and difficulties.

PRAYERS OF THE FAITHFUL

Let us pray that, unlike the young man who turned his back on Christ, we may follow him with courage and generosity. *R*. Lord, hear our prayer.

For all those who call themselves disciples of Christ: that the faith they profess with their words may be borne out with their deeds. (Pause). Let us pray to the Lord.

For government leaders: that they may be unfailing in their efforts to ensure that everybody gets a fair share of the wealth, so that all of God's children can live in dignity. (Pause). Let us pray to the Lord.

For all those who are stifled by their love for the wealth and comforts of us so that we may become his true and authentic followers. to spiritual values. (Pause). Let us pray to the Lord.

That each of us may make whatever sacrifice we feel Christ is asking for us so that we may become his true and authentic followers. (Pause). Let us pray to the Lord.

For local needs.

Let us pray:

Lord, help us to see you more clearly, to follow you more nearly, and to love you more dearly, step by step, and day by day. We make all our prayers to the Father, through you, Christ our Lord.

COMMUNION REFLECTION

Jesus looked at the rich young man with love.
Yet even he failed to touch the man's heart.
So the young man returned to his old life sad,
refusing to share any of his riches with the poor.

Yet how strange that Jesus succeeded in touching
the heart of the corrupt tax-collector Zacchaeus,
and got him to give half of his goods to the poor.

And the night before he died,
he turned and looked at Peter
who had denied him not once but three times,

and what happened?
When Peter felt those eyes looking at him,
he realised that he had betrayed a friend,
and he went outside and wept bitterly.

The look of Christ!
His glance falls on us too,
on you and on me,
It is a glance that comforts and disturbs,
heals and probes,
blesses and beckons at the same time.

What is he saying to me with that look?
One thing for sure:
That he loves me.

TWENTY-NINTH SUNDAY OF THE YEAR
Authority As Service

INTRODUCTION AND CONFITEOR

Most people see authority as a chance to promote their own
honour and glory. But Christ saw it very differently. He saw it as an
opportunity to serve others. This is not easy. We naturally think of
ourselves first. Even the apostles did, as we shall see in today's
Gospel. We are all selfish. (Pause).   Every sin is a sin of selfishness.
Let us ask forgiveness for putting ourselves always before others, and
sometimes even before God.
    I confess to almighty God . . . etc.

HEADINGS AND READINGS

First Reading (Isaiah 53:10-11). This reading tells of a man who takes
on himself all the sins and sorrows of the world in order to remove
them. It found its fulfilment in Christ.

Second Reading (Hebrews 4:14-16). Jesus was like us in all things
except sin. Hence, he knows our weaknesses. This should make it
easy for us to approach him.

Gospel (Mark 10:35-45). (Longer form recommended). Jesus
overturns all our values by declaring that the one who serves is the
greatest. He lived this out to the full in his own life.

HOMILY

People who misuse authority do a lot of damage to those under them. People who are victims of misused authority can be made to feel ignored, stifled, suppressed, used, and humiliated. They are diminished as human beings when those in authority "lord it over them". There is scarcely one of us who has not had first hand experience of this because we have all obeyed.

Nearly everybody likes to be in authority but for different reasons. Some people like bossing others around. It makes them feel important. In other words, they like power. Others like the prestige that it attached to being in authority. They like the glory that goes with it. Then others like the top job because of the high salary that goes with it. All these reasons have one thing in common. Authority is seen as an opportunity to promote oneself and one's own interests. The attitude is: "What's in it for me?" This obviously was the way James and John saw authority when they asked Christ: "Allow us to sit one at your right hand and the other at your left in your glory". Like typical careerists and opportunists they were looking for a comfortable position for themselves.

Now Christ had a completely different understanding of authority. He saw it as an opportunity to serve — to promote the good of others, rather than to promote one's own honour and glory. He said: "Look at the pagan rulers. See how they lord it over their subjects. It must not be like that among you. The one in authority must be the one who serves". Surely this is the most revolutionary thing ever said about authority. It makes for true greatness. After all, any fool can look after Number One.

All of us, except the very young, exercise authority in some shape or form. Parents exercise authority. So do teachers. So do priests. So do employers. So do foremen ... As Christians we should look at how we exercise our authority. Do we exercise it according to the spirit of Christ? Here are some points to consider.

Let us not forget what it was like to obey. It is easy to forget. A young teacher forgets what it is like to be bored, or to be humiliated before one's friends, or the simple fact that all do not learn at the same pace. Parents forget what it is like to be young. Foremen forget what it is like to be down in the trenches. And so on. Now if we forget then we are likely to become insensitive and to hurt, perhaps even to humiliate, those who are under us.

Let us not presume that we are necessarily superior to, or better than, those we command. A uniform, a promotion, a position of authority, these of themselves do not make us better persons. And under no circumstances do they confer on us the right to humiliate those under us. There are some people who cannot believe in their own strength unless they subject others to cruelty (like the school bully). But whoever debases others debases himself. Whoever treats another person like a beast in acting like a beast. If we act like this, then though outwardly people obey us, inwardly they will despise us. If we want the obedience of the heart, rather than mere conformity, we should act not as a superior but as a friend. And obedience of the heart is the only obedience that enobles the person who obeys.

We are not being asked to be easy or soft on those in our charge. Only to set an example. To practise what we preach, in other words. To be the first to obey the laws we lay down. We should not tell others to tighten their belts if we take it easier ourselves. We should not tell them to come in on time if we are late ourselves. No one has a right to demand from others sacrifices he is not prepared to make himself.

By the way you exercise authority over me, you help me to grow, or you repress me and so retard my growth and development. When you act big, you make me feel small. When you ignore me, I cease to count, and in a sense cease to be. When you humiliate me, I shrivel up and hate you and myself too. When you demand total and absolute obedience and loyalty for me, you are turning me into a robot, and you are depriving me of the one thing no one has a right to take away from me, namely, my conscience. But when you praise and encourage me, I forget my pains, I begin to grow, and am able to contribute more. When you consult me, I get a sense of being useful and of being valued. When you make me your partner, I begin to experience my unique dignity, and hopefully I will begin to live up to it.

It is a privilege for a Christian to be in a position of authority and leadership. It is a chance to build people up, not to knock them down or hold them down. It is a chance to help them to grow as human beings and children of God. The welfare of the people under you becomes more important than your own glory or even the success of the project you are engaged in.

As in all things, Christ lived what he preached. He did not seek his own glory. He did not lord it over others. He served others and gave his life to save them.

When you come to think of it, the servant is by far the greatest and most important person. The person in authority makes the plans and give the orders. But who carries them out? The servant. That is precisely why he is the greatest. He is a doer of the word. And yet, we can serve best of all from a position of authority — if we have the spirit of Christ.

PRAYER OF THE FAITHFUL

"The greatest is the one who serves", says Jesus. Mindful of this, let us pray to the Father for a true spirit of service for all the followers of Jesus, especially those in positions of authority. *R*. Lord, graciously hear us.

For the pope and the bishops: that they may be true servants of Christ's flock, guiding it with the same spirit of loving service that Christ showed. (Pause). Lord, hear us.

For all those who hold public office: that they may be people of integrity and humility who sincerely serve those under them. (Pause). Lord, hear us.

For all those who are down-trodden and oppressed, victims of tyrannical authority: that they may achieve their liberation. (Pause). Lord, hear us.

That we may not seek our own honour and glory; rather, after the example of Christ, may we strive to make our neighbour's needs as dear to us as our own. (Pause). Lord, hear us.

For local needs.

Let us pray:

Heavenly Father, help us to learn the value of a humble service of others performed in love. In living like this we become like your Son and we will one day share the glory of his heavenly kingdom. We ask this through the same Christ our Lord.

SIGN OF PEACE

Lord Jesus Christ, you said to your disciples: 'The pagan rulers lord is over their subjects. But this must not happen among you. Anyone who wants to become great among you, must make himself the servant of all'. By this you wanted it known that there are no highs or lows, no firsts or lasts in your community. We are all brothers and sisters. Grant us a spirit of service, so that we may enjoy the peace and unity of your kingdom where you live for ever and ever.

COMMUNION REFLECTION

In plain language James and John
were two opportunists.
Their one aim was to rise in the ranks.
To achieve their end they do not hesitate
to grovel and to beg.
They do not mind how much envy and resentment
they arouse in their companions.

Their aim is to scramble up the career ladder.
But at what price to themselves?
If, in the course of his rise to the top,
a man loses himself, his own soul,
whatever he does or achieves will be worthless.

It's amazing what power and all that goes with it —
money, privilege, rank, status —
can do to a human being,
especially to his heart.
If a person's heart is hardened,
he is no better than a withered tree.

Let us not forget:
it is by giving that we receive,
and it is by this serving that we grow in love.

THIRTIETH SUNDAY OF THE YEAR
Lord, That I May See

INTRODUCTION AND CONFITEOR

Often the blind see more than those who have sight. This is not a contradiction. There are more ways of 'seeing' than through the eyes. In today's Gospel we meet a man called Bartimaeus. He had never set eyes on Jesus — he was blind. Yet he had more faith in Jesus than many of those who saw him. The fact that we have two good eyes does not mean that we see what is important in life. (Pause).   Sometimes the problem is not what we cannot see, but that we won't see. Let us ask Christ to help us to see as he did Bartimaeus.

Lord, you came to open the eyes of the blind.   Lord, have mercy.

You came to open the ears of the deaf.   Christ, have mercy.

You came to set prisoners free.   Lord, have mercy.

HEADINGS FOR READINGS

First Reading (Jeremiah 31:7-9). This reading foretells the return of God's people from exile in Babylon. Even the most helpless will share in the joy of this great event.

Second Reading (Hebrews 5:1-6). This reading sets out the things that are required of a priest and shows how Christ met these perfectly.

Gospel (Mark 10:46-52). Jesus hears the cry of a blind man and gives him back his sight.

"My name is Bartimeaus. I'm just about to attempt the impossible — to tell you what it was like for me to be blind.

"There were times when loneliness enfolded me like a cold mist as I sat at life's closed door. But I was not allowed to enter. To be blind is to be cut off from other people. It means to be in a world of your own. Loneliness caused me untold pain. It almost drove me to despair and suicide. Then there was the sense of deprivation. I was not only cut off from people but from life itself — from all the things that people who can see take for granted. Without sight I was like a bird without wings.

"I was forced to beg for a living. That means I was totally dependent on the charity of others. I was sitting at the roadside of life, going nowhere. My past was made up of many experiences yet there was nothing to remember. My future was a long road, but a road without a goal. I was a man without means or possibilities. I hadn't even a flicker of hope in my life, and that is a terrible way to live. Life would never be any different. I would always be in the dark. I would always be lonely and cut off. Always on the margins of everything that was going on. No one would ever bring me into the banquet hall of life. I would spend my entire life looking in through the window. I longed for one thing — to be able to see. This longing would not leave me. If only it would go away then maybe I would have some peace inside myself.

"Some kind people gave me a coin or two as they passed. But hardly anyone ever stopped to speak to me. Blinded by haste and worry, they went on by. No one entered my lonely world, not even for a minute. The indifference of others, — that is what hurt me most. To be passed by, to be ignored, leaves you with the feeling that you are unimportant, that you don't matter. It's terrible to be treated as if you had no feelings — like a block of wood.

"Not only did the majority of people pass me by, they even speeded up as they approached me and showed down once they were past. This I could tell from the sound of their footsteps. I never could understand why they did this. But it made me feel that I was contaminated. Only later when I got back my sight did I come to realise that a man such as me makes normal people feel uneasy and threatened. The priest too was in darkness. He told me that my blindness was caused by sin. Thus I was made to feel that even God had no time for me, that he too had pushed me to the margins.

"That's how it was for me until one day I heard the noise of a large crowd passing. I enquired and was told that Jesus was passing by. The one thing I had heard about him was that he was compassionate to those in need. Hope flared up inside me. This was my big chance.

"So I began to cry out: 'Jesus, Son of David, have pity on me!' I was surprised at the reaction of the people. They tried to silence me. They said I was an embarrassment. This struck me as very selfish of them. After all, each of them was hoping to get something from the visit of Jesus to their village. Yet they wanted to exclude the one among them who was most in need. In a sense they were as blind as I was, for selfishness causes a terrible blindness. But I refused to be silenced. This was my one chance to break out of my world of darkness. So I just cried all the louder.

"Then I was told that he had heard me and that he wanted me. I threw aside my cloak lest I trip on it, and stumbling and groping I rushed to meet him. I reached out. He took my hand. My heart, which was throbbing within me, slowed down a little. He asked me a question few had ever asked me: 'What can I do for you?' It was music to my ears. Without a moment's hesitation I said: 'Please, help me to see'.

"He asked no further questions. He did not make me beg. He knew that I had done enough begging. He began to touch my eyes. It was a gentle loving touch. Slowly the scales fell from my eyes and light began to filter through. I looked up and I saw his face. He smiled at me and said: 'Go on your way, it was your faith that saved you'.

"How could I go my own way? I followed him along the road. I became an instant disciple of his, though I did not know at the time that the road led to Jerusalem where a shameful death awaited him. But what a joy it was to be able to see! I wanted to reach out and touch everyone. I looked on them all as my friends. In my meeting with Jesus I had felt his love. It was as if I was the sole object of that love. I was not only in from the margins. Jesus had given me a place of honour at the banquet of life".

We all can feel in the dark at times. We can feel lonely and cut off, cut off from much that makes life beautiful, happy, and worthwhile. We find ourselves on the margin of things. We are no longer useful or wanted. People ignore us. Without love the world is very dark. And people want us to keep quiet. And we ourselves are too ashamed to cry out. At those times we are blind, for we lose our way and our hope. We must have courage and the humility to cry out to Christ: "Lord, that I may see". Jesus is the one who brings us in from the cold, from the margins. He tells us that we are precious to the Father. He gives us a seat at the banquet of the Kingdom. The lower we are, the poorer we feel, the more he lifts us up. The more he opens our eyes.

He wants us to do for others what he did for Bartimaeus. We must not pass by the lonely person. We must not leave him or her on the margins. But by our love, our care, our time, we are to let a little light into their world of darkness.

PRAYER OF THE FAITHFUL

Let us pray to Christ our Saviour and our Brother that he may open the eyes of our minds and hearts so that, like Bartimaeus, we may follow him whole-heartedly. *R.* Lord, that we may see.

For Christians: that they may be delivered from the blindness of saying that they believe in Christ while at the same time refusing to follow him. (Pause). Let us pray to the Lord.

For all those in positions of power: that they may be sensitive to the needs of those in their charge. (Pause). Let us pray to the Lord.

For all those who are on the edges of life, the poor, the handicapped, the lonely: that Christians may show them respect and love. (Pause). Let us pray to the Lord.

That Christ may deliver us from the many forms of spiritual blindness that plague our lives and which prevent us from following him. (Pause). Let us pray to the Lord.

For local needs. *THIS WEEK IS PRISONERS AWARENESS WEEK, LET US PRAY FOR ALL PRISONERS, STAFF IN PRISONS,*

Let us pray: *AND VICTIMS OF CRIMES COMMITTED.*

Heavenly Father, our source of life, you know our weakness. May we reach out to grasp with confidence the hand you stretch out to us in Christ your Son, so that we may walk more readily in your ways. We ask this through the same our Lord Jesus Christ, who lives and reigns with you and the Holy Spirit, one God, for ever and ever.

COMMUNION REFLECTION

Lord, many people today
sit at the roadside of life begging,
not for money,
but for love,
for attention,
for companionship,
for a feeling that they are important,
that their life has a meaning.

In a sense they are blind,
for they cannot see a way out of their predicament.
Most of them are to embarrassed
to cry out for help.
They are afraid of being silenced
by the indifference of others.
They need a kind person to stop and ask:
"What can I do for you?"

Lord, that I may see —
see my needy brothers and sisters,
that I may hear their silent cries,
that I may not pass by.
For I too was a beggar,
but you enriched me.
I too was blind,
and you enlightened me.

THIRTY-FIRST SUNDAY OF THE YEAR
The Two Great Commandments

INTRODUCTION AND CONFITEOR

Today's liturgy reminds us of one of the greatest truths in the Bible, namely, that there are really only two commandments. The first is to love God, and the second is to love our neighbour. They are not meant to be separated. But we often do separate them. We like to think that we are on good terms with God, yet how many of us can say that we are on good terms with all our neighbours? We speak to God when we pray, but do we speak to all our neighbours?' (Pause).   Let us ask the Father to forgive us our failues to prove our love for him by loving all our brothers and sisters.

I confess to almighty God . . . etc.

HEADINGS FOR READINGS

First Reading (Deut 6:2-6). Moses reminds the people of the great commandment to love God. To love God means to keep his commandments and to walk in his ways.

Second Reading (Hebrews 7:23-28). This reading shows the superiority of Christ over the priests of the Old Testament.

Gospel (Mark 12:28-34). All of God's commandments can be reduced to two.

HOMILY

Jim knew quite a bit about cars. He owned this old Volkswagen which he wanted to get rid of. It was what is known as a 'banger'. It was worth £400 at the very most. He had been in a bad crash with it in which among other things the back axle had been damaged. But he had a cover-up job done on it. He re-adjusted the clock so that the mileage was cut by half. Then he put an advertisement in the paper and waited for the right buyer to come along. By right buyer he meant someone who needed a car badly but could not afford a new one, and who knew next to nothing about cars. In due time such a man came along. Joe was his name. He paid Jim £1,600 cash down for the old Volkswagen. He took Jim's word for it that it was structurally sound.

Jim felt proud of himself at the way things had turned out. He even gloated over the 'sucker' he had taken in. In the pub he could not help boasting to his mates how he got £1,600 for what he now acknowledged to be just a piece of junk. Of course the thought did go through his head: What if Joe, the father of a young family, were to have a bad accident and he were to get killed? But he quickly chased the thought away again. Meanwhile, with the money and the help of a loan from the bank, he had gone and bought himself a brand-new Mercedes.

A few months later Christmas came around. Jim went to the Sacrament of Penance for the holy season. His confession was along these lines: "Six months, Father, since my last confession. Nothing much to tell — just the usual. I have a habit of cursing and taking the Lord's name in vain. I had distractions during my prayers. Sometimes I even forgot them altogether — the prayers I mean. I missed Mass twice through my own fault. I told a few lies to get myself out of tricky situations. I talked uncharitably about my neighbours on a number of occasions. I took pleasure in listening to smutty jokes and I told a few myself. That's about it . . . And oh, I received once without having fasted the full hour beforehand". The priest waited for a minute but nothing more came. And that was that as far as Jim's confession was concerned.

Two days later he met a friend in the pub. "Jim, I see you were at confession last Saturday", said the friend. "How do you know that?" Jim asked. "Easy! I saw your Mercedes outside the church. By the way — without wanting to interfere of course — but I hope you told him how you cheated your man over the car". "Indeed, I did no such thing", Jim replied. "I told the priest my sins, but I don't have to tell him my business".

If you asked Jim was he happy with the confession he made he would probably say he was. But you wonder — unless of course he is deaf and has never really heard the Gospel. And this can happen — one has only to look into one's own heart. People listen to the Gospel being read every Sunday but never really hear it. As Christ said of some of his followers: "They have ears but they do not hear". We only hear the Gospel, we only understand it, when we begin to live it.

If you look at Jim's list of sins, what do you notice? You notice that on the main they are concerned with his dealing with God: distractions during prayers, missing Mass, taking the Lord's name in vain, cursing . . . and so on. The neighbour hardly gets a look in. When people such as Jim examine their conscience whole fields remain untouched: the conscientious carrying out of one's duty, honesty in business matters, justice, respect and co-operation among those who live under the same roof . . . and so on.

Yet Jim would probably tell you that he is trying to love God and keep his commandments as good as the next man. But is he? For him religion is almost completely divorced from life. Basically it is a private matter between God and himself. Concern for his neighbour is hardly a burning issue for him. Let's face it — it is not an issue at all. This means that his religion has degenerated into mere formalism, mere ritualism. He has allowed rituals (going to Mass, to the sacraments . . .) to take the place of love. Does he love God? If love of God is shown in loving one's neighbour, the answer would have to be a resounding No. According to the Bible, a religion such as Jim's is worse than useless. It is a distortion. It is an abomination.

The danger is real for all of us — that we would separate the two great commandments. It is possible to talk to someone about the love of God and yet never love that person. To do this is like talking to a starving man about bread without giving him some to eat, or it is like talking to a man about warmth while leaving him out in the cold.

In a sense there is only one commandment — the commandment of love. It is like a coin, one entity with two sides. It is impossible to have one without the other.

"Serving God is doing good to man. But praying is thought an easier service and is therefore more generally chosen". (Benjamin Franklin).

"Today, by the grace of God and his beloved Mother, I can honestly say that I love everybody. I might not like everybody, but I love them". (Catherine de Hueck Doherty).

PRAYER OF THE FAITHFUL

Let us pray to the Father who loves all his children, deserving and undeserving, and who wants us to show our love for him by loving others in the same way. *R*. Lord, hear us in your love.

For all the followers of Christ: that they may not be content to declare their love for God in church on Sunday, and then go out and ignore other people during the week. (Pause). We pray in faith.

For all our civil leaders: that God may fill them with a strong and unselfish love so that they may work for the progress of all people. (Pause). We pray in faith.

Without love the world is very dark. For all those who have known little kindness in their lives and who practise even less. (Pause). We pray in faith.

For ourselves: that having experienced the love and mercy of Christ in our own lives, we may generously reach out to others and share these blessings with them. (Pause). We pray in faith.

For local needs.

Let us pray:

Heavenly Father, your Son taught us in word and deed that we are to love you and to love one another. Grant that our lives may bear witness to the faith we profess with our lips. We ask this through the same Christ our Lord.

SIGN OF PEACE

Lord Jesus Christ, you said to your disciples: 'If you are bringing your offering to the altar, and there you remember that someone has something against you, leave your offering there before the altar, go and be reconciled with that person first, and then come back and present your offering'. By this you wanted us to know that we cannot be reconciled with God if we are not reconciled with one another. Lord, help us to seek reconciliation with one another, so that we may enjoy the peace and unity of your kingdom where you live for ever and ever.

COMMUNION REFLECTION

The greatest tragedy in the modern world
is the way we have separated
the two great commandments.
It is clean contrary to the Gospel.

There are some who attend Mass most faithfully
but who are undisturbed
by their neighbour's misfortunes.
Those who brag about their faith
are often the worst offenders.

Then there are others — more numerous —
who do not give a thought for God.
All that matters to them
is that they should succeed in their undertakings.

In other words:
those who have faith often have no love.
Whereas those who love often have no faith.

Thus the Gospel has been torn in two.
Those who have rejected God
are living with the half of the Gospel
we the believers have thrown into the dustbin.

Christ said that we are
to love God with all our hearts,
and to love our neighbour as ourselves.
That is the complete Gospel.

THIRTY-SECOND SUNDAY OF THE YEAR
The Widow's Mighty Mite

INTRODUCTION AND CONFITEOR

  With regard to gifts we have a saying that goes: 'It's the thought that counts'. Yet in practice we often forget this and use a different criterion. We judge a gift by its size, that is, by its cost. But this can be so unfair. Christ did not fall for it. He said that the poor widow who gave exactly one penny gave more than anyone else. We often judge our own contribution and that of others by standards other than those of the Gospel. (Pause). God is generous with his forgiveness. Let us ask pardon for all the unfair and false judgements we make.

Lord, we have sinned against you. Lord, have mercy.

Lord, show us your mercy and your love. And grant us your salvation.

May almighty God have mercy . . . etc.

HEADINGS FOR READINGS

First Reading (1 Kings 17:10-16). In this reading we meet a pagan widow who in the middle of a famine shares the last of her food with a hungry man. In doing so she learns a great lesson, namely, that it is in giving that we receive.

Second Reading (Hebrews 9:24-28). Through his death Christ has taken our sins upon himself and he has opened for us the door of salvation.

Gospel (Mark 12:38-44). (Shorter form recommended). The offering of the widow. In the eyes of others her offering was the least. But in the eyes of Christ it was the greatest.

HOMILY

Once upon a time there was a vixen who had three cubs. On one occasion, worn out from the wearisome business of feeding them, she fell sick. None of them had eaten for two whole days. Reluctantly she had to send the cubs out one dark night in search of food. She warned them to be careful and to use all their cunning. They were to split up and go in different directions.

The first cub, though the strongest, was lazy by nature. He chose the easiest road. He set out eastwards across flat land, keeping close to the hedges for cover. He had a great stroke of luck. He had not gone very far when he heard a rabbit screeching. He entered a small sheltered field that was stirring with rabbits. There he found a fine fat one caught in a trap. He killed it at once, and overcome with hunger, ate it. Then he grabbed another one and made off home with it. On the way home he resolved to tell no one about the field that was stirring with rabbits.

He was home within the hour, without as much as a scratch on him. His mother was delighted. "Oh, back so soon?" she said. "And what a splendid rabbit you've brought back. How did you catch it?" But she answered the question herself. "I bet you had to chase it through thorns, briars, and barbed wire fences? Well done! You're a good cub. I'm proud of you. One day you'll make a very good fox".

The second cub was very clever. He headed southwards across land that was dotted with trees. He used these for cover. Seeing the lights of a farmhouse ahead, he hid in a thicket. Presently an old fox came along. The cub followed it to the farmhouse. The old fox had found a hole in the wire fence which gave access to a house where geese were being fattened for Christmas. Amazingly there was no guard dog. When the old fox had made a kill and gone his way, the cub stole into the house and quickly killed two young geese. He dragged them off with him. When he was at a safe distance he sat down and ate half of the bigger one. The other half he buried, determined to come back next day and finish it off.

He was back home in just over an hour with the other goose, having taken care to wash the blood off himself in a stream. The mother was thrilled. "What a clever young fox you are!" she said.

"Did you have any trouble?" But once again the mother did not allow the cub to tell his story. "No doubt", said she, "you had to contend with savage dogs and angry farmers. Well done! I'm proud of you. You'll make a fine fox when you grow up".

The third cub was rather weak and sickly. He had never been much farther than the edge of the den. He headed northwards across hilly country. Here farmhouses were few and far between. He travelled far, going to no less than six different ones. But each of them was guarded by a ferocious dog that barked and snapped at him. One of them tore him through the wire so that blood streamed down his face. Once an angry farmer fired a shot at him, narrowly missing him. The night went by all too quickly. There was nothing to do but head for home. He had a long way to go and was ready to collapse from exhaustion and hunger. On the way home he came across a dead sparrow under a tree. He had a terrible urge to swallow it but he did not do so. It was not much, but he decided to take it home with him. It would not do to arrive back empty-handed.

Dawn was breaking when he finally reached home. He was covered with mud, and was a mass of scratches, cuts, and bruises. However, the first thing his mother said was: "Look at the cut of you! What kept you anyway?" "I ran into trouble", he answered feebly. "Didn't I warn you to be careful", snapped the mother. "And what have you brought me at the end of it all?" "Not much. This is all I could manage". With that he produced the sparrow. The other two began to laugh. "What's this?" asked the mother. "A sparrow! Surely you're not serious?" "I found it under a tree", said the cub. "You mean you found it dead?" "Yes. It was the best I could do". "You're a nice one! I've obviously wasted my time and energy feeding and caring for you. You'll grow up to be a waster. Take it away from here and get out of my sight at once!" The mother chased him right out of the den. A banquet was then spread. The menu consisted of goose and rabbit. But the little cub was not invited in, because in the eyes of his mother he had contributed nothing.

In one sense the mother was right. Judged by results the little cub had failed. He had come a long way behind the other two. But in another sense the mother was completely wrong. Judged, not by results, but by the effort made and the spirit shown, surely the third cub was a long way ahead of the other two. "It was the best that I could do", he had said. And that was true. But it was not good enough for the mother. Does he not remind you of the widow in today's Gospel. She too could say after putting in her penny: "It's the best that I could do. It's all I have".

However, in the world we live in, prizes and certificates are given, not for trying, but for results. It is the result that counts. According to this line of thinking, the best team is always the one that wins. Best is defined by results, by which side tops the points table, by which company returns a profit or a loss.

But Jesus does not judge according to appearances or by results. He has a different yardstick. He says: "No, it's not the result that counts but the spirit shown. It's not what has been attained but the price that has been paid that matters".

As Mickey Rooney's mother used to say: "Mickey, you don't have to be the biggest to be the best. You just have to try harder". Or as T. S. Eliot said: "It is the trying that matters — the rest is not our business".

PRAYER OF THE FAITHFUL

Let us pray that we may learn the lesson of today's Gospel — that it is not the size of our offering that matters in God's eyes, but the cost of it and the spirit in which we give it. *R*. Lord, graciously hear us.

For the leaders of the Church: that they may teach and practise the values of Christ and not those of the world. (Pause). . Lord, hear us.

For all those who have charge over others: that they may reward people not according to results but according to the effort made and the spirit shown. (Pause). Lord, hear us.

For all those who are involved in menial jobs in which they seldom receive recognition: that they may realise that what they contribute is seen by the Lord. (Pause). Lord, hear us.

That we may not work to win human praise and human rewards; that we may strive rather to please the Lord only. (Pause). Lord, hear us.

For local needs.

Let us pray:

Heavenly Father, help us to show our trust in your care for us by our generosity in sharing our goods with those in need. We ask this through Christ our Lord.

COMMUNION REFLECTION

We give but little
when we give of our goods.
It is only when we give of ourselves
that we truly give.

There are people who have a lot
but who give little.

And the little that they give
is given to win praise from others.
This makes their gift worthless.

But there are people who have little
and who give it all.
These are the really great.
Through the hands of such people
God cares for his people,and through their eyes
he smiles on the world.

We may feel that we have not much to give.
Let this not deter us.
We can give little things,
and give them with great love.

Then we will be imitating the poor widow,
who was able to look beyond her own need,
because she placed all her trust in God.

THIRTY-THIRD SUNDAY OF THE YEAR
My Words Will Remain

INTRODUCTION AND CONFITEOR

During the course of a single week we hear a lot of words, but how many of them are worth remembering? Here each Sunday we hear the words of Christ, words that were written down by the people who knew him, and were preserved for us over the centuries by the Church. Thus Christ's promise has come true: "All things will pass, but my words will remain". How well do we listen to his words, and how hard do we try to practise them in our lives? (Pause).   Let us ask pardon for the way we fail to let his words transform our lives.

Your word, Lord, is a lamp for our steps and a light for our path.   Lord, have mercy.

Blessed are those who hear your word and who do it.   Christ, have mercy.

No one ever spoke like you spoke; you alone have the words of eternal life.   Lord, have mercy.

First Reading (Daniel 12:1-3). This contains a vision of the prophet Daniel about the end of time. It introduces the belief in a resurrection of the dead and the notion of retribution after death.

Second Reading (Hebrews 10:11-14, 18). This reading insists on the superiority of the sacrifice made by Christ over all the sacrifices of the old law.

Gospel (Mark 13:24-32). This talks about the destruction of Jerusalem and the second coming of Christ. Certain signs will precede the first, but the time of the second is known only to God.

HOMILY

A missionary working in a remote area had two very promising men under instruction. Suddenly he was called home. The two were very upset on hearing that he would be away a long time. However, before leaving the priest gave each of them a copy of the Gospels, saying: "It's all here — everything you need for your lives. Here you have the words of the Master himself. This book will be to you a teacher that will never lead you astray. Its incredible wealth is all yours for free. You don't really need me". They promised him that they would study the book diligently, and they bore it away with enthusiasm and love.

As soon as the first man got home he put a leather cover on the book to preserve it from wear and tear. He kept it in a central spot in his bookcase. He had such reverence for it that he seldom used it! Only when misfortune visited his house did he take it down. Then he would look through its pages in search of comforting passages. And as he put it away again, it often happened that there would be tears in his eyes.

On the whole, however, it remained largely unused. It became for him an object of veneration. Sometimes he would take it down and show it to guests, boasting that he had a copy of 'The Book'. But he lost sight of the most important thing — his promise to study its message and to put it into practice in his life. He never examined his life against the words of the book. It was a personal consolation to him, like a private devotion, but none of his neighbours caught any of the warmth from the fire that it should have kindled in his heart. So, if the truth were told, he would not have been very much the poorer if he had never been given the book.

Let us turn to the second man. On the way home, typical of the kind of man he was, he went to the aid of a neighbour whose house had gone on fire. In his eagerness to help, he left the book down and completely forgot about it. Afterwards, when he went to look for it,

226 of the Year

he could not find it. It had been destroyed in the fire. He felt very bad about this. He experienced a great sense of loss. His most precious possession was gone. He had been so looking forward to studying it and trying to live his life according to its teachings. He felt guilty also. What would he be able to say to the priest? How would he be able to explain his carelessness?

But then calm returned. He sat down and tried to recall as much of its contents as he could. It was hopeless trying to recall the words in detail. He simply had not had a chance to familiarise himself with them. The best he could do was try to recall the core, the essence of what the book said and above all its spirit. He came to a simple conclusion: he recalled having heard the priest say that the book contained only those things that were the best and the deepest in life. He would live his life in that spirit.

He was as good as his word. Whenever he was faced with a difficult decision he would ask himself: what would the book say? The answer would come back from deep inside him: you must do what is right and best. Thus, though he never had a chance to read it, the book had an enormous influence on him. It strengthened him in moments of weakness. It inspired him in moments of generosity. It shamed him in moments of cowardice. At times it shook him like the wind shakes a tree. But he always listened to it, and in the end did what it said. He had grasped the essential thing: that the Gospel had to be lived. If it was not lived, it was no good. It was like an unplanted seed. His neighbours wondered where he got his strength and hope and inspiration. And he would tell them that it was from the book. When asked to show them the book he would reply: "I can't. You see, the book only exists inside me".

Jesus promised us that, no matter how much trouble and confusion there would be, his words would remain with us. "Though heaven and earth were to pass away, my words will never pass away". The Gospel is the handbook of every Christian. It should be the inspiration of our lives. We should be familiar with what it says through a prayerful reading of it, or at least through an attentive listening to it when it is read out at Mass. Without the words of Jesus what are we left with? A babble of conflicting opinions.

Today's Gospel gives us a timely message about the end of the world. Between now and the end of the century we are likely to have to put up with a multiplicity of 'prophets' telling us that the end is nigh. Some of them will no doubt presume to know the time and the number of the last bus! Jesus tells us that no one knows when the end will come except the heavenly Father. We should take that very seriously and pay no heed to the false prophets.

And with regard to the end — we should be hopeful, rather than fearful. This is the only attitude worthy of a Christian. God made us for salvation, not for damnation. His love and mercy are at the heart of the Good News Jesus preached. Jesus said that we should live as if the end was about to happen at any moment. But he also said he should look forward to the end, as prisoners and slaves look forward to the day of their freedom.

The words of Jesus that have been handed down to us are enough, provided of course they are alive in our hearts and active in our lives. They will give sufficient light and hope to get by, and we will shed light around us so that those who are now in darkness will also be able to find their way home.

"My words will remain", said Jesus. They do. But of what use are they unless we listen to them and live by them?

"No matter how well I think I know the Gospel, everytime I open it everything is new to me". (Catherine de Hueck Doherty). That's the way to read the Gospel.

PRAYER OF THE FAITHFUL

"My words will remain", said Jesus. Let us pray that his words may not only be in our hearts and on our lips but active in our lives.
R. Lord, hear our prayer.

For the Church: that all its members may give effective witness to the truth of the Gospel by the way they live. (Pause).   Let us pray to the Lord.

For all those in charge of civil affairs: that the teaching of the Gospel may inspire them in their efforts to ensure justice for all their brothers and sisters. (Pause).   Let us pray to the Lord.

For the unemployed, and for all those who are in pain or distress: that the words of Christ may give them strength and hope. (Pause).   Let us pray to the Lord.

That we may not be mere nominal believers, creating for ourselves a thousand false gods, and living by values that we do not even remotely resemble those of the gospel. (Pause).   Let us pray to the Lord.

For local needs.

Let us pray:

Lord, grant that what we have said with our lips, we may believe with our hearts, and practise in our lives. We ask this through Christ our Lord.

COMMUNION REFLECTION

The Lord's words remain with us
just as he said they would.

"What good will it do you to gain the while world
if you lose your soul?

"Love your enemies;
pray for those who persecute you.

"The greatest among you
is the one who serves.

"There is joy in heaven
when a sinner repents.

"Woman, has no one condemned you?
Then neither will I condemn you.

"'Seek first the kingdom of God,
and all these other things that you fret about
will be given to you".

Lord, your words challenge and inspire,
they guide and comfort us.
They turn our values upside down.

Once heard, we cannot forget them.
We anchor our lives to them.
For though heaven and earth should pass away,
your words will never pass away.

THIRTY-FOURTH SUNDAY OF THE YEAR
Christ Our King

INTRODUCTION AND CONFITEOR

Today the feast of Christ our King brings us to the end of the liturgical year. We have travelled a long road since the first Sunday of Advent. Christ has been on that road with us as the invisible Companion of our journey. Let us hope that during it we have grown to know him better, to trust him better, and to love him better, so that today we can rejoice in calling him our King. (Pause). Christ's kingdom is a very special kingdom. It calls for special qualities.

Lord Jesus, your kingdom is a kingdom of truth and life. Lord, have mercy.

Your kingdom is a kingdom of holiness and grace. Christ, have mercy.

Your kingdom is a kingdom of justice, love, and peace. Lord, have mercy.

HEADINGS FOR READINGS

First Reading (Daniel 7:13-14). The prophet Daniel forsees in a vision the coming of one who will have dominion over all peoples. That person is Christ.

Second Reading (Apocalypse 1:5-8). The risen Christ is the ruler of all the earth. But it is only at the end of time that he will take full possession of his kingdom.

Gospel (John 18:33-37). Questioned by Pilate, Jesus declares that he is indeed a King, but that his kingdom is not like the kingdoms of this world.

HOMILY

The new prisoner arrived quietly at Mount Simon State prison. His name was Pastor. Nobody knew what crime, if any, he had committed. To the warders he was just another criminal. He settled in at once. At first he was unusually quiet. But then he began to make his presence felt — simply by the kind of life he led. He did not fight for the first place in queues. He did not go chasing after the jobs. He did not try to win favour with the warders. He did not get involved in any of the shady rackets that were going on around him. Yet he was no softie. He could endure solitary confinement as well as any other. He could face ill-treatment without flinching.

He also soon won a reputation for generosity, a kind of generosity rarely witnessed among prisoners. He would share his meagre ration of bread, not just with a mate of his who might be expected to return the compliment, but with anyone who was hungry. When someone was struggling under a heavy load, Pastor's willing shoulder was always available. But all this he did so unobtrusively that much of it went unnoticed.

During evening recreation a little group of fellow prisoners would gather around him. Why? They just knew that it was good to be with him. Soon they began to bring him their problems. His replies were always honest and truthful. They poured out their sad stories to him. He proved to be a very good listener. They did not feel judged. They felt understood. Up to this, nobody had ever taken them seriously. Pastor did.

As their confidence in him grew, they unburdened on him all their fears, hates, hurts, worries, wounds, and sorrows. Life had bent them into all sorts of shapes. To the authorities they were grotesque and beyond redemption. But not to Pastor. He convinced them that it was possible for them to straighten themselves out and to make something worthwhile of their lives. There was a quiet authority about everything he said. But it was above all the way he treated them that had the greatest effect on them.

His influence continued to grow. As it did so, incredible things happened. Some he rescued from the clutches of loneliness and despair. Others he rescued from the claws of bitterness and hatred. At his touch many of them began to live again. He opened their minds and led them to a new way of seeing and of judging. He had the gift of being able to unlock people who were closed up. He made them feel that they were important, that they mattered.

Inevitably, some of the warders grew jealous of him. Most of these were decent men. But there was a small number of bullies among them who took satisfaction out of making life difficult for the prisoners. It was the latter who especially began to resent the influence Pastor had over an increasingly large number of what they regarded as highly dangerous men.

A time came when the whole prison was talking about him. Yet Pastor himself was untouched by his fame. He went about calm and self-assured but without a trace of arrogance. But his days were clearly numbered. He was proving to be a threat to the system, not by his badness, but by his goodness. His enemies confined him to his cell. Then on a trumped-up charge they had him brought before the prison governor. "What crime have you committed?" the governor asked. "My only crime", Pastor answered, "is that I have loved my fellow prisoners". The governor could find nothing to pin on him. However, he did not want to let his subordinates down. Besides, he wanted a quiet last year as governor. He was coming up to retirement and a handsome pension awaited him, provided he did not blot his copybook in the meantime.

Pastor spent his last night in solitary. As the next day dawned a sense of foreboding gripped the prison. Everybody to some degree was affected by it. It was is if it was they, not Pastor, who were on trial. And in a sense this was true. Pastor's presence was like a light that showed up where everybody stood. It judged them all — prisoners, warders, and the governor alike. And because each of them had something to hide, each felt uneasy. Deep down they knew that a great injustice was being committed, and that they were all involved in it. Towards evening a single shot rang out. News spread that Pastor was dead. The official explanation: he was shot while trying to escape.

In one sense Pastor was a nobody. Yet in another sense he was a 'king'. He was the greatest source of goodness, light, and hope in that dark world. He is a figure of Christ — the Christ who in today's liturgy we call our King. Christ was indeed a King, but not in the ordinary sense of the word. He had no army or territory. He had no throne or crown. Yet he came on earth to establish a kingdom — the kingdom of God. To let people know that they had royal blood in them. More than that. That they were sons and daughters of God.

He himself showed us how to live up to our dignity — by a blameless life. He also showed us how to treat others, even the very least, in a way that encouraged them to believe in their dignity and to live up to it. But the light of his goodness was so bright that it blinded some, showing up their darkness. Like Pastor he had to be killed. Unwilling to follow his light they were determined to extinguish it.

By the way we live, especially by our attitude to truth and justice, we declare each day where our loyalty lies — whether we are on the side of Christ and his kingdom, or whether like Pilate we take the way of evasion and cowardice, thus betraying him. It is not possible to remain neutral. But what a joy it is to belong to Christ and his kingdom. To let our lives be ruled by his spirit, and in our own small way to work for the spread of his kingdom — a kingdom of justice, truth, and love.

PRAYER OF THE FAITHFUL

Let us pray that God's kingdom may come and that his will may be done on earth as it is in heaven. *R*. Lord, may your kingdom come.

For the Church: that all its members may work with courage and faith for the spread of the reign of God in the world by striving to live good and holy lives. (Pause). Let us pray to the Lord.

For all world leaders: that they may realise that they are working to build up the kingdom of God whenever they work to promote a more just and a more human world. (Pause). Let us pray to the Lord.

For all those who are suffering persecution because of their allegiance to Christ; that God may sustain their hope and their love. (Pause). Let us pray to the Lord.

That of all our loyalties, our loyalty to Christ and his Gospel may come first in our lives. (Pause). Let us pray to the Lord.

For local needs.

Let us pray:

Heavenly Father, help us to be loyal and true followers of Christ your Son, so that we may come to share his glory in the kingdom of heaven, where he lives and reigns with you and the Holy Spirit, one God, for ever and ever.

OUR FATHER

Let us pray to our heavenly Father for the coming of his kingdom as Jesus taught us.

SIGN OF PEACE

Lord Jesus Christ, you said to Peter in the garden: 'Put away your sword, for all who live by the sword will die by the sword'. Help us to put away the weapons of war and to take up those of peace instead, so that we may enjoy the peace and unity of your kingdom, where you live for ever and ever.

COMMUNION REFLECTION

Last Judgement

Don't wait for the last judgement.
It takes place every day.
Long before the end,
people will already have judged themselves.
In a thousand ways
they will have already chosen
for or against themselves,
for or against their brothers,
for or against the truth.

As an X-ray shows up the hidden black spots,
so God's judgement will show up what already is:
the goat among the sheep,
the weeds among the wheat,
the guest without the wedding garment.

Lord, let us never forget, however,
that the Father's love and mercy
are at the heart of the Good News.
You never said that we were to fear the last day,
only that we should be ready for it.
You even told us to look forward to it.
as slaves look forward to the day of their liberation.

Lord, may your kingdom come,
now and hereafter.

Festivals

THE IMMACULATE CONCEPTION

INTRODUCTION AND CONFITEOR

Today we celebrate the feast of Mary's Immaculate Conception. What we are celebrating is the radical holiness of Mary, the Mother of God. She was never subject to Satan, the Prince of Darkness. From the very moment of her coming into existence she belonged to the kingdom of God. We too are called to belong to that kingdom. Let us start by calling to mind our sins and our need of God's grace and mercy. (Pause).   As we confess our sins to the heavenly Father and to one another, let us ask the Blessed Virgin to pray for us.

I confess to almighty God . . .

HEADINGS FOR READINGS

First Reading (Genesis 3:9-15,20). When man and woman disobeyed God and fell into sin, God promised salvation from sin through another man and woman, namely, Christ and his Mother.

Second Reading (Ephesians 1:3-6, 11-12). In his love for us God has adopted us as his sons and daughters. Hence we too are called to a holy and blameless life.

Gospel (Luke 1:26-38). Mary's greatness and holiness are due to God's grace and her cooperation with that grace.

HOMILY

Gold was one of the first metals to attract human attention. It was known and highly valued by the earliest civilisations. What makes it so valuable and so sought after? First of all there is its brilliant yellow colour. Then, when pure, gold is the most malleable of all metals. It can be beaten to .00001mm. in thickness. Thin sheets of pure gold become translucent. Traces of other metals reduce its malleability. Again pure gold is ideal as a conductor of electricity. But once again traces of impurities affect this. Pure gold is said to be 24 carat.

For centuries men had been looking for gold in the hills above a certain western town. When they found some they would bring it down into the town. Sometimes their find consisted of a handful of specks and flakes which they had laboriously panned from a mountain stream. Occasionally, however, a man would come down with a nugget that he had found embedded in a rock. This would cause a new flock of prospectors to take to the hills.

Naturally occurring metallic gold has variable amounts of base metals in it. Now in the town there was a mint and a refinery. It was the job of the experts to determine whether a chunk of ore was low-grade or high-grade. Usually they could tell by the colour, for the characteristic yellow is greatly affected by alloying with other metals. If it was bright yellow it meant that the gold content was high. But if it had a greenish tint this meant that it contained a lot of silver. If it was redder than usual this betrayed the presence of copper. A whitish tint denoted the presence of platinum. A purple tint meant there was aluminum present. And so on. Many a prospector discovered to his bitter disappointment that all that glitters is not gold.

One day a young shepherd arrived in the town with a large lump of yellow ore. Though its surface had traces of earth on it, when the experts examined it they were flabbergasted.

"This is impossible!" they said. "Everything on this earth is impure and contaminated in some way."

"Do you mean it's pure gold?" asked the shepherd.

"Yes. We can't find a trace of impurity in it. It's 24 carat. Just look at the way itt shines."

And they showed him how to look at it, and he marvelled at what he saw.

"Where did you find it?" they asked him.

"I stumbled across it up in the mountains as I was looking for one of my sheep that had strayed," the shepherd replied.

"You're a very lucky man," they said. "We can do anything with this or make anything out of it. It has absolutely no need to be put through the refinery. If all ore was like this we would be out of business."

When we say that Mary was conceived without original sin we are saying that she was pure gold. Right from the moment of her conception she was radically holy. Though made of 'the stuff of this earth' she had no impurities in her. From the beginning of her life she belonged totally to the kingdom of God. Never, not even for a moment, did she belong to the kingdom of Satan. And all this she owed to a special act of God. In order to prepare her to be a worthy mother for his Son, he allowed her to enjoy in advance the benefits of Christ's redemption.

This does not mean that Mary's life was easier than ours, or that it was sunshine all the way. If anything, the opposite is nearer the truth. Her sinlessness made her more vulnerable, just as exceptionally beautiful flowers are very frail. But, like pure gold, she was more pliable in the hands of God. She was more ready to do his will rather than her own. She did not offer resistance to what his grace wanted to do in her and through her. And like pure gold she was an excellent conductor of God's light and love.

Just as all metals, even rocks, have traces of gold in them, so we have gold in us. But it is not yet of the 24 carat variety. We have impurities mixed in with it that dim its lustre, and which make it more resistant to the hands of the Craftsman, and a more imperfect conductor of his light and love. Because of this we are less available to God. But Christ has redeemed us. He has made it possible for us to refine the gold in us. This process was begun at our Baptism, and will go on right through life. It will entail a lot of pain, sacrifice, and struggle. But Mary our Mother will help us. She shows us what it means to be redeemed. In her we see what we are called to become — radically holy and totally free.

We have no need to go chasing all over the world in search of gold. We all have gold inside us. It just needs a little refining. We need to rid ourselves of self-righteousness, hypocrisy, selfishness, greed, pride . . . so that God can act in us and through us. The lovely thing is — no one can rob us of this gold. The only tragedy would be that we might never discover it.

PRAYER OF THE FAITHFUL

As we praise God for the holiness of Mary, let us pray to him that we may overcome our sinfulness and live up to our dignity as his sons and daughters. *R.* Lord, hear our prayer.

For the pope and the bishops: that they may continually remind the People of God of their call to holiness of life. (Pause). Let us pray the Lord.

For all of humankind: that they may see the holiness of Mary as a model for all that is best and beautiful in humanity. (Pause). Let us pray to the Lord.

For all women, and especially for mothers: that they may experience the help of Mary the Mother of Jesus in all their difficulties. (Pause). Let us pray to the Lord.

For all of us: that Mary our Mother may help us to persevere in the

struggle against temptation and sin. (Pause).   Let us pray to the
Lord.

For local needs.

Let us pray:

Lord, at the angel's message, Mary, the immaculate Virgin, became
the temple of God, and was filled with the light of the Holy Spirit.
Grant that after her example we may humbly and steadfastly follow
your will. We make our prayer through Christ our Lord.

COMMUNION REFLECTION

A mother is everything.
She is our consolation in sorrow,
our hope is misery,
our strength in weakness.
The person who loses a mother
loses a pure soul,
a constant source of blessing and protection.

Everything in nature speaks of a mother.
The sun is the mother of the earth,
nourishing it with light and heat.
It never leaves the universe at night
until it has put everything to sleep,
to the songs of the birds and the brooks.
And the earth, in its turn,
is the mother of trees and flowers.
Then the trees in their turn
become mothers of their fruits and seeds.

And Mary is our spiritual Mother,
the Mother Jesus gave us as he died.

Holy Mother, pray for us now and at the hour
of our passing from this world to the Father.
Keep us free from sin,
and help us to walk in the bright light
Jesus your Son brought into the world.

THE BODY AND BLOOD OF CHRIST
The Church As The Body of Christ

INTRODUCTION AND CONFITEOR

This is the feast of *Corpus Christi* — the Body of Christ. St Paul continually reminds us that *we are* the Body of Christ. The Eucharist is not a private devotion, it is a great act of common worship. Here we become conscious of our unity. Here the Body of Christ becomes visible. The one thing which above all others would make us unfit to be part of the Eucharist is if we were not reconciled with one another. Are we? (Pause). We ask God's forgiveness for our sins and for the grace to be reconciled with one another.

I confess to almighty God ... etc.

HEADINGS FOR READINGS

First Reading (Exodus 24:3-8). This reading describes the solemn ratification by Moses and the people of the covenant God made with them on Mount Sinai.

Second Reading (Hebrews 9:11-15). Through the redeeming work of Christ God has entered into a new and eternal covenant with his people.

Gospel (Mark 14:12-16, 22-26). This describes the preparation and the celebration of the Passover meal Jesus ate with his disciples the night before he died.

HOMILY

During World War II the Russians and the Germans fought for two weeks for possession of a few hundred yards of ground. During this time the Russians made a surprising discovery. They discovered that there were Russians fighting for the Germans. These were men who were so desperate to get rid of Stalin that they had changed sides in the hope of achieving their aim. These fought with a desperation all their own. They could not afford to be captured as they would be looked upon as renegades and would be treated accordingly.

It was December 1943 and the weather was bitterly cold. Snow covered the ground and both sides were wearing camouflage — white cloaks that covered their overcoats and caps. An interesting encounter took place. As the soldiers dashed back and forth among the forest trees things got very confused. Two soldiers lay down close to one another. They felt rather lost but nevertheless continued firing at shadowy figures some distance away among the trees. Both had Russian pistols. They shared their ammunition, encouraged one another, and together swore when the cold caused their pistols to freeze up. Finally the pistols refused to fire at all so they decided to take a break from the war. The first took out a packet of cigarettes and offered one to the second. The second took out a bar of chocolate and gave half of it to the first.

After a while they decided to really relax. They pulled back their white hoods and in the same instant each noticed the other's cap. One of the caps had the eagle of Germany on it. The other had the star of Russia, which meant that they were actually on opposite sides. So what did they do? They jumped to their feet at once, drawing their pistols as they did so. But these still refused to work. Then, grabbing them by the barrels and swinging them like clubs, they set upon one another like two primitive cavemen. This was not politics. Nor was it love of the Motherland. It was just like two crabs, victims of blind mistrust. If I pity my enemy he will kill me.

We are not told how the incident finished up. But there is a lesson in it for us. We come here each Sunday to celebrate the meal Christ asked us to celebrate in his memory. While in church we behave like the two soldiers before they discovered they were on opposite sides. We pray to the one Father. We call each other brothers and sisters. We offer one another a sign of peace. We eat from the same loaf. But once we leave the church what happens? Is it not true that we take off the camouflage, and we revert to being private individuals. We no longer recognise the ties that exist between us, the followers of Christ. We go our own way, ignoring one another, and sadly in some cases, turning against one another. Surely this is not what Christ intended?

Everything here speaks to us of community, of togetherness, and of love. During the week we are scattered by circumstance over which we have no control. But here we are reassembled, we become the Body of Christ made visible. During the week we can and ought to pray individually or in small groups. Here we pray as a community, as members of a large family — the family of God's children, brothers and sisters in Christ. St Paul says: "We form a single body because we all share in the one loaf". (1 Cor 10:17).

Here we experience our unity. Here we have everything in common. We are part of a great people — the People of God on pilgrimage to the Promised Land of eternal life. Here we are fed with food that is far more precious than the manna the Israelites ate in the desert. Here we are also fed with the Word of God, which is a lamp for our steps and a light for our path. We are fed with Christ himself who comes to us as the food of our souls. Christ is like bread to us his followers. We need him if we are to live lives that are worthy of children of the Father.

Love and trust must be the very atmosphere we breathe here. In this context what meaning the words of the priest take on: "Pray, my brothers and sisters, . . ." "Lift up your hearts . . ." "Let us pray to the Father in the words Jesus gave us". "Let us offer one another a sign of peace".

The one thing that would seriously damage the witness of what we do is if there were divisions among us. But we must also guard against a certain coldness, a certain indifference, perhaps even just a certain shyness which prevents us from experiencing and expressing our unity.

And we must make sure that when we depart from here we take away with us some of the warmth we have experienced here. We take it out with us into a world where there is a lot of coldness — the coldness of indifference, mistrust, and hostility. All those who come into contact with us will know that we have been sitting at a warm fire. We have so much to share with one another, things that are so vital — faith in God, trust in one another, love, and hope.

PRAYER OF THE FAITHFUL

Christ is the head of his Body, the Church, and we are the members of that Body. Gathered together on this day we pray to the Father in his name. *R*. Lord, hear our prayer.

For the Church: that it may be a light for all the nations, a sign of unity, and a force for reconciliation among all peoples. (Pause). Let us pray to the Lord.

For all the leaders of the world: that God may grant them the gifts of unity, of love, and of peace. (Pause). Let us pray to the Lord.

For the poor, the sick, the lonely, and the unloved: that we the followers of Christ may befriend them and show them that Christ cares about them. (Pause) Let us pray to the Lord.

That as we celebrate this Eucharist we may experience the bonds of love Christ wanted to see among his followers, and that these bonds may be strengthened. (Pause). Let us pray to the Lord.

For local needs.

Let us pray:

Heavenly Father, may our celebration of Christ's farewell meal of love mould us into a caring community. We ask this through the same Christ our Lord.

OUR FATHER

Let us pray to God our Father that all his children may have sufficient bread for body and spirit. Let us pray in the words Jesus gave us:

COMMUNION PRAYER

Prayer before the Blessed Sacrament.

Outside this church the noisy traffic flows past.
People rush hither and thither.
But I have left that world behind
and I am here before you.

I do not exclude my brothers and sisters.
I bring them with me,
for I know that they are equally dear to you.

I have nothing.
But I feel that I have everything
since I have you.

I close my mind and open my heart,
and so I am at peace.
There are so many people in the world
with whom one feels at peace.
But I feel at peace here with you.

Here I experience my true worth, which consists,
not in my possessions or achievements,
but in knowing that I am loved by you.
Here I grow like corn in the sun.

In this oasis I encounter you, Lord.
Here I am nourished with that mysterious food
which alone can satisfy the hunger
the heavenly Father has put in my heart.

FINAL PRAYER

Father, here in your house our roads come together and our paths meet. Here we lay down our differences and become one family. Here we are in from the cold and experience a little of the warmth of human friendship and community. Grant that as we leave we may not take up our differences again. Rather let us try to live as brothers and sisters who care about one another. We ask this through Christ our Lord.

THE ASSUMPTION OF THE BLESSED VIRGIN MARY

INTRODUCTION AND CONFITEOR

In celebrating the feast of Mary's Assumption into heaven we are celebrating the fact that she now shares fully in the Easter victory that Christ her Son gained over death. As Mother of the Saviour it is right that she should have a very special place at the eternal banquet. And it is right that we should be happy on this day for she is our Mother too.

Mary attained to the glory of heaven because she was a humble person who sought to do the will of God at all times. Often we deliberately choose to do our own will rather than that of God. This means that we sin. Let us pause to call to mind our sins. (Pause).

We turn to the God who as Mary said is rich in mercy.

Lord, your mercy reaches from age to age for those who revere you.   Lord, have mercy.

Lord, you send the self-sufficient away empty-handed, but the hungry you fill with good things.   Christ, have mercy.

Lord, you cast down the mighty from their seats of power, but the poor and the lowly you lift up.   Lord, have mercy.

HEADINGS AND READINGS

First Reading (Apocalypse 11:19; 1-2:1-6, 10). As the Mother of the Redeemer, Mary was at the very centre of the struggle between good and evil, between God and Satan. However, God took special care of her.

Second Reading (1 Cor 15:20-26). Christ is the new Adam who undoes all the harm done by the old Adam.

Gospel (Luke 1:36-56). Mary had no doubt about the importance of the role she had been given by God. However, she takes no credit for herself but gives all the glory to God.

HOMILY

You cannot fully understand or appreciate the end of a play or film without knowing what went before. You have to know the story that led up to it. At the end of her earthly life Mary was taken up body and soul into heavenly glory and exalted by God as queen of heaven. This is the feast we celebrate today. I feel, however, that we cannot appreciate it properly without briefly looking at 'where she came from'. Let me tell you a little story. It's about a drop of water called Daisy.

Daisy started life as a snowflake on top of a high mountain. She lay there, pure and white, in the freezing cold until the sun came along and melted her. Then, pulled by an invisible force outside herself, she began to move down the mountain. As she did so she joined up with a host of other drops to form a small but fast-flowing stream.

Daisy was like all the other drops in that she was small, weak, and insignificant. Yet she was different. She had a greater consciousness of her dependence on the mysterious 'outside power' that was pulling them all to the ocean, and she was more prompt in responding to it than any of the others. She was also conscious that she had been given a special role to play, though what that role was she didn't know at this stage. One day part of her broke off and formed a new droplet. Thus it was that her son was born. She called him Lux, for there was a radiance about him.

At first life was exciting for her and her son because it was full of movement. Yet at times it could be frightening, like when they were bounced off rocks and other hard objects. Finally, however, they reached the bottom of the mountain and the now greatly swollen stream slowed down. Life became very peaceful. Sometimes it appeared that the stream was going nowhere. Yet it was nice sometimes to lie in shallow pools and bask in the sunshine.

In time the stream merged with other streams and became a river. It was at this stage that Lux left her. He told her that he had work to do, and went on ahead of her. She was sorry to see him go but knew that this was the way things were meant to be. The pools got larger and deeper. Daisy knew moments of great anxiety and depression as she and her companions lay for days at the bottom of deep and dark pools, where only a faint glimmer of light filtered through.

However, everywhere she went she discovered that Lux had been there before her. It was also becoming clear to her that through him a new element had been introduced into the river. He had given new direction, meaning, and hope to all seekers of the ocean. He had blazed a trail for them to follow. The thought of him lit up her darkest moments. In her heart she heard his gentle voice calling her to trust, to hope, and to follow. The worst danger she encountered came from the various pollutants that were dumped into the river. It was no joke trying to keep oneself uncontaminated by these, for their poison was everywhere. But once again she drew strength and comfort from knowing that Lux had also encountered these dangers, and had successfully negotiated them.

At last a vast expanse of water opened up ahead of her. The pull was now irresistible. At the sight of the broad ocean a new sense of excitement gripped her. It was marvellous to be part of something so great. Thus it was that she reached the ocean.

But this is not the end of her story. The climax is still to come. One day as she lay on the surface of the ocean a wonderful thing happened to her. Under the bright rays of the sun she began to vaporise, and was slowly lifted up into the air, above the tops of the highest mountains, right up into the clouds in fact. It was an incredible feeling. As she looked down from her lofty perch on the meandering and often rocky course she had travelled, a glow of satisfaction came over her. Hard-won victories give more joy. Then out of the cloud she heard a familiar voice calling to her, saying: "Welcome home, mother!" It was her son Lux. Now her joy was complete.

Daisy of course stands for Mary, and Lux for Jesus. During her life on earth Mary knew happy times when her life went along joyfully and peacefully. Though she was privileged by God in not suffering the contamination of sin, she was spared none of the trials of life. Yet at all times she sought to do, not her own will, but the will of God. It was through her obedience that Christ our Saviour came into the world.

On this day the Church invites us to celebrate her final triumph. We are in a better position to do so now that we have looked briefly at her lifestory. This is the day the humble Mary was assumed into heaven to share fully in the glorious victory her Son won over sin and death. She had attained to the fulness of that redemption which we hope will one day be ours too. It was the same power that raised Jesus from the dead that brought glory to Mary.

Each one of us has to make the same journey from mountaintop to ocean, and we, hope, beyond. We are straining towards the glorious state Mary has arrived at. Today is a day to renew our hope. It is also a day to renew our confidence that Mary will watch over us at every turn in our journey. She will understand when we are going through a rough patch. She will help us to persevere in following her Son. He too whispers in our hearts: "Trust, hope, and follow me. For where I now am, I want you too to be".

PRAYER OF THE FAITHFUL

We are all straining towards the glorious state Mary has arrived at. Christ left her to us to be our Mother. Let us then with confidence pray to him. *R*. Give us a share in Mary's joy.

For all Christians: that they may hear the gentle voice of Jesus calling them to trust, to hope, and to follow him. (Pause). Let us pray to the Lord.

For the world and all mankind: that all God's people may see heaven as their final goal and come to share in Mary's glory. (Pause). Let us pray to the Lord.

For all those whose lives are hard, hidden, and meaningless: that they may find faith and hope. (Pause). Let us pray to the Lord.

That we may be thankful to God when life is joyful and peaceful; that we may seek his help when life is dark and difficult. (Pause). Let us pray to the Lord.

For local needs.

Let us pray:

Heavenly Father, as we journey through this life towards the goal of you Kingdom, may we always experience in our lives the protection of Mary the Mother of your Son. We ask this through the same our Lord Jesus Christ, your Son, who lives and reigns with you and the Holy Spirit, one God, for ever and ever.

COMMUNION REFLECTION

Mary was a very humble person.
A humble person is a transparent person,
and cares nothing for acclaim.
He or she receives praise and honour
the way a clean window takes in the light of the sun.
The brighter and more intense the light is,
the less you see of the glass.
It attracts no attention to itself,
for it retains nothing of the light for itself
but lets it shine through.

Humble people know that without the light of God
they themselves would be in darkness.
Such an attitude makes it possible for them
to receive the help and gifts of God.

So it was with Mary.
"All generations will call me blessed", she said,
"because God has done great things for me".
Hence her soul was filled with joy and serenity, and the light of God shone through her.

Mary, teach us to be humble and trustful before God,
and we will find rest for our souls,
and the light of God will shine through us.

FINAL PRAYER

Father, Mary was full of grace at all times, from the very beginning of her life to the last moment. May she be with us at every moment of our lives: in the calm moments when our lives flow along like a singing brook or a gurgling stream; and in the troubled moments when our lives are full of turbulence. May she be with us now and at the hour of our death, so that that moment may become the moment of our glory. We ask this through Christ our Lord.

ALL SAINTS

INTRODUCTION AND CONFITEOR

Today we do not concentrate on the spiritual heroes of the Church, the canonised saints. Instead we concentrate on those who became saints in little, ordinary, and hidden ways, and who will never be canonised. We are celebrating those who, inspired by the Gospel, made the interests of others more important than their own. Let us pause to remember one genuinely holy person we have known. (Pause). That is what we are called to — holiness, which means being like Christ.

Lord, you call us to holiness by helping us to love one another in every everyday lives.   Lord, have mercy.

You call us to holiness by helping us to care for others in our everyday lives.   Christ, have mercy.

You call us to holiness by helping us to forgive those who offend us in our everyday lives.   Lord, have mercy.

HEADINGS FOR READINGS

First Reading (Apocalypse 7:2-4, 9-14). Here we have a vision of the victorious followers of Christ rejoicing in his presence in the heavenly kingdom. They come from every nation, and race, and tribe, and language.

Second Reading (1 John 3:1-3). St John tells us that in heaven we shall see God as he is. However, if we want to attain to this vision we must try to live like Christ.

Gospel (Matthew 5:1-12). Here Jesus stresses the qualities he wishes to see in his disciples, qualities we see exemplified in the lives of the saints.

It was a Saturday afternoon. The streets were full of people going about their business. Yet in spite of the hustle and bustle and din, there was a certain calm and order and peace about the whole scene.

But all of a sudden the peace was shattered. Some hooligans coming home from a football match went on a rampage. They began to fight with rival fans. Missiles were thrown, and then with a loud shattering noise they knocked in the front window of a large store. Bedlam broke loose. People panicked and began to scream. The traffic stopped. The pavement in front of the store was littered with broken glass. The police arrived but the hooligans had fled, melting into the crowd. The panic subsided and things gradually got back to normal.

About an hour later two repairmen arrived on the scene. The first thing they did was to sweep up the broken glass. Then they tackled the window itself. They mounted their tall ladders carefully. It was not a pleasant job. In fact it was quite dangerous. They had to remove all the remaining jagged fragments of glass without cutting themselves or letting anything fall on the passersby. Then the old putty had to be removed. Next the window had to be carefully measured, after which they phoned their office to send out a new pane. It duly arrived and they proceeded to put it in. They knew their job and did it thoroughly. Yet they went about it quietly and without fuss. Any noise they made was quickly drowned by the traffic. All the time they worked on the window not a single passerby stopped to watch them. By now those who had actually witnessed the breaking of the window were probably at home. Only the store manager knew the job those two men did.

Next day's newspapers had headlines about the hooligans who had smashed the window and went on a rampage. There were even photos of the broken window. The papers made a meal out of it. But there was not a single line about the two repairmen who had done such a splendid job that by the end of the day everything was back to normal.

We live in a world where, thanks largely to the mass media, the 'window-breakers' get all the attention and the 'repairmen' are frequently ignored. A visitor from another planet might well get the impression that the former were the more important people around and far and away in the majority, whereas we know that this is far from being the case. The Church sets aside one day to honour all the 'repairmen' and 'repairwomen' who do such an excellent job, and who do it quietly and anonymously. We call it All Saints day.

An evil act, whether witnessed or read about, can cause momentary surprise or shock. But evil and evil people are dull, empty, and leave us cold. Besides, they leave a trail of darkness behind them, causing others to stumble and fall. Goodness, on the other hand, touches something inside us. It inspires us. And so it is that the saints are the most interesting people of all. Every time we read the life of one of the saints we cannot but experience a powerful call to conversion, that is, to a better and a more authentic life. The saints leave a trail of light behind them. In that light we see the way we ought to go, and we feel a strong pull in that direction. We are like a swimmer returning to shore who is helped on by an in-coming tide.

And so today we honour and rejoice in the little people, the forgotten heroes and heroines, people who in their own humble ways have followed Christ, and followed him to the end. We have all known some of them, for God sees to it that saints live among us all the time. The daily life of many people is made up of great sacrifices and acts of quiet heroism. Think of the parents of a severely handicapped child. Think of those who do obscure and routine jobs, such s cleaning a floor, and who do them cheerfully and well. Think of those quiet, gentle people to whom their neighbour is as dear as themselves, and who give God and his Kingdom first place in their lives.

Saints are witnesses to the love of God, and there is no higher vocation in all the earth than that. It is our vocation too. In honouring the hidden saints let us be inspired by them to follow our own vocation in our own humble way.

As one writer put it: "In spite of all its sham, drudgery, and broken dreams, it is still a beautiful world. Many people strive for high ideals, and everywhere life is full of heroism". Saints make the world beautiful. They fill it with light, hope, and warmth.

"At a particular moment each day the sexton's love of God becomes a love of lighting candles". (Antoine de Saint-Exupery).

PRAYER OF THE FAITHFUL

Let us pray that we may hear the call to holiness of life, and respond to it in faith, in hope, and in love.   R. Lord, hear us in your love.

For Christians: that they may seek to know the will of God and to do it with all their strength, thus imitating Christ and his saints. (Pause).   We pray in faith.

For men and women of goodwill: that they may persevere in the path of goodness, truth, honesty, and integrity — for that is the path of holiness. (Pause).   We pray in faith.

For all those who are weighed down by troubles and disappointments: that the example of the saints may inspire them. (Pause). We pray in faith.

That we may be able to overcome our weakness, selfishness, and cowardice, and imitate the generosity and courage of the saints. (Pause). We pray in faith.

For local needs.

Let us pray:

Father, to be a saint is to be a witness to your love in our lives. There is no higher vocation than this. Help us to follow it with all our hearts. We make all our prayers through Christ our Lord.

SIGN OF PEACE

Lord Jesus Christ, you looked with compassion on Mary Magdalen, the sinner, and you said to her: 'Your sins are forgiven; go in peace'. Thus Mary Magdalen the sinner became Mary Magdalen the saint. Look not on our sins, but on the faith of your Church, and grant us the peace and unity of your kingdom where you live for ever and ever.

COMMUNION REFLECTION

Isn't it strange that princes and kings,
And clowns that caper in sawdust rings,
And ordinary folks like you and me,
Are builders of eternity.

To each is given a bag of tools,
And hour-glass and a book of rules,
And each must build ere his time is flown,
A stumbling block or a stepping stone.

(Anon).